fiona beddall

nicholas murgatroyd
julie penn
howard smith
adrian tennant
nick witherick

move

pre-intermediate

teacher's book

MACMILLAN

Macmillan Education
Between Towns Road, Oxford OX4 3PP
A division of Macmillan Publishers Limited
Companies and representatives throughout the world

ISBN-10: 1-4050-0316-2
ISBN-13: 978-1-4050-0316-2

Text by Fiona Beddall
Resource materials by Nicholas Murgatroyd, Julie Penn, Howard Smith, Adrian Tennant and Nick Witherick.

First published 2006

Cover by Macmillan Publishers Limited
Designed by eMC Design
Illustrated by Stephen Elford, Tim Kahane, Robin Lawrie, Kath Walker and Sholto Walker

Printed and bound in Spain by Edelvives

2010 2009 2008 2007 2006
10 9 8 7 6 5 4 3 2 1

Contents

Coursebook contents

Module 1 Vision

Unit	Topic	Language study	Vocabulary	Main skills
1 **I know what I like** pages 2–5	• Nature or nurture (three gifted young women) • Speed-dating	• Likes and dislikes, agreeing and disagreeing	• Phrasal verbs: growing up • Sports, leisure activities, types of film and styles of music	• **Reading:** understanding main information • **Speaking:** discussing child development; asking for and giving personal information • **Listening:** identifying key information
2 **Innovation** pages 6–9	• Great minds (Steve Jobs and Steve Wozniak, co-founders of Apple Computers) • Tokyo gizmo (innovative gadgets from a Japanese toymaker)	• Talking about past events (past simple and past continuous)	• *make* and *do*	• **Listening:** identifying main information • **Pronunciation:** regular past tense endings (*-ed*) • **Reading:** understanding main information • **Speaking:** discussing the importance of inventions
3 **The sixth sense** pages 10–13	• Psychic powers • Your lying ways (sleeping positions)	• Expressing necessity and advice (*must(n't), (don't) have to, should(n't), ought to, don't need to*)	• Character adjectives	• **Reading:** understanding gist • **Writing:** an email to a friend • **Speaking:** discussing psychic powers; describing people • **Listening:** identifying particular information
4 **What do you do?** pages 14–17	• Any volunteers? (experiences of a volunteer working in China) • Volunteers needed	• Making promises, requests and predictions: *will*	• Work experience • Occupations	• **Reading:** identifying main information • **Listening:** identifying key information • **Speaking:** talking about jobs and career choices; making promises, requests and predictions

5 **Review unit** pages 18–21
• **Extra practice** pages 22–25 • **Grammar reference and wordlist** pages 26–28 • **Listening scripts:** pages 30–31 • **Communication activities:** pages 29, 32

Module 2 Taste

Unit	Topic	Language study	Vocabulary	Main skills
1 **Don't breathe a word!** pages 34–37	• Gossip • You didn't hear it from me	• Talking about recent events (past simple and present perfect simple) • Phrases to talk about time and quantity	• Phrases about friendship and rumour	• **Reading:** identifying key information • **Listening:** completing details of events • **Speaking:** listening and responding to news about other people
2 **Pass the popcorn, please** pages 38–41	• Mad about movies • Movie mistakes message board	• Asking for and giving opinions	• Types of film • Describing elements of a film	• **Reading:** identifying main ideas • **Listening:** identifying descriptions • **Pronunciation:** emphatic stress in description phrases • **Speaking:** discussing strengths and weaknesses of a film • **Writing:** a film review
3 **You must try it** pages 42–45	• A question of taste (response to blue food) • Good manners cost nothing (politeness in restaurant conversations) • Doing the right thing (cultural expectations)	• Quantifiers with countable and uncountable nouns	• Food • Ordering food in restaurants	• **Reading:** understanding main ideas • **Speaking:** role-play between customer and waiter; discussing good and bad manners • **Listening:** identifying correct information
4 **Followers of fashion** pages 46–49	• Looking good (beauty contest) • Body art	• Recognising and using phrasal verbs	• Describing appearance and things you wear	• **Reading:** identifying main ideas • **Speaking:** discussing beauty and body decoration • **Listening:** understanding descriptions of body art • **Writing:** an email explaining a decision

5 **Review unit** pages 50–53
• **Extra practice** pages 54–57 • **Grammar reference and wordlist** pages 58–60 • **Listening scripts:** pages 62–63 • **Communication activities:** pages 61, 64

Module 3 Motion

CD-ROM contents

Location	Activities for each unit	Features
Modules 1–3, Units 1–4	• Language activity • Vocabulary activity • Common European Framework linked activity • Language game	• Markbook – helps you to record and update your marks. • Bookmark – helps you to save your favourite activities. • Wordlist – helps you to create your own wordlists. • You can back up, restore and print out your Markbook, Bookmarks and Wordlists. You can also send saved files as emails.

For more information use the Help feature, read the CD-ROM leaflet or visit www.macmillanenglish.com/move

Introduction

Welcome to *Move*

Adult learners have a wide variety of reasons for choosing to learn English. Some, for instance, do so as part of a foundation course for university or other course of studies; others do so for career reasons in order to gain promotion or perhaps to seek a new job. Yet others are planning to travel and wish to improve their English, or they are studying English as part of their holiday. Some students choose short, intensive courses of study, while others are studying perhaps two or three hours a week over a longer period.

Move recognises that to meet this wide variety of learning needs and teaching contexts, the key feature of a course for adults must be that it builds in a great deal of flexibility, allowing teachers to select from both core and optional material.

Each level of *Move* contains a core course of three modules, and with that there is an extensive range of optional materials, in the Coursebook and Class CD, and also in the CD-ROM and this Teacher's Book. There are five levels of *Move*, and it is suitable for use with adult students from an elementary level through to an advanced level of English.

The aim of this introduction is to explain both the methodological approach taken by *Move* as a language course, and the features that make up the core course, and the optional materials.

Methodology

Move recognises that the best way that most students learn is through a discovery approach. Throughout *Move*, language is presented in context and students are encouraged to notice its use, meaning and form before plenty of practice is given.

Move attaches great importance to the accessibility of topics through engaging reading and listening texts. Throughout *Move*, students are given the opportunity to present personalised and meaningful responses and to discuss their own ideas and opinions as a means of encouraging learning.

Move recognises that students are primarily looking to use their language in communicative situations. Therefore, central to *Move* are exercises and activities that encourage students to communicate their ideas, in particular through speaking and listening.

Move recognises that learning a language means a lot more than studying tenses or other isolated grammatical features and individual lexical items. Just as important is the ability to recognise, for example, language chunks such as collocations and fixed phrases, and to develop an awareness of the importance of naturalness and register. *Move* covers aspects of these language features throughout.

Each unit of *Move* has a Language study section, which focuses on a key area of language. The section starts with examples of the language in context taken from a preceding text or listening activity and then guides the students, encouraging them to notice its use and then work out meaning and form. Plenty of practice is then given through activities which allow the students to engage with the language on a personal level. Grammar reference pages support the Language study sections.

Each unit of *Move* has at least one Vocabulary section and many units have more than one. The students are encouraged to notice how the vocabulary is used in a preceding text or listening activity and it is then extended and practised, again allowing the students to engage with the language on a personal level.

Throughout *Move*, language is recycled and revised throughout each module. Additionally, the Review units at the end of each module bring language together from each of the preceding units and provide more overt revision. For further recycling and revision, *Move* has stimulating Extra practice material for each of the main units at the end of each module and the Teacher's Book includes photocopiable resource activities and end of unit and end of module tests. There are also CD-ROM activities for each unit (see below).

Move recognises the importance and value of self-study. The Extra practice activities are designed for use as homework or in class. The Grammar reference and Wordlist pages help students to review and keep a record of the language they have studied as they go through the course. The CD-ROM, which can be used on PC or Macintosh platforms, can be used either in school computer rooms or privately at home.

Coursebook organisation

Each level of *Move* contains three stand-alone teaching modules, each of which focuses on one overall topic, such as 'Taste' or 'Motion'. The language is recycled and tested within the module. The main advantage of this is that students joining the course at a later stage are not disadvantaged if, for instance, they start their studies from the second module.

Each module contains four main teaching units and a review unit. The four main teaching units each take one aspect of the module's overall topic. So, for instance, the 'Taste' module has topics that include films, food and clothes.

The key features of the main teaching units are:

A **Lead-in activity** at the start of every unit. The purpose of the Lead-in is to activate the topic by drawing on students' knowledge and curiosity.

Stimulating **reading texts**. These occur at least once in each unit and include a mixture of global, gist and detailed information tasks. Recognising the importance of authenticity, the texts are based on authentic sources such as magazine and internet articles and book extracts, and are chosen to be appropriate for use with Pre-intermediate students. Students are encouraged to engage with and react to the texts on a personal level. The main reading texts in each unit are recorded to give you the flexibility to use an alternative means of presentation, or for the students to listen and read simultaneously. This can consolidate pronunciation features such as word and sentence stress and intonation, as well as helping students to adjust to the normal speed at which English is spoken.

Stimulating **listening activities**. These occur at least once in each unit and include carefully graded main listening tasks as well as student-to-student listening and speaking interaction. Skills covered include prediction, global and gist listening as well as listening for detail. The Listening scripts are reproduced at the end of each module. There are also dedicated pronunciation tasks for all modules.

A **Language study section**. This draws from the reading and listening texts and follows a guided discovery approach. As well as work on traditional grammar such as tenses and word order, the Language study sections also cover broader language considerations such as politeness and register, how to express particular ideas or how to modify language. The sequence of tasks moves from more controlled to freer practice.

Vocabulary input and practice sections. These occur at least once in each unit and draw from the reading and listening texts. They include topic-based lexical sets and other useful language items such as phrasal verbs, phrases, expressions and collocations.

Speaking activities. These occur in a number of sections within every unit and include pairwork and small and larger group discussion opportunities. The speaking activities give the students the chance to respond personally to texts and issues. There are also more substantial speaking activities such as role-plays and presentations.

Writing activities. There is at least one major task in every module, and in most cases there are two. The writing tasks are integrated with other skills work in order to help students to plan and prepare for the written task. There is a variety of writing genres, which are chosen as practical examples of writing tasks students are likely to come across in everyday life. These include emails and film reviews.

CD-ROM practice at the end of each main teaching unit. This includes four corresponding activities for each unit. (For more details see below.)

The sequence of activity types within units varies to reflect the nature of the material.

The **Review units** focus on the main language presented in the preceding four main teaching units and recycle it through reading and listening texts, speaking activities and games. Review units also feature a song related to the module theme, with a short factfile about the singer / writer. There is also an extended production task, such as a role-play or survey, using language from the module.

Extra practice pages, which are at the end of each module, offer a chance for further practice and consolidation of the grammar and vocabulary in each unit.

Grammar reference sections, which support each Language study section, are at the end of each module.

A **Wordlist** for each unit with phonetic spellings, is at the end of each module.

Flexibility

One of the key benefits of *Move* is that as teachers you can combine the core and additional course material to suit your teaching situation and the needs and interests of your students. Each module contains 15 hours of core teaching material (three hours per unit). Therefore using just the core material for each level provides a course of around 45 hours' study. But in addition, you can supplement this with the following additional materials and resources and potentially expand the course to over 90 hours:

Extra practice pages. These can be completed for homework or in class, during or at the end of each unit.

CD-ROM (see below).

Teacher's Book optional activities. Throughout this Teacher's Book there are suggestions for additional optional activities to consolidate and extend the language being taught.

Teacher's Book resources. For each of the main teaching units there are two photocopiable worksheets offering different kinds of practice (see below).

Tests. There are photocopiable progress tests for the end of each unit, and more substantial tests for the end of each module. There is also a placement test (see below).

Common European Framework (CEF) links

There is a dedicated section in this Teacher's Book which explains how *Move* links to the CEF (see pages 9–20). Essentially, this section explains what the CEF is, introduces a photocopiable, detailed mapping document and photocopiable student checklists for each unit that students can use as part of their Biography. These checklists also draw on the 'Can do' learning aims which appear at the start of each unit of the Coursebook.

The CD-ROM contains one activity per unit which expressly links to the student checklists. Additionally the Markbook feature allows marks for each of the activities to be recorded and printed so that students can add these to their dossiers, and you can also check progress. The Bookmark and Wordlist features also allow students to save their own wordlists or to access particular activities directly. Again, this can be used to contribute towards the student's Biography, and it encourages learner independence.

Other components

Class CD set

There are two CDs in the set. CD1 contains the listening material for the first and second modules, while CD2 contains material for the third module. All recorded listening material for the core course, which includes listening and pronunciation activities, is shown with the symbol, with the corresponding track number set out alongside the activity in the Coursebook. Optional listening activities, ie the main reading tasks, are shown by the symbol. The Listening scripts are set out in the reference material at the end of each module in the Coursebook and, for convenience, in the teaching notes in this Teacher's Book.

CD-ROM

There are four activities for each of the main units. These provide further practice of language presented in the unit:

Language study activity – focusing on language presented in the Language study.

Vocabulary – recycling language presented in the Vocabulary sections.

'Can do' activity – focusing on one of the main 'Can do' statements in the Common European Framework student checklists. These include reading, listening and writing activities.

Language game – drawing on language from the unit, these are highly interactive, fun activities in which students have to perform tasks such as beating the clock, chasing a villain, or saving someone from meeting a terrible fate.

The CD-ROM contains a useful Help section which shows students how to use it. Additionally, the Markbook feature allows students to record and update their results, as well as to print them out. The Bookmark feature is a space for students to create shortcuts to their favourite activities. The Wordlist feature helps students to create and organise their own wordlists. The Help section shows students how to create bookmarks and build their own learning resource.

Teacher's Book

This Teacher's Book contains a range of useful sections:

The Common European Framework section sets out how *Move* links with the CEF (see page 9).

The Teaching tips is an invaluable four-page section providing useful teaching ideas. These include suggestions for five-minute lesson warmers before opening the Coursebook, lesson closing activities and revision activities. Tips include ideas for varying speaking activities such as different ways of organising pairwork, how to lead whole class discussions and lots more.

The teaching notes provide straightforward and clear procedural notes, with answer keys and listening scripts inserted in the body of the notes for easy reference. You'll also find useful optional activities to add extra practice, cultural background notes and help with pronunciation of difficult words and phrases. The summary at the start of each unit sets out the main learning aims and content of each unit, as well as a preparation checklist for some of the optional activities. The reference section at the end of each unit shows where to find additional study material in the Coursebook and this Teacher's Book.

The Teacher's resource section comprises two parts: a Resource pack section, and a Test section:

The Resource pack contains 24 photocopiable worksheets, two for each of the main teaching units. These comprise a stand-alone discussion lesson based on the topic of the unit, and a language-oriented activity, which consolidates and extends the language presented in the unit. The discussions are deliberately intended to be challenging, so make sure you read them and check they are suitable for your class before photocopying them.

The Test section comprises three kinds of tests. The pre-course placement test is flexible and contains a half-hour multiple-choice grammar and vocabulary test, which is easily marked. It includes a suggested additional spoken interview and written task for a more comprehensive assessment of a student's level. The complete test can be administered in under one and a half hours, and is the same test for all levels of *Move*. The end of unit tests are flexible, quick tests which contain grammar, vocabulary and reading skill elements drawn from the unit. The three end of module tests are more substantial tests which assess students' progress against the main learning points in each of the preceding four main teaching units. These can be used instead of the end of unit tests or in addition to them. The end of module test also contains a listening element. All of the tests are easily marked.

We very much hope you and your students enjoy using *Move*. The range of material and resources it offers make it a unique course with enough space within each unit for students to get an impressive range of practice, and plenty of variety in their learning experience.

Jon Hird

The Common European Framework and *Move*

Introduction

The Common European Framework (CEF) is a document which has been drawn up by the Council of Europe. Its main purpose is to provide an 'open, neutral framework of reference' to help students, teachers, institutions and employers describe the stages of learning that students typically go through when they are learning a foreign language, and to establish benchmark levels of language proficiency. A range of international language qualifications can also be mapped against these benchmark levels of proficiency.

The Framework sets out six levels of language proficiency. These are A1, A2, B1, B2, C1, and C2. A1 learners are just starting to learn the language. The B1 level represents the threshold level of English and C2 learners are at a very advanced level of proficiency. Each of these levels incorporates a series of statements that describe a wide range of language skills and sub-skills. The main advantage of this is that it enables the individual student to assess their own progress in order to build up a profile of their own learning, and to set learning objectives for the future.

The series of level statements can be made more specific to the course of learning by generating a series of language descriptors that correlate to the level statements. The CEF sets out clear guidelines about how these descriptors should be formulated in Chapter 9, Assessment (pp177–196) of the *Common European Framework of Reference*, and in Appendix A: developing proficiency descriptors (pp205–216). This document can be downloaded in all European languages from:
www.coe.int.

The three criteria of assessment that the guidelines set out are:

1 Validity: what is actually assessed is what should be assessed;
2 Reliability: the accuracy of decisions; and
3 Feasibility: the assessment has to be practical.

Additionally, the guidelines advise that descriptors should be set out as follows:

- Positiveness: although it is easier, particularly at low levels, to describe what a learner can't do, rather than what they can do; if levels of proficiency are to serve as objectives rather than just an instrument for screening candidates, then it is desirable to use positive descriptors.
- Definiteness: descriptors should describe concrete tasks and / or degrees of skill in performing tasks.
- Clarity: descriptors should be transparent, not jargon laden.
- Brevity: no individual student is typical. A range of shorter descriptors helps both students and teachers to identify what is being assessed. Descriptors that are longer than a two-clause sentence cannot realistically be used accurately. Teachers also consistently prefer short descriptors.
- Independence: descriptors that are likely to describe a behaviour about which one can say 'Yes, this person can do this' can be used as independent criteria statements in checklists, self-assessment or teacher continuous assessment. Independent descriptors offer greater integrity to those forms of assessment.

The CEF also introduces the concept of a student portfolio. A student portfolio can consist of three strands. Firstly, a language 'Passport' will incorporate the formal qualifications that a student has successfully completed, along with details of courses completed. Secondly, the portfolio contains a personal 'Biography' which can contain notes about what the student found easy or difficult and a record of his or her learning experience. The third element is a 'Dossier', which can contain individual pieces of a student's writing in a foreign language as well as recordings of the student speaking it.

The approach used in *Move*

The key point is that no coursebook can accurately claim that by completing the activities contained within it a student will have attained a given level of the CEF. *Move* is a short course which has been comprehensively mapped against appropriate levels of the Framework. In completing the course, students are offered a range of activities that are consistent with the aims of the Framework, and which contribute significantly towards the learning progress that a student will make.

CEF mapping document

In the case of *Move Pre-intermediate*, the course has been mapped against statements at the A2 / B1 levels of attainment. The photocopiable mapping document which follows this introduction uses statements taken from the CEF and provides instances from the course where each skill and sub-skill is presented and practised. The main purpose of this is to provide teachers with a detailed overview of how *Move* relates to the various skills and sub-skills identified in the CEF.

CEF student portfolio checklists

The second set of documents is a series of photocopiable student portfolio checklists, one for each of the main teaching units of the course. We have followed the guidelines contained within the CEF to generate the descriptors within each of these checklists, and these are linked in turn to the level statements. The purpose of these checklists is to enable students to reflect at the end of each unit in the Coursebook, and related CD-ROM activities, on the level of proficiency that they have reached for each of the skills and sub-skills that are set out. The main purpose of the checklists is to provide the students with a record of their ongoing self-assessment, as part of their portfolio Biography.

In completing the student portfolio checklists students can assess how successful they have been, what they need more practice in, and what specific help they could ask their teacher for.

Levels of learning:

1 = a very low level of understanding. The student may recognise the item but not be able to use it at all.
2 = understands and can use a little.
3 = understands and can manipulate the item fairly well.
4 = understands, can self-correct and manipulate the item appropriately most of the time.
5 = the learner has passive understanding, appropriate selection and accurate active use of the item.

How to use the checklists:

1. Once you have completed a unit, give your students a photocopy of the relevant checklist. Avoid giving the impression that you are testing them.
2. Ask students to take the list home and think it over.
3. In the following lesson discuss any points that the students raise.
4. After each review unit ask students to look at the four checklists for that module again and update their assessments.
5. Ask students to keep their checklists and file them with their self-assessment documentation as part of their portfolio.

Coursebook links to the CEF

As well as the photocopiable material contained within this section of the Teacher's Book, there are a number of other 'tools' that *Move* incorporates as part of an integrated approach towards the European Framework. Each module of the course begins with a Contents map which sets out the content of each of the syllabus strands of the course. *Move* has a multi-stranded syllabus which is consistent with the range of skills and sub-skills set out in the CEF.

Additionally, the main learning aims of each of the teaching units are expressed as 'Can do' descriptors. These are replicated in the student portfolio checklists, thus ensuring that what is presented is also what is being assessed.

Revision and testing

The importance of revision work in recycling new language cannot be underestimated. Each module of *Move* contains a review unit, and we recommend that as part of the review process students revisit their student portfolio checklists and re-evaluate their self-assessment after completing each review unit.

This Teacher's Book also contains a comprehensive, photocopiable test section. The placement test provides a benchmark pre-course record of attainment, and there are end of unit and end of module progress tests which can contribute either towards an overall end of course grade, as part of the student portfolio Passport, or, alternatively be integrated into the student's Dossier.

CD-ROM links to the CEF

The CD-ROM contains at least one activity for each unit which has been specifically written to provide further support for one of the descriptors set out in the student portfolio checklists. Other activities for each unit are also consistent with the learning aims recorded on the checklists.

The Markbook feature of the CD-ROM allows students to print out their end scores for the activities, and provides a further record of how the student is performing against the descriptors set out in the student portfolio checklist as well as an invaluable document for the student's Dossier.

Concluding remarks

The comprehensive approach in *Move* to the Common European Framework reflects the overall aim of the Framework to provide an ongoing practical and accurate assessment of the level of language proficiency that a student has attained. The 'tools' provided for both teachers and students to record progress allow for a flexible approach which can be tailored to reflect the level of detail needed by individual students and educational institutions.

CEF mapping

Descriptor	Page of CEF	Pages of *Move Pre-intermediate* containing practice for this descriptor
GLOBAL		
Range (vocabulary)		
A2: Can produce brief everyday expressions in order to satisfy simple needs of a concrete type: personal details, daily routines, wants and needs, requests for information.	110	4, 7, 9, 22, 23, 35, 40, 54, 55, 83, 86, 87
A2: Has a limited repertoire of short memorised phrases covering predictable survival situations; frequent breakdowns and misunderstandings occur in non-routine situations.	110	2, 9, 22, 23, 40, 41, 54, 55, 86, 87
B1: Has enough language to get by, with sufficient vocabulary to express him / herself with some hesitation and circumlocutions on topics such as family, hobbies and interests, work, travel, and current events, but lexical limitations cause repetition and even difficulty with formulation at times.	29, 110, 112	9, 13, 15, 18, 19, 24, 25, 47, 50, 56, 57, 78, 83, 88, 89
Accuracy (grammar)		
A2: Uses some simple structures correctly, but still systematically makes basic mistakes, eg tends to mix up tenses and forget to mark agreement; nevertheless, it is usually clear what he / she is trying to say.	114	4, 7, 9, 12, 16, 22, 23, 36, 43, 54, 55, 68, 75, 86, 87
B1: Uses reasonably accurately a repertoire of frequently used 'routines' and patterns associated with more predictable situations.	29, 114	7, 9, 12, 16, 18, 24, 25, 43, 47, 48, 51, 56, 57, 76, 80, 83, 88, 89
Pronunciation		
A2: Pronunciation is generally clear enough to be understood despite a noticeable foreign accent, but conversational partners will need to ask for repetition from time to time.	117	7, 40, 69
B1: Pronunciation is clearly intelligible even if a foreign accent is sometimes evident and occasional mispronunciations occur.	117	7, 40, 69
Sociolinguistic appropriateness (function / register)		
A2: Can handle very short social exchanges, using everyday polite forms of greeting and address.	122	5, 37, 40
A2: Can make and respond to invitations, suggestions, apologies, etc.	122	4, 12, 37, 40
B1: Is aware of the salient politeness conventions and acts appropriately.	122	12, 16, 44, 45, 78, 81
B1: Is aware of, and looks out for signs of, the most significant differences between the customs, usages, attitudes, values and beliefs prevalent in the community concerned and those of his or her own.	122	45, 66, 69, 81
Fluency		
A2: Can make him / herself understood in very short utterances, even though pauses, false starts and reformulation are very evident.	29	2, 5, 6, 9, 37
A2: Can expand learned phrases through simple recombinations of their elements.	124	2, 5, 9, 18, 37
B1: Can exploit a wide range of simple language flexibly to express much of what he / she wants.	124	53, 81
Interaction		
A2: Can answer questions and respond to simple statements.	29	2, 5, 9, 41
B1: Can initiate, maintain and close simple face-to-face conversation on topics that are familiar or of personal interest.	29	53, 67
B1: Can repeat back part of what someone has said to confirm mutual understanding.	29	53, 67, 76
Coherence		
A2: Can link groups of words with simple connectors like 'and', 'but' and 'because'.	29, 125	9
A2: Can tell a story or describe something in a simple list of points.	125	5, 6, 7
B1: Can link a series of shorter, discrete simple elements into a connected, linear sequence of points.	29, 125	66, 80
B1: Can reasonably fluently relate a straightforward narrative or description as a linear sequence of points.	125	76
B1: Can convey simple, straightforward information of immediate relevance, getting across which point he / she feels is most important.	129	81

Descriptor	Page of CEF	Pages of *Move Pre-intermediate* containing practice for this descriptor
LISTENING		
General		
A2: Can understand phrases and the highest frequency vocabulary related to areas of most immediate personal relevance (eg very basic personal and family information, shopping, local area, employment).	26	5, 9, 37, 40, 69
A2: Can catch the main point in short, clear, simple messages and announcements.	26	37
B1: Can understand the main points of clear standard speech on familiar matters regularly encountered in work, school, leisure etc, including short narratives.	26, 66	6, 16, 18, 45, 50, 76, 78, 85
Conversation between native speakers		
B1: Can generally follow the main points of extended discussion around him / her, provided speech is clearly articulated in standard dialect.	66	16, 18, 49, 50, 76, 78, 85
As member of live audience		
B1: Can follow in outline straightforward short talks on familiar topics provided these are delivered in clearly articulated standard speech.	67	21
Audio media and recordings		
A2: Can understand and extract the essential information from short, recorded passages dealing with predictable everyday matters which are delivered slowly and clearly.	67	5, 6, 13, 37, 40, 45, 69
B1: Can understand the main points of radio news bulletins and simpler recorded material about familiar subjects delivered relatively slowly and clearly.	68	13, 16, 18, 20, 45, 49, 50, 52, 76, 78, 84, 85
READING		
General		
A2: Can find specific, predictable information in simple everyday material such as advertisements, prospectuses, menus and timetables and understand short simple personal letters.	26	12, 14, 34
A2: Can understand short, simple texts containing the highest frequency vocabulary, including a proportion of shared international vocabulary items.	69	2, 8, 10, 34, 66
B1: Can understand texts that consist mainly of high-frequency everyday or job-related language.	26	11, 14, 20, 38, 42, 46, 52, 74, 84
B1: Can read straightforward factual texts on subjects related to his / her field and interest with a satisfactory level of comprehension.	69	11, 14, 20, 38, 42, 46, 52, 74, 79, 84
B1: Can extrapolate the meaning of occasional unknown words from the context and deduce sentence meaning provided the topic discussed is familiar.	72	11, 14, 20, 38, 42, 46, 48, 52, 74, 79
Correspondence		
A2: Can understand short simple personal letters.	69	12
B1: Can understand the description of events, feelings and wishes in personal letters well enough to correspond regularly with a pen friend.	69	14, 74
For orientation		
A2: Can find specific, predictable information in simple everyday material such as advertisements, prospectuses, menus, reference lists and timetables.	70	34
B1: Can find and understand relevant information in everyday material, such as letters, brochures and short official documents.	70	79
For information and argument		
A2: Can identify specific information in simpler written material he / she encounters such as letters, brochures and short newspaper articles describing events.	70	2, 11, 34, 38
B1: Can recognise significant points in straightforward newspaper articles on familiar subjects.	70	14, 38, 42, 79, 84
SPOKEN INTERACTION		
General		
A2: Can identify what he / she means by pointing to it (eg 'I'd like this, please').	64	10, 67
A2: Can communicate in simple and routine tasks requiring a simple and direct exchange of information on familiar and routine matters to do with work and free time.	26, 74	3, 5, 6, 9, 13, 69
A2: Can handle very short social exchanges but is rarely able to understand enough to keep conversation going of his / her own accord.	26, 74	2, 5, 6, 9, 35, 67

Descriptor	Page of CEF	Pages of *Move Pre-intermediate* containing practice for this descriptor
B1: Can deal with most situations likely to arise whilst travelling in an area where the language is spoken.	26	16, 17, 44, 75, 77, 78, 81
B1: Can initiate, maintain and close simple face-to-face conversation on topics that are familiar or of personal interest.	29	15, 18, 46, 53, 85
B1: Can repeat back part of what someone has said to confirm mutual understanding.	29	17, 21, 75, 76, 77, 85
B1: Can work out how to communicate the main point(s) he / she wants to get across, exploiting any resources available and limiting the message to what he / she can recall or find the means to express.	64	9, 15, 17, 21, 41, 53, 77
Understanding a native speaker		
A2: Can understand what is said clearly, slowly and directly to him / her in simple everyday conversation; can be made to understand, if the speaker can take the trouble.	75	5, 37, 40
B1: Can follow clearly articulated speech directed at him / her in everyday conversation, though will sometimes have to ask for repetition of particular words and phrases.	75	16, 18, 50, 78
Conversation		
A2: Can handle very short social exchanges but is rarely able to understand enough to keep conversation going of his / her own accord, though he / she can be made to understand if the speaker will take the trouble.	76	5, 6, 9, 35, 37, 69
A2: Can make and respond to invitations, suggestions and apologies.	76	37
A2: Can say what he / she likes and dislikes.	76	4, 6, 9, 50
B1: Can follow clearly articulated speech directed at him / her in everyday conversation, though will sometimes have to ask for repetition of particular words and phrases.	76	16, 53
B1: Can maintain a conversation or discussion but may sometimes be difficult to follow when trying to say exactly what he / she would like to.	76	15, 46, 53
Informal discussion (with friends)		
A2: Can discuss everyday practical issues in a simple way when addressed clearly, slowly and directly.	77	3, 5, 7, 9, 35, 37, 69
B1: Can give or seek personal views and opinions in discussing topics of interest.	77	9, 17, 39
B1: Can make his / her opinions and reactions understood as regards solutions to problems or practical questions of where to go, what to do, how to organise an event.	77	17
B1: Can express belief, opinion, agreement and disagreement politely.	77	4, 9, 13, 17, 39
Goal-oriented co-operation		
A2: Can indicate when he / she is following and can be made to understand what is necessary, if the speaker takes the trouble.	79	6, 9
A2: Can communicate in simple and routine tasks using simple phrases to ask for and provide things, to get simple information and to discuss what to do next.	79	3, 6, 7, 9
B1: Can generally follow what is said and, when necessary, can repeat back part of what someone has said to confirm mutual understanding.	79	17, 21, 75, 77, 85
B1: Can invite others to give their views on how to proceed.	79	21, 53, 75, 85
Transactions for goods and services		
A2: Can give and receive information about quantities, numbers, prices, etc.	80	43
A2: Can order a meal.	80	44
B1: Can deal with most transactions likely to arise whilst travelling, arranging travel or accommodation, or dealing with authorities during a foreign visit.	80	17, 44, 77
B1: Can make a complaint.	80	78, 81
Information exchange		
A2: Can communicate in simple and routine tasks requiring a simple and direct exchange of information.	81	2, 3, 5, 6, 7, 9, 35, 37
A2: Can ask for and provide personal information.	81	5, 7, 13, 35, 37, 53
B1: Can find out and pass on straightforward factual information.	81	21, 53, 77, 85
Interviews		
A2: Can answer simple questions and respond to simple statements in an interview.	82	5, 7, 35, 38, 41
B1: Can take some initiatives in an interview / consultation (eg to bring up a new subject) but is very dependent on interviewer in the interaction.	82	18, 21, 53, 77, 85

Descriptor	Page of CEF	Pages of *Move Pre-intermediate* containing practice for this descriptor
Turntaking		
A2: Can ask for attention.	86, 124	5, 6, 9, 35, 69
B1: Can initiate, maintain and close simple, face-to-face conversation on topics that are familiar or of personal interest.	86, 124	53, 85
Clarification		
B1: Can ask someone to clarify or elaborate what they have just said.	87	17, 21, 53, 76, 77, 85
SPOKEN PRODUCTION		
General		
A2: Can give a simple description or presentation of people, living or working conditions, daily routines, likes / dislikes, etc as a short series of simple phrases and sentences linked into a list.	58	4, 6, 9, 37
B1: Can connect phrases in a simple way in order to describe experiences and events, dreams, hopes and ambitions.	26	17, 21, 53
B1: Can briefly give reasons and explanations for opinions and plans.	26	17, 21, 53
Sustained monologue		
A2: Can describe his / her family, living conditions, educational background, present or most recent job.	59	6
B1: Can give straightforward descriptions on a variety of familiar subjects within his / her field of interest.	59	21, 53
B1: Can reasonably fluently relate a straightforward narrative or description as a linear sequence of points.	59	21, 53
B1: Can give detailed accounts of experiences, describing feelings and reactions.	59	17, 21
Addressing audiences		
A2: Can give a short, rehearsed, basic presentation on a familiar subject.	60	6, 9, 37
B1: Can give a prepared straightforward presentation on a familiar topic within his / her field which is clear enough to be followed without difficulty most of the time, and in which the main points are explained with reasonable precision.	60	17, 21, 53
WRITING		
General		
A2: Can write a very simple personal letter, eg thanking someone for something.	26	12
A2: Can write a series of simple phrases and sentences about their family, living conditions, educational background, present or most recent job.	62	7
B1: Can write simple connected text on topics which are familiar or of personal interest.	26	41, 49
B1: Can write straightforward connected texts on a range of familiar subjects within his field of interest, by linking a series of shorter discrete elements into a linear sequence.	61	41, 49, 81
Written interaction		
A2: Can write short, simple formulaic notes relating to matters in areas of immediate need.	83	3, 12
Correspondence		
B1: Can write personal letters describing experiences, feelings and events in some detail.	83	49
Notes, messages and forms		
A2: Can write short, simple notes and messages relating to matters in areas of immediate need.	84	3, 12
B1: Can write notes conveying simple information of immediate relevance to friends, service people, teachers and others who feature in his / her everyday life, getting across comprehensibly the points he / she feels are important.	84	21
Processing text		
A2: Can pick out and reproduce key words and phrases or short sentences from a short text within the learner's limited competence and experience.	96	12
B1: Can collate short pieces of information from several sources and summarise them for somebody else.	96	81
B1: Can paraphrase short written passages in a simple fashion, using the original text wording and ordering.	96	66
Spelling		
B1: Can produce continuous writing which is generally intelligible throughout.	118	49

CEF student checklists

Module 1 Unit 1 I know what I like

Complete the checklist. Add an extra activity you have done in class or at home.
1 = I can do this with a lot of help from my teacher 2 = I can do this with a little help
3 = I can do this fairly well 4 = I can do this really well 5 = I can do this almost perfectly

Competences	Page	Exercise	Your score
Language quality			
I can understand and use very common phrasal verbs.	2	Reading and vocabulary 4–5	1 2 3 4 5
Spoken interaction			
I can discuss child development.	2–3	Reading and vocabulary 3, 6–8	1 2 3 4 5
I can agree and disagree.	4	Language study 1–3, 6–7	1 2 3 4 5
I can discuss a familiar topic in simple terms.	2	Lead-in 1	1 2 3 4 5
Spoken production			
I can express likes and dislikes.	4	Language study 2–5, CD-ROM	1 2 3 4 5
I can talk about sports and leisure activities.	4–5	Vocabulary 1–2, Listening 2	1 2 3 4 5
I can talk about types of film and styles of music.	4–5	Vocabulary 1–2, Listening 2	1 2 3 4 5
I can ask for and give personal information.	5	Speaking 1–3	1 2 3 4 5
Reading			
I can understand the main information in simple texts.	2	Reading and vocabulary 1–2	1 2 3 4 5
Listening			
I can identify key information in a simple conversation.	5	Listening 1–3	1 2 3 4 5
Strategies			
I can rank and classify vocabulary to remember it better.	3	Reading and vocabulary 7–8	1 2 3 4 5
Your own extra activity			1 2 3 4 5

Module 1 Unit 2 Innovation

Complete the checklist. Add an extra activity you have done in class or at home.
1 = I can do this with a lot of help from my teacher 2 = I can do this with a little help
3 = I can do this fairly well 4 = I can do this really well 5 = I can do this almost perfectly

Competences	Page	Exercise	Your score
Language quality			
I can distinguish the past simple and past continuous tenses.	7	Language study 1–3	1 2 3 4 5
I can correctly pronounce regular past tense endings.	7	Pronunciation 1–3	1 2 3 4 5
I can make phrases using *make* and *do*.	9	Vocabulary 1–3	1 2 3 4 5
Spoken interaction			
I can discuss the relative importance of a range of factors.	6	Lead-in 2	1 2 3 4 5
I can discuss the importance of inventions.	9	Speaking 1–2	1 2 3 4 5
Spoken production			
I can talk about admirable people.	6	Lead-in 1–2	1 2 3 4 5
I can connect simple sentences to tell a story.	6	Listening 5	1 2 3 4 5
I can talk about past events.	7	Language study 1–3, Pronunciation 1–3	1 2 3 4 5
Reading			
I can understand the main information in a short article.	8	Reading 1–3	1 2 3 4 5
Listening			
I can identify the main information in a factual radio interview.	6	Listening 1–5	1 2 3 4 5
I can recognise regular past tense endings (*-ed*).	7	Pronunciation 1–3, CD-ROM	1 2 3 4 5
Strategies			
I can predict the meanings of words from their context.	9	Reading 4–5	1 2 3 4 5
Your own extra activity			1 2 3 4 5

Module 1 Unit 3 The sixth sense

Complete the checklist. Add an extra activity you have done in class or at home.
1 = I can do this with a lot of help from my teacher 2 = I can do this with a little help
3 = I can do this fairly well 4 = I can do this really well 5 = I can do this almost perfectly

Competences	Page	Exercise	Your score
Language quality I can use modals of obligation.	12	Language study 1–6	1 2 3 4 5
Spoken interaction I can discuss psychic powers.	10	Reading 3	1 2 3 4 5
Spoken production I can express necessity and advice. I can describe people using character adjectives.	12 13	Language study 1–6 Vocabulary and speaking 1–2, CD-ROM	1 2 3 4 5 1 2 3 4 5
Reading I can understand the gist of a questionnaire and the explanation of its results. I can understand simple definitions. I can read a simple personal email.	10 10–11 12	Lead-in 1–2 Reading 1–2 Writing 1	1 2 3 4 5 1 2 3 4 5 1 2 3 4 5
Listening I can identify particular information in a lengthy radio report.	13	Listening 1–4	1 2 3 4 5
Writing I can write a simple personal email.	12	Writing 1–2	1 2 3 4 5
Strategies I can fix new vocabulary by applying it to my own situation.	13	Vocabulary and speaking 1–2	1 2 3 4 5
Your own extra activity			1 2 3 4 5

Module 1 Unit 4 What do you do?

Complete the checklist. Add an extra activity you have done in class or at home.
1 = I can do this with a lot of help from my teacher 2 = I can do this with a little help
3 = I can do this fairly well 4 = I can do this really well 5 = I can do this almost perfectly

Competences	Page	Exercise	Your score
Language quality I can use *will* and *won't* appropriately.	16–17	Language study 1–7	1 2 3 4 5
Spoken interaction I can make promises, requests and predictions.	17	Speaking 1–3	1 2 3 4 5
Spoken production I can talk about jobs and career choices. I can rehearse and perform a short role-play.	15 17	Lead-in 1, Reading 1–4, Vocabulary 1–4 Speaking 1–4	1 2 3 4 5 1 2 3 4 5
Reading I can understand texts about work experiences. I can identify main information in a text.	14 15	Reading 1, CD-ROM Reading 2	1 2 3 4 5 1 2 3 4 5
Listening I can make predictions about the context of an informal conversation between native speakers. I can identify key information in a conversation.	16 16	Listening 1–3 Listening 1–3	1 2 3 4 5 1 2 3 4 5
Writing I can write a short dialogue together with a partner.	17	Speaking 1–4	1 2 3 4 5
Strategies I can use images to help me predict the content of a text.	14	Reading 1	1 2 3 4 5
Your own extra activity			1 2 3 4 5

Module 2 Unit 1 Don't breathe a word!

Complete the checklist. Add an extra activity you have done in class or at home.
1 = I can do this with a lot of help from my teacher 2 = I can do this with a little help
3 = I can do this fairly well 4 = I can do this really well 5 = I can do this almost perfectly

Competences	Page	Exercise	Your score
Language quality			
I can distinguish and use the past simple and the present perfect simple.	36–7	Language study 1–9	1 2 3 4 5
Spoken interaction			
I can respond appropriately with rehearsed phrases to surprising information.	37	Listening and speaking 5	1 2 3 4 5
I can discuss my own habits and values in simple terms.	34	Lead-in 1	1 2 3 4 5
Spoken production			
I can use phrases to talk about quantity.	34	Reading 3	1 2 3 4 5
I can talk about friendship and rumour.	35	Vocabulary 1–5	1 2 3 4 5
I can talk about recent events.	36–7	Language study 1–9	1 2 3 4 5
I can use phrases to talk about time.	36–7	Language study 1–9	1 2 3 4 5
Reading			
I can identify key information in a brief report.	34	Reading 1–4	1 2 3 4 5
I can understand simple statistical information.	34	Reading 1–4	1 2 3 4 5
Listening			
I can complete details of events from a recorded telephone conversation.	37	Listening and speaking 1–7	1 2 3 4 5
I can listen and respond to news about other people.	37	Listening and speaking 1–7, CD-ROM	1 2 3 4 5
Strategies			
I can notice which words combine into common phrases and then use those phrases.	35	Vocabulary 1–5	1 2 3 4 5
Your own extra activity			1 2 3 4 5

Module 2 Unit 2 Pass the popcorn, please

Complete the checklist. Add an extra activity you have done in class or at home.
1 = I can do this with a lot of help from my teacher 2 = I can do this with a little help
3 = I can do this fairly well 4 = I can do this really well 5 = I can do this almost perfectly

Competences	Page	Exercise	Your score
Language quality			
I can use appropriate intonation in expressing a strong opinion.	40	Listening and pronunciation 1–4	1 2 3 4 5
I can qualify adjectives with reinforcing adverbs.	40	Listening and pronunciation 1–4	1 2 3 4 5
I can use appropriate expressions for agreeing and disagreeing.	40	Language study 1–5	1 2 3 4 5
Spoken interaction			
I can ask for and give opinions.	40	Language study 1–5	1 2 3 4 5
I can use appropriate register in an informal discussion.	40	Language study 1–5	1 2 3 4 5
I can discuss the strengths and weaknesses of a film.	41	Speaking and writing 1–3	1 2 3 4 5
Spoken production			
I can describe different elements of a film.	38; 41	Lead-in 1–3, Reading 1–7; Vocabulary 1–4	1 2 3 4 5
I can use a range of common functional expressions to express personal opinions.	40	Language study 1–5	1 2 3 4 5
Reading			
I can understand the main ideas of a simple film review.	39–40	Reading 1–7	1 2 3 4 5
Listening			
I can identify descriptions.	40	Listening and pronunciation 1–4	1 2 3 4 5
Writing			
I can write a film review.	41	Speaking and writing 2, CD-ROM	1 2 3 4 5
Strategies			
I can follow a model text when writing a text of my own.	41	Speaking and writing 2	1 2 3 4 5
Your own extra activity			1 2 3 4 5

Module 2 Unit 3 You must try it

Complete the checklist. Add an extra activity you have done in class or at home.
1 = I can do this with a lot of help from my teacher 2 = I can do this with a little help
3 = I can do this fairly well 4 = I can do this really well 5 = I can do this almost perfectly

Competences	Page	Exercise	Your score
Language quality			
I can use quantifiers to talk about food.	43	Language study 1–9	1 2 3 4 5
I can distinguish countable and uncountable nouns.	43	Language study 1–9	1 2 3 4 5
I can use appropriate polite language.	44	Vocabulary 1–5	1 2 3 4 5
Spoken interaction			
I can predict and then obtain personal information in a simple prepared interview.	43	Language study 5–9	1 2 3 4 5
I can order food in restaurants.	44	Vocabulary 1–5, CD-ROM	1 2 3 4 5
I can make an effort to adapt to new cultural situations.	45	Listening and speaking 1–2	1 2 3 4 5
I can discuss good and bad manners.	45	Listening and speaking 3	1 2 3 4 5
Spoken production			
I can talk about food.	42	Lead-in 1, Reading 3	1 2 3 4 5
Reading			
I can understand main ideas in a text.	42	Reading 1–3	1 2 3 4 5
Listening			
I can identify correct information from a recording.	45	Listening and speaking 1–2	1 2 3 4 5
Writing			
I can complete sentences to build a summary of a short article.	42	Reading 2	1 2 3 4 5
Strategies			
I can work with others to practise appropriate responses.	43–44	Language study 6–9	1 2 3 4 5
Your own extra activity			1 2 3 4 5

Module 2 Unit 4 Followers of fashion

Complete the checklist. Add an extra activity you have done in class or at home.
1 = I can do this with a lot of help from my teacher 2 = I can do this with a little help
3 = I can do this fairly well 4 = I can do this really well 5 = I can do this almost perfectly

Competences	Page	Exercise	Your score
Language quality			
I can understand how to work out the meanings of phrasal verbs from a dictionary.	47–48	Language study 1–7	1 2 3 4 5
I can recognise and use phrasal verbs.	48	Language study 9	1 2 3 4 5
I can understand the syntax of phrasal verbs.	48	Language study 4–9	1 2 3 4 5
I can use a dictionary to distinguish transitive from intransitive verbs.	48	Language study 5, 8	1 2 3 4 5
Spoken interaction			
I can discuss beauty and body decoration.	46; 47	Lead-in 1; Reading 3	1 2 3 4 5
I can discuss personal style and body decoration.	47; 49	Vocabulary and speaking 3; Listening and speaking 5	1 2 3 4 5
Spoken production			
I can describe appearance and clothing.	47	Vocabulary and speaking 1–3	1 2 3 4 5
Reading			
I can understand a text about beauty and decoration.	46–7	Reading 1–2, CD-ROM	1 2 3 4 5
Listening			
I can identify correct information from a recording.	49	Listening and speaking 1–4	1 2 3 4 5
I can understand descriptions of body art.	49	Listening and speaking 1–5	1 2 3 4 5
Writing			
I can write an email explaining a decision.	49	Writing 1–2	1 2 3 4 5
Strategies			
I can categorise vocabulary items in order to talk more accurately about myself and my experiences.	47	Vocabulary and speaking 1–3	1 2 3 4 5
Your own extra activity			1 2 3 4 5

Module 3 Unit 1 Get down to the rhythm

Complete the checklist. Add an extra activity you have done in class or at home.
1 = I can do this with a lot of help from my teacher 2 = I can do this with a little help
3 = I can do this fairly well 4 = I can do this really well 5 = I can do this almost perfectly

Competences	Page	Exercise	Your score
Language quality			
I can use the correct prepositions with very common verbs.	66	Reading 3	1 2 3 4 5
I can use *for* and *since* with the present perfect.	68	Language study 1–8	1 2 3 4 5
I can use time expressions correctly.	68	Language study 4–5	1 2 3 4 5
Spoken interaction			
I can identify cultural differences as expressed through styles of music.	66	Lead-in 1–4	1 2 3 4 5
Spoken production			
I can talk about musical instruments.	67	Vocabulary and speaking 1–2	1 2 3 4 5
I can produce simple questions and answers with a natural intonation and stress pattern.	69	Pronunciation 1–3	1 2 3 4 5
I can talk about music and festivals.	69	Speaking 1–2	1 2 3 4 5
Reading			
I can order a text summary.	66	Reading 4	1 2 3 4 5
Listening			
I can recognise strong and weak forms in sentences.	69	Pronunciation 2, CD-ROM	1 2 3 4 5
I can listen for the correct links between given pieces of information.	69	Listening 1–2	1 2 3 4 5
I can identify main information.	69	Listening 1–2	1 2 3 4 5
Strategies			
I can scan a long text for specific information.	66	Reading 2	1 2 3 4 5
Your own extra activity			1 2 3 4 5

Module 3 Unit 2 Just do it

Complete the checklist. Add an extra activity you have done in class or at home.
1 = I can do this with a lot of help from my teacher 2 = I can do this with a little help
3 = I can do this fairly well 4 = I can do this really well 5 = I can do this almost perfectly

Competences	Page	Exercise	Your score
Language quality			
I can use *play*, *do* and *go* with the names of sports.	70	Vocabulary and speaking 1–4, CD-ROM	1 2 3 4 5
I can make comparative and superlative statements.	71	Language study 1–5	1 2 3 4 5
I can use phrases with *get*.	73	Vocabulary 1–3	1 2 3 4 5
Spoken interaction			
I can discuss the advantages and disadvantages of a proposal.	72	Reading 3	1 2 3 4 5
I can discuss sport and exercise.	70	Lead-in 1	1 2 3 4 5
Spoken production			
I can report what I learned about someone in a discussion.	73	Vocabulary 4	1 2 3 4 5
Reading			
I can select an appropriate title for a text.	72	Reading 1	1 2 3 4 5
I can understand narrative sequence and contrast.	73	Writing 1–4	1 2 3 4 5
Listening			
I can understand key information from an informal recorded interview.	70	Listening 1–3	1 2 3 4 5
I can understand the gist of short spoken messages.	71	Language study 4–5	1 2 3 4 5
Writing			
I can apply simple spelling rules.	71	Language study 2	1 2 3 4 5
I can write a short story using sequencers.	73	Writing 3–4	1 2 3 4 5
Strategies			
I can use visual clues to predict the context of spoken language.	70	Listening 1–3	1 2 3 4 5
Your own extra activity			1 2 3 4 5

Module 3 Unit 3 On the road again

Complete the checklist. Add an extra activity you have done in class or at home.
1 = I can do this with a lot of help from my teacher 2 = I can do this with a little help
3 = I can do this fairly well 4 = I can do this really well 5 = I can do this almost perfectly

Competences	Page	Exercise	Your score
Language quality			
I can use prepositions of place.	75	Vocabulary 1–3	1 2 3 4 5
I can make phrases using *say* and *tell*.	76	Language study 1–3	1 2 3 4 5
I can report what has been said using direct or indirect speech.	76	Language study 1–3	1 2 3 4 5
Spoken interaction			
I can discuss travel and holiday preferences.	74–75	Lead-in 1, Reading 5	1 2 3 4 5
I can read and respond to written information in an interview situation, responding to the other person's answers.	77	Listening and vocabulary 5–6	1 2 3 4 5
Spoken production			
I can talk about location, accommodation and holiday activities.	77	Speaking 1–3	1 2 3 4 5
Reading			
I can understand key details of a short anecdote.	74	Reading 1–2	1 2 3 4 5
I can summarise a story.	75	Reading 3, CD-ROM	1 2 3 4 5
Listening			
I can understand the main information from a brief interview about preferences.	76–77	Listening and vocabulary 1–4	1 2 3 4 5
Strategies			
I can arrange vocabulary in tables to reveal language patterns.	75	Vocabulary 1	1 2 3 4 5
Your own extra activity			1 2 3 4 5

Module 3 Unit 4 Out and about

Complete the checklist. Add an extra activity you have done in class or at home.
1 = I can do this with a lot of help from my teacher 2 = I can do this with a little help
3 = I can do this fairly well 4 = I can do this really well 5 = I can do this almost perfectly

Competences	Page	Exercise	Your score
Language quality			
I can talk about real and imaginary situations (conditionals).	80	Language study 1–5	1 2 3 4 5
Spoken interaction			
I can buy and return goods.	81	Reading 1	1 2 3 4 5
I can make a complaint	81	Writing and speaking 1	1 2 3 4 5
I can discuss consumer issues and buying habits.	78, 79	Listening and vocabulary 6; Reading 6	1 2 3 4 5
Spoken production			
I can talk about possibility.	80–81	Language study 1–7	1 2 3 4 5
I can use shopping vocabulary.	78; 79	Listening and vocabulary 3–5, Reading 2, CD-ROM	1 2 3 4 5
Reading			
I can understand the gist of a text giving advice.	79	Reading 1–4	1 2 3 4 5
Listening			
I can understand mood and manner in a recorded dialogue.	78	Listening and vocabulary 1–2	1 2 3 4 5
Writing			
I can write a short dialogue.	81	Writing and speaking 1	1 2 3 4 5
Strategies			
I can select language appropriate to particular emotion adjectives.	81	Writing and speaking 1	1 2 3 4 5
Your own extra activity			1 2 3 4 5

Teaching tips

Starting lessons

Start the lesson with an interesting opener related to the topic of your lesson, before students open their books. The Teacher's notes give ideas for lesson warmers, for example using an opening discussion question. You could also use one of these ideas:

- Show students realia (everyday objects) related to the topic but not too obviously. Ask students to guess the topic of the lesson (for example, for Module 3, Unit 3, holidays, you could bring in a passport and rucksack).
- Ask students to describe and speculate about a magazine picture that is related to the subject of the lesson in some way.
- Write the unit title or the subject of the lesson on the board and ask students to brainstorm words connected with it. You can do this with the class for more control, or with teams of students as a competition for more fun.
- Write a word related to the unit topic on the board (for example, *home, mother, health*) and ask students what they associate with that word. This is a good way to discuss how things are seen in different cultures and the differing importance attached to them.
- Write one or two controversial statements relating to the topic on the board (for example, for Module 1, Unit 4: *There are some jobs that women shouldn't do*). Ask students to discuss the statement(s).
- Write a jumbled list of topic-related verb+noun collocations (for example, for Module 2, Unit 1 *make – friends, lose – touch*), or adjective+noun collocations (*close – friend*) on the board and ask students to match them.

Whole class work

Whole class work needs to address the needs of each student as far as possible. Here are some tips for large or mixed ability classes.

- Make sure that you know the names of everybody in the class! Ask students to make a desk name card.
- The best classroom layout of desks is usually a horseshoe shape so that all students can see and be seen.
- Ensure that every student has the chance to speak. Most students are quite happy to contribute when asked directly but some students will not offer information voluntarily.
- Make sure that everyone has understood the instructions. For more complex tasks, demonstrate the steps with a stronger student. Allow students thinking time before answering or performing a task.
- Ask weaker students easier questions so that they feel encouraged to participate in discussions.
- Do not allow stronger or more outgoing students to dominate. Encourage students to listen and show respect for each other.
- Ensure whatever you write on the board is clear and clearly visible to everybody in the class.
- Try to provide a variety of tasks that will appeal to all learning styles: visual tasks (for example, picture description and speculation, TV and video extracts, newspaper cartoons); physical response tasks (mime, drawing, acting out); audio tasks (songs, sound recognition, dictations, pronunciation tasks, rhymes); mechanical tasks (comprehension questions, gap-fills, rewriting sentences); problem-solving tasks (ranking activities, group discussion tasks requiring agreement, logic puzzles); tasks requiring creativity and imagination (role-plays, writing brochures, making posters, interpreting poems).
- If you have a wide range of ability, make sure that you have prepared extension tasks for students who work more quickly (extra questions, extra tasks, checking tasks, etc) and provide extra support for weaker students while they are doing tasks (checking, offering help, etc).

Pairwork and groupwork

Pairwork and groupwork allow students to speak more and exchange ideas and information with other students. Use these tips to ensure that students work effectively in pairs and groups.

- It is usually easier to let students work with their neighbour or neighbours. However, you can swap pairs and groups round for variety now and then by asking them to work with someone else in the class.
- To pair students randomly: make cards with pairs of words and distribute them. Students have to find their partner by asking questions or showing their card. You can use for example, two words that make a compound word (*foot, ball*); pairs of names (*Jekyll, Hyde / David, Beckham*), synonyms (*rich, wealthy*) or opposites (*rich, poor*).

For group work: give every student a letter from a set of, say, four letters (*A, B, C, D*) and then ask all *A*s to work together, all *B*s, etc.

- Always make sure students know what they have to do. Present the task clearly, using an example. You can demonstrate the tasks using open pairs: ask two students to perform the task or part of the task to the class. Check students have understood the task and allow time for questions.
- Set a time limit for the task. Make sure students know they have to stop when the time limit has been reached, even if they have not quite finished. About a minute before time runs out, warn students to try and complete their task.
- Monitor discussions. Sort out any problems, praise students and make a note of recurring errors for later discussion and correction.

Always ensure whole class feedback so that students feel their activity had a point or an end result. Ask students to report back to the class, discuss their results or ask individual pairs or groups to perform their role-play, etc to the class.

Correcting and praising

Students need to feel that they are making progress and achieving something. Encourage students as much as possible by praising them, both for effort and for achievement:

- Smile and make positive comments.
- Always begin by focusing on what students have done well before correcting mistakes.

The level of language correction necessary will depend on the type of activity you are using. Explicit and frequent correction will be necessary in accuracy tasks such as controlled grammar, pronunciation and vocabulary activities. In fluency activities and warmers, it is unnecessary to correct every mistake if students are able to convey their message. In these cases, you can correct indirectly as follows:

- Correct students by adding a comment which repeats the correct formulation or pronunciation, rather than drawing attention to the mistake directly.
- Make a note of frequent mistakes and correct them on the board with the whole class after the activity has finished.
- Ignore minor mistakes completely!

Dealing with cultural differences

The huge advantage of having multilingual or multicultural classes is that students bring a wealth of different experiences and opinions to the language class. Exploit this by:

- asking students to compare the material in their Coursebook with their own country and customs as much as possible. Ask, for example: *Do you have this tradition / type of house, etc in your country? How is the further education system different in your country?* Discussing idioms and popular sayings is often a good way to discuss the importance of things in different cultures.
- asking students to reflect on their own experiences and compare them with those of students from different countries. Ask in Module 1, Unit 2, for example: *Do you have an iPod? When did you get it? Do all young people in your country have iPods?*

However, be aware that not all students will possess the same degree of awareness about popular culture, such as famous people, famous buildings and places, music, sports, technology, etc. You can get students to share knowledge by:

- mixing students from different countries and backgrounds when doing pairwork and groupwork.
- asking the class to define potentially problematic terms or explain proper names that come up in the Coursebook material. Scan texts for these in advance.
- doing specific cultural recognition activities (for example, in Module 2, Unit 4, by asking students to give examples of what clothes are currently fashionable).

Using reading materials

- Before reading a text, students can use the photos, the title and the general look of the text to predict the content of the text and the text type. If students already have some ideas about the text before they read it, they will be able to deal with it more confidently. Predicting also motivates students to read the text to find out if their ideas are correct. Ask questions such as: *Look at the title: what does it tell you about the subject of the text? Look at the photos: who is the text about? Where does this text come from – a teenage magazine, a newspaper, a travel brochure?*
- Pre-teaching vocabulary can give students extra support when reading a text. You can pre-teach particular items from the text by deciding in advance which items might cause difficulty and writing them on the board. Or you can choose a vocabulary set which covers several items in the text, for example in Module 1, Unit 4 there is a text on working abroad which includes the words *challenges* and *homesickness*. You could pre-teach / elicit a 'working abroad' set which also includes *skills, voluntary*. You can also do word building exercises (focusing on verbs, nouns, adjectives) which include words from the text (for example, in Module 1, Unit 4, *home – homesick*, where *homesickness* is the word in the text).
- All *Move* reading texts are recorded on the CD, which means that students can listen to the text while they read it. This helps learners who prefer learning orally rather than visually and is a good pronunciation help for all students. It also means that learners have to read at a certain speed; you can let students listen and read the first time they see a text and perform a gist-reading task. Simply listening to a reading text can also be a useful alternative, particularly for 'spoken' texts such as interviews.
- Jigsaw reading tasks are a good way of exploiting reading texts in pairs and groups. Divide a text into sections; ask students to read one section, find out information and then share this information orally with their partner or group members.

- Reading texts often contain a lot of unknown vocabulary. Emphasise again and again that students don't have to understand every word! Students need to understand enough to complete the main task. Advise students to always try and work out the meaning of the word from the context if they can – by looking at the type of word (adjective, noun, verb, etc) and 'clues' about the meaning of the word in the lines before and after.
- If students need to look up the meanings of unknown words, encourage them to use a good monolingual learner dictionary. This type of dictionary gives a simple definition in English as well as an example, making the meaning clearer than a translation – which may well have several meanings. You can build dictionary work into your class (finding definitions, discussing different forms of a word, explaining dictionary abbreviations, etc) so that students can get the maximum help out of their dictionaries and become more independent learners.

Speaking

- Encourage students to speak as much as possible and stress that they should not worry about making mistakes.
- Make sure students speak with correct pronunciation and intonation. Ask students to repeat new words in class, in chorus and individually; ask students to repeat sentences from listening and reading texts or their own sentences, with correct rhythm and sentence stress.
- Speaking about concrete, personal topics is easier than discussing abstract situations. Personalise tasks as much as possible, so that all students have the chance to say something.
- Train students to use strategies to help them make the best use of the language they have. For example, you can train students to describe things when they don't know an English word using phrases such as '*It looks like a …, It's made of …, It's used for …*' (practice task: *You are in a chemist's and want to buy plasters and mouthwash, but you don't know the English words. Explain to the chemist what you need*). Teach the use of fillers such as *'Well, Actually, Anyway, What I mean to say is …'* which allows students to keep a conversation going while looking for the language to express something.
- Use pairwork for checking and comparing answers to tasks, so that students have more opportunities to speak.

Using listening materials

- Before listening, as before reading, exploit the pictures in the book and any other clues to the content of the listening text.
- Tell students not to panic if they can't understand some of what they hear. Make sure students understand that they are listening to perform a task and if they can complete the task, they have been successful.
- Encourage students to use clues in people's voices which show their feelings, age, attitudes, etc to reinforce understanding of the content.
- Allow students to listen to the material more than once, if they wish.
- You can direct students to use the listening scripts in the Coursebook to support their understanding and check answers.
- Encourage students to watch English-language TV, listen to radio and interact in English as much as possible outside their classes in order to 'tune their ear' to the English language.

Writing

- Brainstorm ideas on the board before students write to make sure all students have something to write about.
- Tell students to use any similar texts in the Coursebook as models.
- Tell students to think carefully about what they write and revise their work when they have finished: *Is it interesting? Are there any repetitions or unclear parts? Is it grammatically correct?*
- Make sure somebody reads or listens to written work: check writing tasks individually yourself; ask students to read a partner's work and check it; ask students to read out an answer or task to the whole class and the class to comment.
- The Optional activities in the Teacher's notes contain extra writing tasks which can be used both for language consolidation and for practising writing skills.

Reviewing and revising

Build in regular revision of structures and vocabulary. The Teacher's notes contain suggestions for unit-related revision activities at the end of each unit. Students can use the Grammar reference to revise or check structures at any time. They can revise vocabulary by studying the Wordlist and playing these word games:

- **Explain it:** Students work in teams of four. They write out all the nouns / adjectives / verbs in the Wordlist on small pieces of paper. They then work with another team. Teams take turns explaining words. Each member of a team must pick up a word and explain it to their team while the other team times them (1 minute). If the team gets the word in time, they get a point.
- **Categories:** Write umbrella nouns from the Wordlist on the board (for example: *sports, accessories*). Students work individually or in teams and make a list of as many words as possible which fit this category.
- **Countdown:** Write a (long) word from the Wordlist in jumbled form on the board. Teams of students try and make a word using all the letters. Follow up with students making a new word with the same letters (the team with the longest word wins).

- **Collocations:** Write a noun from the Wordlist on the board. Teams of students make lists of verbs that go with the noun (set a time limit for this). Check the collocations on the board. The team with the most correct ones wins (for example: *chess: play, watch, understand, practise, compete at, win at, lose at, like, dislike, hate, enjoy …*). You can also practise other collocations, such as noun+noun (*chess board, chess champion, chess match, chess set …*).
- **Pictionary:** Students choose a word from the Wordlist and draw a picture on the board. The class or their team guesses.
- **Comparisons:** Write two nouns from the Wordlist on the board. Students work individually or in teams. They have to compare the two things (for example, in Module 3, Unit 2: *cycling – ice hockey – Ice hockey is more exciting than cycling*).
- **Crosswords:** Students work in pairs. They make a completed crossword grid using ten words from the Wordlist. Then they make an empty, numbered grid and write clues for the words. Pairs exchange their crosswords with another pair and complete them.
- **Headlines:** Students make headlines using only the words in the list and prepositions (for example, in Module 3, Unit 4: *Fake designer angry at online auction*). They then write a short story for the headline.

Ending or filling in lessons

Sometimes you will need a short activity or game to change the pace of the lesson, end a lesson on a positive note or just provide a bit of fun. Here are a few ideas that can be used with different topic and language areas:

- **Charades:** Students mime a film, book, item of vocabulary or phrase for the class or their team to guess.
- **Bingo:** Write 20 large numbers (over 100) on the board. Students choose five and write them down. Call out the numbers on the board at random. The first student to tick off their numbers is the winner. You can also play this with categories of words or a list of unit-related words.
- **Find someone who …:** Write a list of questions on the board (*find someone who was born in the same month as you, find someone who likes cats, find someone who knows what (a word from the Wordlist) means*, etc). Students move around the class asking questions, and find at least one name for each question.
- **Picture dictation and drawing:** Describe a scene or a person. Students draw a picture. Students then compare pictures with a partner and discuss any differences. Students can also dictate pictures to each other.
- **Student's book picture dictation:** Students choose a picture in one of the units already covered in their book and describe it to the class or to a partner without showing them the picture. The class or their partner listens and then has to find the correct picture in their book.
- **Five things:** Ask students to think of five things …
  - they do well / badly
  - they hate to eat / love to do
  - that are small / disgusting / beautiful / blue / …
  - that make people embarrassed / angry / happy / … etc

Students discuss their ideas with a partner.

- **Memory game:** Bring ten objects from home or collect ten things from students in class. Hold the objects up to the class to memorise first and then put them in a dark bag or put them on the teacher's desk and cover them with a blanket. Students have to say what is in the bag or under the blanket, giving a description of each object.
- **Chinese whispers:** Whisper a fairly complex sentence to a student at the front of the class. Students take it in turns to whisper the sentence to another student. The last student writes it on the board. Whisper different sentences at intervals, so about five sentences are circulating in a clear progression. Compare the sentences on the board to the original sentences.
- **Stand in line:** Write the words of a long sentence on individual cards. Give out the cards at random to students. Students with cards go to the front of the class in turn. They show the class their word and take their place in the sentence, moving around until students form the correct sentence.
- **General knowledge quiz:** Students work in teams. They write ten general knowledge questions on the topic of the unit. Teams take turns to ask their questions.

Emergency lessons

The *Move Pre-intermediate* Teacher's Book contains 24 photocopiable resource sheets (see pages 88–117). 12 of these are one-page games and communicative activities and 12 are 45-minute discussion lessons requiring little or no preparation. Both types are linked to the topic of the units in the Coursebook and can be used as emergency lessons or activities.

Below is an idea for an emergency lesson, built around a single, simple activity. It requires no preparation and can be used at any point in the book, with any topic.

Storytime

- Explain that students are going to write a story using ten words from their Coursebook.
- Students work in small groups. Each group chooses ten words from the previous two units: three nouns, three verbs, three adjectives and one adverb. They can do this using the Wordlists for the correct module. Check the groups' lists to ensure that they have complied with the instructions.
- The groups discuss and write their story.
- Each group checks its story carefully. Encourage students to revise their work.
- The groups present their story to the class. The group can nominate one person to read out the story or they can take it in turns to read a section. They can draw pictures, use realia or make sound effects to add interest.

UNIT 1

I know what I like

Topic	Language study	Vocabulary	Main skills
• Nature or nurture (three gifted young women) • Speed-dating	• Likes and dislikes, agreeing and disagreeing	• Phrasal verbs: growing up • Sports, leisure activities, types of film and styles of music	• **Reading:** understanding main information • **Speaking:** discussing child development; asking for and giving personal information • **Listening:** identifying key information

Learning aims

- Can express likes and dislikes
- Can agree and disagree
- Can ask for and give personal information

Ideas for preparation

- photos of celebrities who became famous as children (see Warmer below)

Warmer

- Bring in photos of celebrities who became famous as children, eg Prince William, Michael Jackson, Daniel Radcliffe. If you don't have photos, write their names on the board.
- Ask: *Who are these people? What do they have in common?* (They all became famous as children.)
- Ask: *Is it good or bad to be famous when you are young?* Elicit short answers, if possible giving conflicting views, eg *You have a more interesting childhood than other children; you get rich. / You become arrogant and spoiled; it's hard to make friends because you're different.*

Nature or nurture

Lead-in

1

- Ask students to open their books on page 2. Read out the questions. Check that students understand the words *talent* and *gifted.*
- Students work in small groups and discuss the questions.
- Discuss question 3 with the class.

Reading and vocabulary

1

- **01** This text is recorded on the CD. You can use it as an alternative or in addition to the teaching notes below.
- Students look at the photos on page 3. Ask: *What talent do these people have, do you think?*
- Students read the text and check their ideas.
- Check the answers with the class.

Answers

Flavia: writing Keira: acting Marla: painting

2

- Read out the task. Check comprehension of vocabulary such as *origin* /ˈɒrɪdʒɪn/, *treat.*
- Students work individually. They read the text again and tick the boxes.
- Check the answers with the class.

Answers

1 Marla 2 Flavia 3 Keira 4 Flavia, Keira, Marla
5 Flavia, Keira 6 Flavia, Keira, Marla

3

- Students work in pairs and discuss the question.
- Students report back to the class. Do most students have similar ideas?

4

- Students work individually and match the phrasal verbs to the definitions. Encourage them to find the words in bold in the text on page 3 and use the context to help them.
- Check the answers with the class.

Answers

1 take after 2 hang out 3 go into 4 look after
5 grow up

5

- Students read the statements. Check comprehension of vocabulary such as *entertainment industry.*
- Students complete the sentences.
- Check the answers with the class.

Answers

1 grow up 2 hang out 3 go into 4 look after
5 take after

6

- Read the task and example with the class. Elicit more responses like the example, preferably agreeing and disagreeing with it.
- Students work in pairs and talk about the statements in Ex 5. Encourage them to give reasons for their answers.

Optional activity

Childhood

- Write these sentences on the board:
  1 Famous children grow up too fast.
  2 In big families with more than three children, parents can't look after all their children properly.
  3 Most children want to go into showbusiness when they grow up.
  4 Children shouldn't hang out in the streets with their friends after dark.
  5 Girls usually take after their mothers.
- Ask: *Do you agree or disagree with these statements?*
- Students discuss the sentences in small groups.
- Ask some students to report back to the class.

7

- Students read the list of conditions. Check comprehension of vocabulary such as *frequently, miss breakfast, supportive, strict.*
- Students work in pairs. In their notebooks, they copy the table and write each item from the list of conditions in either the *Helpful* or the *Unhelpful* column.
- Write *Helpful* and *Unhelpful* as column headings on the board. Go through the list and ask individual students to tell you which column to write the items in. Encourage them to give reasons for their choices, and other students to disagree with any controversial answers, especially *having a lot of money, going to bed early* and *having very strict parents.*

Suggested answers

Helpful: having a lot of money, travelling to other countries, having supportive parents, mixing with other children, going to bed early, taking regular exercise, having a lot of friends
Unhelpful: changing schools frequently, missing breakfast, eating a lot of fast food, watching a lot of TV, having very strict parents

8

- Read out the task. Rank your own top three conditions as an example and give reasons for your choices.
- Students work individually. They rank the items in their *Helpful* list, writing *1* beside the most important, *2* beside the second most important, and so on.
- Students compare their rankings with their partner. They discuss any differences and give reasons for their answers.
- Ask some students to report back to the class.

Optional activity

Pyramid discussion

- Put two pairs together to make groups of four. In their groups, students compare their rankings from Ex 8 and try to reach agreement.
- Put two groups together to make groups of eight. Again, they compare their rankings and devise a ranking that they can all agree on.
- Have a whole class discussion. See if students can decide on a final ranking that everyone is happy with.

Language study

Likes and dislikes, agreeing and disagreeing

1

- Check that students understand *agree* and *disagree.*
- Ask two students to read out dialogue 1 to the class. Ask: *Does A like painting?* (yes). *Does B like painting?* (no).
- Explain that there are two ways of pronouncing *neither:* /ˈniːðə/ or /ˈnaɪðə/.
- Ask two other students to read out dialogue 2. Ask: *Does A like fantasy novels?* (no). *Does B like fantasy novels?* (no).
- Students answer the questions.
- Check the answers with the class.

Answers

1 disagreeing 2 agreeing

2

- Students read the table and complete the gaps with *agree* or *disagree.*
- Check the answers with the class.

Answers

1 agree 2 disagree

3

- Students answer the questions individually, then compare their answers with a partner.
- Check the answers with the class.

Answers

1 *-ing* form 2 Me too. 3 Me neither. 4 *-ing* form

4

- Write the three headings, *Positive, Negative, Neutral* on the board.
- Students work in pairs and choose the correct heading for each verb.
- Check the answers with the class.

Answers

Positive: enjoy, like, love, really like
Negative: can't stand, don't like, hate, really don't like
Neutral: don't mind

5

- Check comprehension of problematic vocabulary by eliciting examples of a place on the *coast,* an *action movie,* a *horror film* or a *ball game.* Refer students to the sentences in Ex 2 to check that they are using the correct verb form.
- Students work individually and complete the sentences.
- Check the answers with the class.

Answers

1 going 2 reading 3 listening 4 watching
5 studying, learning 6 playing

6

- Read out the task.
- Students tick or cross the statements in Ex 5.

7

- Ask two students to read out the example. Then elicit a disagreement for the same statement, or give one yourself, eg *Really? I don't. I prefer going to the mountains.*
- With a weaker class, write on the board: *I really hate going to the coast.* Elicit agreement and disagreement for the statement and write them on the board.
- Refer students to the table in Ex 2. They work in pairs and complete the task.
- Ask some students to report back to the class.

Vocabulary

1

- Draw four columns on the board, with headings at the top: *Sports, Leisure activities, Types of film, Styles of music.*
- Students copy the table into their notebooks and add the words in the box.
- Write the words in the correct columns on the board as you check the answers with the class. Alternatively, ask the students to write the words on the board.
- Practise pronunciation of *reggae* /'regeɪ/, *karate* /kə'rɑːti/, *science fiction* /'saɪəns 'fɪkʃn/.

Answers
Sports: basketball, karate, tennis
Leisure activities: hanging out with friends, reading, watching TV
Types of film: comedy, horror, science fiction
Styles of music: hip-hop, rap, reggae

2

- Read out the task. Say: *I really love playing tennis* and ask one student to agree with you and one to disagree as an example.
- Students work in pairs and talk about their likes and dislikes. Go around the class and note errors.
- Ask some students to report back to the class.
- Write on the board and discuss any recurring errors.

Optional activity

Class likes

- Students work individually or in groups. They prepare a short presentation about their interests.
- Give help by breaking the presentation into stages, and asking questions to elicit information, eg *When did you start? What equipment do you need? How often do you play?* etc.
- Ask students to present their interests to the class.

Speed-dating

Listening

1

- Students work in pairs and discuss the question.
- Ask some students to report their ideas to the class.

Answer
Speed-dating is where an equal number of men and women attend a venue; each person spends a short time chatting to each member of the opposite sex. At the end, each person decides which people he / she would like to see again. The organisers facilitate an exchange of details if there is a match.

Background information

Speed-dating agencies try to have equal numbers of men and women at their events. But it is hard to find enough men to match female demand, even when women have to pay for a ticket to the event and men are paid to attend.

Interestingly, online dating agencies don't have this problem – there are more male online daters than female.

2

- **02** Explain that students are going to listen to two conversations at a speed-dating event. Make sure they understand that the first time they listen they only have to write the names in the table and answer the question.
- Students listen and write in the names at the top of the table.
- Check the answers with the class.

Answers
1 Ben 2 Layla 3 Ian
Ben and Layla could have a second date.

Listening script 02
(B = Ben, L = Layla, I = Ian)
B: Hi. What's your name?
L: Hi. I'm Layla.
B: Nice to meet you, Layla. I'm Ben. So, what do you do?
L: I'm at university at the moment.
B: Me too. What's your subject?
L: Business. It's a bit boring, but the job opportunities are good. What about you?
B: Art and design. It's OK, but I'm more into music, actually.
L: What sort of music do you like?
B: All sorts, but I'm in a band and we play a mix of reggae and hip-hop stuff. Those are our favourites, anyway.
L: Oh, really? I'm, like, the world's biggest reggae fan.
B: You should come and see us.

L: I'd love to.
B: Good, I'll give you the details later. So, what else do you like doing?
L: Well, um, when I'm not studying, I like hanging out with my friends and … [bell rings] oh …
B: I like hanging out with my friends, too. Let's talk a bit more later.
L: OK. See you later.
B: Ciao.
I: Hello, hello. My name's Ian. And you are?
L: Hi, Ian. I'm Layla.
I: Nice to meet you. I work in scientific research. It's very interesting. At the moment we're working on the DNA of a …
L: That is interesting. I'm studying business at university.
I: Ah, student days. The happiest days of your life. I remember when I was at university, I …
L: Do you have any hobbies, Ian?
I: I love going to the cinema.
L: Oh, me too. What kind of films do you like?
I: My favourite type of film is science fiction. Do you know, I even have a Stormtrooper's uniform from *Star Wars* …
L: I prefer comedies. Science fiction is not really my thing. And horror – I really like that.
I: Yes, I like old comedies. But horror, dear me, no. I can't stand horror films. They are not clever, they are not funny and they are not scary.
L: Oh, I also really like reading. I'm reading a story at the moment about a family living in …
I: Mm, I don't like reading that much. I prefer watching TV to relax. I … [bell rings] … oh, what a shame. I was enjoying that. Um, I'll see you again later, though, I hope.
L: Bye then.

3

- Check students understand the words in the table.
- Students listen again and complete the table. They don't need to put a tick or cross in every section.
- Students compare their answers with a partner.
- Check the answers with the class.

Answers

	Ben	Layla	Ian
Reggae music	✔	✔	
Hip-hop music	✔		
Hanging out with friends	✔	✔	
Science-fiction films		✘	✔
Comedies		✔	✔
Horror films		✔	✘
Reading		✔	✘
Watching TV			✔

Optional activity

Vocabulary extension

- Write on the board some useful expressions from Listening script 02:

  1 I'm more into …
  2 … is not really my thing.
  3 I don't like … that much.
  4 I'm the world's biggest … fan.

- Students categorise the expressions: *like* (1, 4) or *dislike* (2, 3).
- Check the answers with the class.
- Students work in pairs and talk about their likes and dislikes using these expressions.

4

- Check that students understand the questions, especially *be attracted to someone.*
- Students work in pairs and discuss the questions. Go around the class giving help as necessary.
- Ask some pairs to report back to the class.
- Ask: *Why do you think speed-dating is becoming popular in some countries?*

Speaking

1

- Read out the task. Check students understand that they can complete the questions however they want, and that they will be answering the questions themselves. They should make their questions as interesting as possible.
- Students work individually and complete the questions.

2

- Students give their questions to a partner, who asks the questions.
- Set a time limit of three minutes for the conversation.
- Students ask and answer their questions. Encourage them to give as much detail in their answers as possible.

3

- Students repeat Ex 2 with a new partner.
- Elicit suggestions for the most interesting question and answer. Write suggestions on the board and have a class vote for the best.
- Ask: *Do you still agree with the answers you gave in Listening Ex 4? Does anyone feel differently about speed-dating now?*
- Write on the board and discuss any recurring errors.

Optional activity

Dialogue writing: speed-dating disaster

- Explain that students are going to write a dialogue between themselves and the most incompatible person they can imagine meeting at a speed-dating event. If necessary, explain: *If two people are incompatible, they have such different characters that it is difficult for them to have a good relationship.*
- Students work individually. They note down some of the habits and interests that they find particularly unattractive in a potential girlfriend / boyfriend.
- Ask a few students to tell the class their ideas.
- Students write a dialogue between themselves and their most incompatible speed-date, using the questions in Ex 1 to help them. This activity could be set for homework.
- Select a few students to act out their dialogues for the class.

Revision activity

The alphabet game

- Copy this table onto the board. You could add one or two more columns with other vocabulary areas you want to revise, eg countries, clothes, jobs.

	sports	leisure activities	types of film	styles of music
H				

- Divide the class into teams of three or four students. Explain that they are going to play a game. They have one minute (or more if you have more than four columns) to write one word in each column, beginning with the letter on the left. If they write a correct word, they get a point. If they write a correct word that no other group writes, they get two points. They can use their dictionaries but should not refer to the words in Vocabulary Ex 1 on page 4.
- Do letter H with the class as an example. Elicit suggestions for each category, eg *hockey*, *hanging out with friends*, *horror*, *hip-hop*.
- Start playing the game. Good letters to use are C (*cycling*, *chess*, *comedy*, *classical*) and S (*swimming*, *shopping*, *science fiction*, *salsa*). Write a letter in the left column, then immediately start timing. When the time is up, write the teams' words on the board and allocate points.
- After three or four rounds of the game, work out which team is the winner.

Extra practice

Students complete the Extra practice material on page 22, either in class or for homework.

Extra practice answers

1 1 up 2 after 3 out 4 after 5 into

2 1 Really 2 studying 3 neither 4 too 5 stand 6 hate 7 prefer 8 you

3 1 watching / *individual answer* 2 listening / *individual answer* 3 reading / *individual answer* 4 eating / *individual answer*

4 1 rap 2 basketball 3 science fiction 4 hip-hop 5 reading 6 tennis 7 reggae 8 comedy 9 karate

5
1 What kind of music do you like?
2 Who is your favourite film star?
3 How many brothers have you got?
4 How often do you eat in restaurants?
5 Where do you like hanging out?

References

Grammar reference Unit 1: Coursebook page 26
Wordlist Unit 1: Coursebook page 28
Photocopiable resources: Teacher's Book pages 88–89
Unit 1 test: Teacher's Book pages 121–122

CD-ROM

Unit 1 I know what I like
Language exercise: Nice to meet you
Vocabulary activity: Growing up
CEF-linked activity: I can express likes and dislikes
Game: Neighbourhood (personal information)

UNIT 2 Innovation

Module 1

Topic	Language study	Vocabulary	Main skills
• Great minds (Steve Jobs and Steve Wozniak, co-founders of Apple Computers) • Tokyo gizmo (innovative gadgets from a Japanese toymaker)	• Talking about past events (past simple and past continuous)	• *Make* and *do*	• **Listening:** identifying main information • **Pronunciation:** regular past tense endings (*-ed*) • **Reading:** understanding main information • **Speaking:** discussing the importance of inventions

Learning aims

- Can talk about past events
- Can make phrases using *make* and *do*
- Can discuss the importance of inventions

Ideas for preparation

- students' favourite gadget or toy (see Warmer below)

Warmer

Favourite gizmo

- In the previous lesson, ask students to bring into class their favourite technological gadget or toy.
- Write on the board:
  What is it? What does it do? When do you use it? How long have you had it? Why do you like it?
- Students present their object to their classmates, answering the questions on the board. If they couldn't bring their object into class, they can describe a picture of it.

Great minds

Lead-in

1

- Ask students to open their books on page 6. Ask: *What do you know about the people at the top of the page?*
- Students read the task. Check pronunciation of *musician* /mjuːˈzɪʃn/, *politician* /pɒləˈtɪʃn/, *scientist* /ˈsaɪəntɪst/. Ask: *Which two people in the pictures match categories in the list?* (Nelson Mandela – politician; Marie Curie – scientist; Confucius was a philosopher.)
- Students work in groups of three and choose a 'greatest' in each category.
- Ask each group to report back to the class. Did any groups choose the same people?

2

- Ask a pair of students to act out the example. Check comprehension of *qualities* /ˈkwɒlətiz/, *results*.
- Students rank the qualities individually, then discuss them in pairs.
- Ask some pairs to report back to the class. Alternatively, turn this activity into a pyramid discussion (see Unit 1, page 26).

Listening

Background information

Apple is based in California. Their Macintosh computers ('Macs') were the first to use an interface with windows on a desktop and mouse control – now standard in all computers. Macs are particularly popular in education and with creative professionals such as graphic designers. Apple also produces the iPod, a digital audio player on which videos and photos can be stored, along with music.

1

- Ask: *What do you know about Steve Jobs / Apple? What do the photos at the bottom of the page show?*
- **03** Read out the task. Check comprehension of *co-founder* and *mentioned.*
- Students listen and tick the qualities they hear.
- Check the answers with the class.

Answers

b, c, e

Listening script 03

(I = Interviewer; K = Kathryn Yates)

I: … and on this evening's *Great Minds* we're talking to Kathryn Yates, who has studied the life of the inventor and businessman, Steve Jobs. Kathryn welcome.

K: Thank you. Good to be here.

I: OK, I guess the first question is: Who is Steve Jobs?

K: Steve Jobs is co-founder of Apple. He and his friend Steve Wozniak invented the personal computer.

I: Wow. A couple of clever guys. How did they meet?

K: They met for the first time when they were working at the same company during the summer holidays. Steve Jobs was just 13 years old and Steve Wozniak was 18. They discovered that they both had the same interests and both had dreams about making the world a better place, and that was the beginning of a great partnership.

I: And later they started to build this personal computer?

K: Right, and when it was finally ready, they named it Apple 1 …

I: By the way, why did they call the company Apple?
K: Well, the story I heard was that Steve Jobs had the idea for a home computer when he was picking apples in an orchard in Oregon. He looked at the apple in his hand and decided to call his future company Apple.
I: Beautiful. So, is this the perfect success story, then?
K: Well, not quite. Apple grew very fast. Three years after they started the company, it was worth $100 million. But soon afterwards the new management pushed Steve out of his own company. You see, Steve Jobs had a different way of thinking and the business people didn't really understand him.
I: Mm, not such a happy ending after all, then?
K: Well, it didn't actually end there. Years later, after trying a few different presidents, the Apple management realised that they needed Steve after all. Steve was making the movie *Toy Story* with his new company, Pixar, when Apple asked him to come back.
I: So he went back?
K: He did.
I: Incredible.
K: Yes, and from the moment he returned he started adding colour to the company. Until 1998, all computers were grey or beige. Steve changed all that with the brightly coloured iMacs. Then came iTunes and the iPod. Apple became a popular company once again.
I: Amazing. Kathryn, can I stop you there for a moment? We're going to take a short break but join us again in a few moments to hear more about this …

2

- Students read the statements. Check comprehension of vocabulary such as *invented, was pushed out of.*
- Students choose whether the sentences are true or false.
- Students listen again and check their answers.
- Check the answers with the class.

Answers
1 T 2 F (Steve Jobs was 13) 3 T 4 F (Steve Jobs chose the name) 5 T 6 F (He returned many years later) 7 T

3

- Students read the events in the box. Check comprehension of *was valued at, brightly-coloured.*
- Students work in pairs to complete the task.
- Check the answers with the class.

Answers
1 Steve Jobs: c, e, f, g 2 Apple: a, d, h
3 Steve Jobs and Steve Wozniak: b

4

- Students look again at the phrases in Ex 3 and write a–h in the graph.
- Students compare their answers with a partner.
- Check the answers with the class.

Answers
1 c 2 b 3 h 4 g 5 f 6 e 7 d 8 a

5

- Students work in pairs and retell the story of Steve Jobs. Go around the class giving help and noting any errors.
- Ask some students to report back to the class.
- Write on the board and discuss any recurring errors.

Optional activity

Writing a biography

- Ask: *What words did you use to help you order the events in Steve Jobs' life?* Write students' suggestions on the board and add more, eg *after that, at the same time, a few years later.*
- Students choose a famous person, such as one of their 'great minds' from the Lead-in. They need to know, or be able to find out, some facts about the person's childhood as well as adult life.
- They write a biography of their famous person, using the sequencers on the board to help them.
- Display biographies on the wall for the class to read.

Language study

Talking about past events

Past simple and past continuous

1

- Read out the example. Ask: *Which of the verbs in bold is in the past simple?* (met). *Which is in the past continuous?* (were working).
- Briefly revise the formation of the two tenses.
- Students look at the diagram. Check comprehension and pronunciation of *circumstances* /ˈsɜːkəmstænsɪz/ and *main event* /meɪn ɪˈvent/.
- Students answer the questions in pairs.
- Refer students to the Grammar reference on page 26, where they can check their own answers.
- Check the answers with the class.

Answers
1 past simple 2 past continuous 3 were working

2

- Read out the task. Check comprehension of *pick.*
- Students complete the sentences individually, referring to the Grammar reference on page 26 if necessary.
- They compare their answers with a partner.
- Check the answers with the class. For each sentence, ask: *Which verb talks about the main event? Which verb talks about the circumstances?*

Answers
1 had, was picking 2 was making, asked

3

- 04 Students read through the task. Check comprehension of *break down, doorbell.*
- Students listen to the first situation and read the example sentence. Ask: *Which action started first?* (having lunch, ie the past continuous verb).
- Students write sentences to describe the situations they hear.
- Check the answers with the class.

Suggested answers
1 He was having lunch when the doorbell rang.
2 She was walking (down the road) when it started to rain.
3 She was brushing her teeth when her mobile rang.
4 She was driving when her car broke down.
5 He was sleeping when the alarm clock rang.

Optional activity

Memorable moments
- Tell the class about a memorable moment in your life and what you were doing at the time. For example: *My boyfriend asked me to marry him while I was eating a pizza in the living room.*
- Students write three similar sentences about memorable moments in their lives, using the past simple and past continuous. Encourage them to write sentences that are interesting or surprising.
- Students work in groups. They read out their sentences. Everyone in the group votes for the most surprising sentence.
- Ask each group to read out their most surprising sentence for the class.

Pronunciation

Regular past tense endings (*-ed*)

1

- 05 Students listen to the first three verbs. Ask them to repeat the verbs, paying attention to the different *-ed* pronunciations.
- Students complete the table with the rest of the verbs.
- They listen to the rest of the verbs and correct any mistakes in their table.
- Ask: *What type of verbs have an /ɪd/ ending?* (verbs that end in /t/ or /d/).
- You could explain that for verbs ending in the sounds /k/, /tʃ/, /ʃ/, /s/, /p/ and /f/, *-ed* is pronounced /t/ in the past simple. For other verbs, it is pronounced /d/.

Answers
/d/ changed, discovered, returned /t/ asked, looked, pushed /ɪd/ decided, invented, started

2

- 06 Students work in pairs. They read out the verbs in the box and work out the correct *-ed* pronunciation.
- Students listen, check the *-ed* pronunciation of the verbs, and add them to their table.
- Check the answers with the class.
- Play the recording again. Students repeat each verb.

Answers
/d/ lived, loved /t/ watched, worked
/ɪd/ departed, wanted

3

- Read out the task. Ask two students to read out the example.
- Say three sentences about yourself. Ask students to guess the false sentence, giving reasons for their choice.
- Students complete the task in pairs.
- Ask some students to report back to the class. Ask: *Did you all guess the false statements?*

Reading

1

- 07 This text is recorded on the CD. You can use it as an alternative or in addition to the teaching notes below.
- Students look at the title *Tokyo Gizmo* and the photos. Ask: *What does 'gizmo' mean?* (It's a small technological gadget or toy.) Check pronunciation of *gizmo* /ˈgɪzməʊ/.
- Students describe the objects they see. Pre-teach necessary vocabulary such as *globe, jellyfish, robot.*
- Ask: *Are any of these objects useful? Would you like to own them? Why? / Why not?*
- Students read the task. Set a time limit of two minutes to find the answer. Tell them not to worry about language they don't understand at this stage but to answer the question as quickly as possible.
- Check the answer with the class.

Answer
the jellyfish

2

- Students read the questions. Encourage students to use the context to help them with meanings.
- Students read the text again and answer the questions.
- Check the answers with the class.

Answers
1 Toys like Japanese Barbie and Transformer robots.
2 a It was shaped like a banana.
b It could talk.
c It dropped from the ceiling to wake you up.
3 Because the company wasn't making money with his son as president.
4 It tells you what your cat is saying.
5 You can drive the full-sized versions of the toy cars.
6 He wanted to dream that he was playing football for Japan in the World Cup.
7 He dreamed that he was watching the game on TV on his own, eating crisps.

3
- Students work in pairs and discuss the questions.
- Ask some students to report back to the class. Discuss any differences of opinion.

4
- Students read through the sentences. Check comprehension of *industry*, *government*.
- Students complete the sentences individually, using the context of the text on page 8 to help them.
- Check the answers with the class.

Answers
1 produces 2 scent 3 innovative 4 retirement 5 policy

5
- Read out the task and the example. Make sure students understand that they are changing not the gapped words, but other parts of the sentences.
- Students write their sentences then compare their answers in pairs.
- Students report back to the class. Did many students express the same opinions?

Vocabulary

make and *do*

1
- Ask two students to read out the example sentences. Ask: *Are 'make someone laugh' and 'do well' expressed in your languages with the same verb, or different ones?* Explain that the English verbs *make* and *do* have similar meanings but are used in different expressions. Suggest that students keep a page of their notebooks for recording expressions with *make* and *do*.
- Students copy the table into their notebooks and work individually to complete it using the words and phrases in the box.
- Students compare their answers with a partner and check in a dictionary if they are unsure of any.
- Check the answers with the class.

Answers
make: a decision, a mistake, a phone call, money, someone angry, someone laugh / cry
do: an exam, business, some damage, someone a favour, well / badly, your homework

2
- Students read the sentences. Check comprehension of vocabulary such as *admit*.
- Students complete the questions.
- Check the answers with the class.

Answers
2 makes 3 made 4 done 5 make 6 done

3
- Ask a student to read out question 1 from Ex 2 as an example. Ask another student for an answer.
- Students work in pairs and ask and answer the questions in Ex 2.
- Ask some students to report back to the class.

Most important for the world

Speaking

1
- **o8** Read out the task. Explain that the players in the game have to argue that their object is more important for the world than their opponent's object.
- Students listen to the example and discuss their answer in pairs.
- Ask some students to report back to the class.

Listening script o8
(T = Teacher, J = Jose, W = Wanlee)
T: José, what are you going to talk about?
J: Toothbrushes.
T: And Wanlee?
W: Chickens.
T: OK, when you're ready.
J: Toothbrushes are much more important than chickens – you can eat anything: beef, vegetables, fruit, but you can only clean your teeth with one thing – a toothbrush.
W: That's not true. You can brush your teeth with a stick or even with chewing gum, but chickens give us eggs. You can eat eggs, paint with eggs (like Leonardo da Vinci), or even throw eggs at politicians. If someone comes to your house, you need eggs to make them a delicious cake …
J: But without toothbrushes you wouldn't …

2

- Check students understand the rules.
- In a weaker class, discuss what to say about another object, eg a dog. Write useful language on the board: *Without an X, you can't …, You need an X to … .*
- Divide the class into three groups, A, B and C and say: *Turn to page 29 to find your object.* As students prepare what they are going to say, go around the class giving help as necessary.
- When they have prepared their arguments, say: *Each student from group A find a partner from group B, and a judge from group C.* The As and Bs have their discussion and the Cs choose a winner. Then the As find new partners from group C, with Bs as judges, and so on. Walk around the class as they talk and note down any errors.
- Ask some students to argue their case for the whole class to hear.
- Write on the board and discuss any recurring errors.

Revision activity

Dice game

- You will need a dice for each group of four or five.
- Write on the board:

  1 a sentence with a past continuous verb
  2 a sentence with a past simple verb with an /ɪd/ ending
  3 a sentence with a '*make*' expression
  4 a sentence with a '*do*' expression
  5 a great sports personality or musician and why he / she is famous
  6 a great politician or scientist and why he / she is famous

- Students work in small groups. They throw the dice and give an answer according to the list on the board. If they throw 1, they have to give a sentence with a past continuous verb, eg *We were waiting at the bus stop when it started to rain.* They get a point for every correct answer. Be at hand to adjudicate if there are any disagreements.
- Play for about five minutes, then find out who has the most points.

Extra practice

Students complete the Extra practice material on page 23, either in class or for homework.

Extra practice answers

1 1 become 2 met 3 wasn't 4 didn't go 5 get 6 worked 7 give 8 didn't earn 9 were

2 1 was cycling, saw 2 didn't break down, were driving 3 were eating, heard 4 didn't buy, was shopping 5 started, was sitting 6 wasn't listening, asked 7 was looking, found 8 was sleeping, called

3 1 was drinking 2 decided 3 was looking for 4 discovered 5 was working 6 complained 7 weren't 8 loved 9 was experimenting 10 drank 11 didn't think 12 liked

4 1 do, made 2 do, make 3 make, made 4 made, do, made 5 make, does / did / is doing

References

Grammar reference Unit 2: Coursebook page 26
Wordlist Unit 2: Coursebook page 28
Communication activities: Coursebook page 29
Photocopiable resources: Teacher's Book pages 90–91
Unit 2 test: Teacher's Book pages 123–124

CD-ROM

Unit 2 Innovation
Language exercise: From fish to birds
Vocabulary activity: Innovations and technology
CEF-linked activity: I can recognise regular past endings (*-ed*)
Game: The big squeeze (*make* and *do*)

UNIT 3

The sixth sense

Module 1

Topic	Language study	Vocabulary	Main skills
• Psychic powers • Your lying ways (sleeping positions)	• Expressing necessity and advice (*must(n't), (don't) have to, should(n't), ought to, don't need to*)	• Character adjectives	• **Reading:** understanding gist • **Writing:** an email to a friend • **Speaking:** discussing psychic powers; describing people • **Listening:** identifying particular information

Learning aims

- Can express necessity and advice
- Can describe people using character adjectives
- Can discuss psychic powers

Ideas for preparation

- pictures of places that have particular rules: a theatre / cinema, a school, a plane (see Optional activity: *Do*'s and *don't*'s page 37).

Warmer

- Write on the board: *The senses.* Ask: *What are our senses?* Write students' answers on the board (*sight, touch, hearing, smell, taste*).
- Ask: *So, how many senses do we have?* (five). Tell students to look at the title, *The sixth sense*, and guess what it means. When they have come up with some good answers, write *psychic* on the board, and under it things that psychic people can do, such as see ghosts, predict the future, read people's minds.
- Students work in groups and discuss whether there are psychic powers that they would like to have.
- Discuss the answers with the class.

Background information

Psychics in the UK

Many people are willing to pay up to £100 for a session with a medium (a person who can 'communicate' with the dead). There are also a number of popular paranormal shows on television. If you want to find someone to read tarot cards or predict your future, their phone numbers are often listed at the back of women's magazines.

Psychic powers

Lead-in

1

- Ask students to open their books on page 10. Ask: *Do you think you are psychic?* Explain that students are going to do a questionnaire to find out. Check pronunciation of *psychic* /ˈsaɪkɪk/.
- Read out the task. Students complete the questionnaire.

2

- Students work in pairs. They compare their answers and read their psychic rating on page 29.
- Discuss the meaning of problematic vocabulary such as *in touch with your spiritual side, meditation, relaxed, the back of your mind* and *awareness*.
- Students discuss their responses to the analysis.
- Students report back to the class. Ask: *Who is more psychic than they thought?*

Reading

1

- **09** This text is recorded on the CD. You can use it as an alternative or in addition to the teaching notes below.
- Read out the task. Set a time limit of two minutes to complete it. Tell students not to worry about language they don't understand at this stage. They are simply trying to match the paragraphs with the pictures as quickly as possible.
- Check the answers with the class.

Answers

1 pendulum 2 aura 3 tarot cards 4 dreams

2

- Students read the descriptions. Check comprehension of *rock, experienced*.
- Students read the text again and answer the questions. Encourage them to use the context to help them with the meanings of difficult words.
- Check the answers with the class.

Answers

2 dreams 3 aura 4 pendulum 5 tarot cards 6 aura 7 dreams 8 tarot cards

3

- Students work in pairs and discuss the questions.
- Ask some students to report back to the class. Which method has been tried by the most students?

Optional activity

Vocabulary extension

- To focus on some useful expressions from the reading text, write on the board:

1	the palm	a	motion
2	seven cards	b	your mind
3	turn the lights	c	down
4	clear	d	in a row
5	in a circular	e	direction
6	in the opposite	f	of your hand

- Students match the two columns.
- Check the answers with the class and discuss the meanings of any problematic expressions.
- Ask: *Can you remember where these expressions were in the text?*

Answers

1 f 2 d 3 c 4 b 5 a 6 e

Language study

Expressing necessity and advice

1

- Explain that you are going to look at ways of saying things are necessary or a good idea.
- Students match the examples to the questions.
- Check the answers with the class.

Answers

1 must 2 should 3 don't have to

2

- Read out the question and discuss the answer with the class.

Answer

Infinitive without *to*

3

- Students complete the matching activity.
- Check the answers with the class.

Answers

1 ought to = it's a good idea 2 have to = it's necessary
3 don't have to = it's not necessary

4

- Students work individually and complete the table.
- Check the answers with the class. Ask: *Which verbs have 'to' after them?* (have, need, ought). *Which don't have 'to' after them?* (must, should). Check students understand too that *must*, *should* and *ought* don't change in the *he / she / it* form.

Answers

It's necessary to do something: *must, have to*
It's not necessary to do something (but you can if you want to): *don't have to, don't need to*
It's a good idea to do something: *should, ought to*

5

- Read out the task. Check comprehension of vocabulary such as *improve, bite, fingernails, upset.*
- Students work in pairs to complete the statements.
- Check the answers with the class.

Answers

2 should / ought to 3 don't have to / don't need to
4 shouldn't 5 mustn't

6

- Students turn to the activity on page 32 and read the task. Check comprehension of vocabulary such as *uniform, junk food, make an effort, keep in touch, give up,* and *violent* /ˈvaɪələnt/.
- **Step 1:** Students work individually to write their questions.
- **Step 2:** Explain that students are going to interview their classmates to find a different person who can answer *yes* to each question. Read out the example questions. Encourage students to ask similar questions and find out as much information as possible.
- Students complete the task.
- **Step 3:** Students report back to the class with their most interesting piece of information.
- Alternatively, in a large class, students work in groups for step 3.

Writing

1

- Read out the task and the questions. Check comprehension of *religious, offend.*
- Students read the email and answer the questions.
- Check the answers with the class.

Answers

1 No – it's warm.
2 No, but you must cover your arms and legs.
3 Yes – Ma'mar Masjid Mosque.
4 You must cover your arms and legs in the mosque. You mustn't photograph it. You shouldn't refuse an offer of tea or coffee. You ought to try to learn one or two words of Arabic.

2

- Read out the task. Ask: *How will your email start?* (Dear Marco). *And how will it end?* (Best wishes, …).
- Students find expressions in Mahmoud's email that show how he's feeling about Marco's visit: *I'm really pleased that you're coming*; *I'm sure you'll really like it*; *I'm looking forward to seeing you.* Write them on the board.
- Ask: *Where does Mahmoud start his answers to Marco's questions?* Write *To answer your questions …* on the board.

- Students write their emails.
- Students swap emails with a partner and check for errors. Encourage them to focus in particular on verbs of necessity and advice.

Optional activity

***Do*'s and *don't*'s poster**

- Bring in some pictures of different places that have particular rules: a theatre / cinema, a school, a plane. Students identify the locations.
- Students discuss the *do*'s and *don't*'s of each place.
- Each pair chooses one of the locations, or an idea of their own, and creates a poster clearly displaying the place's rules. Go around the class as they work, giving help as necessary.
- Display the posters around the class and give students time to read them all.
- Ask: *Which poster is the most attractive / funniest?*

Character adjectives

Vocabulary and speaking

1

- Ask: *What's your best friend like?* If necessary, explain that this question is asking about the person's character, not his / her appearance (for which the correct question is *What does he / she look like?*). Write on the board a few of the character adjectives that students mention. Encourage them to keep a separate page in their notebooks for character adjectives.
- Check comprehension of *emotions*, *attention*, *reasonable*, *practical*, *pleasant* /ˈplezənt/, *nervous*, and *embarrassed*.
- Students work individually and complete the descriptions.
- Check the answers with the class.

Answers

2 helpful 3 quiet 4 demanding 5 selfish
6 confident 7 sensible 8 friendly 9 over-sensitive
10 suspicious 11 shy 12 boring

Optional activity

Word stress

- Students mark the stressed syllables in the words in Ex 1.
- Ask: *Which two adjectives don't have the stress on the first syllable?* (suspicious /səˈspɪʃəs/, demanding /dɪˈmɑːndɪŋ/).
- Students practise saying the words.
- Students tap out the rhythm of the words for their partners to guess.

2

- Students underline the character adjectives in the example.
- Students describe their friends. Encourage them to talk about friends that both people know.
- Ask some students to report back to the class.

Your lying ways

Listening

1

- Students work in pairs. They look at the pictures and discuss the questions.
- Ask some students to report back to the class.

2

- **10** Read out the task. Make sure students know that the first time they listen, they only have to write two adjectives under each picture.
- Students listen and write the adjectives.
- Students compare their answers in pairs.
- Check the answers with the class.

Answers

Foetus: sensitive, shy Log: friendly, selfish Yearner: sensible, suspicious Soldier: quiet, demanding Freefaller: confident, over-sensitive Starfish: helpful, boring

Listening script 10

(N = Newsreader, S = Simon)

N: Can our sleeping position tell us something about our character? According to recent research, yes. Let's go over to our science reporter, Simon Ward, to hear more about it. Simon?

S: Fiona, according to research by Professor Chris Idzikowski, director of the Sleep Assessment and Advisory Service, there are six common sleeping positions and each one is linked to a particular personality type. The most common position is the Foetus. 41% of us sleep in this position, mostly women. A person who sleeps like this is sensitive – they care about others – but they are also quite shy, especially when meeting people for the first time. But people from this group make very good, and loyal, friends.
The next most popular position, for 15% of us, is the Log. It's called the Log because, lying with you arms and legs straight, you look like a fallen tree. These sleepers are friendly and mix easily with others. However, they sometimes think only about themselves and can actually be quite selfish. So, friendly but not always a good friend.
13% of us are Yearners. The sleeping position is like the Log except both arms are out in front of them. These people are sensible, and never do anything too crazy, but they don't trust people easily and tend to be quite suspicious by nature. They are slow to make decisions but once they do, they are unlikely to change them.
If you sleep lying on your back with both arms by your sides, then you are a Soldier. As a Soldier, you are a quiet person and generally speak only when someone speaks to you. However, you expect a lot from other people and you can be difficult to please, in fact rather demanding. Apart from personality, if you sleep in this position you will probably snore.

The Freefaller is a confident person, or certainly seems confident, but they don't like to be criticised and can become quite emotional. This oversensitivity only shows itself in particularly extreme situations.
The Starfish is the final category. These sleepers make good friends and are always ready to offer help. They don't like to be the centre of attention and they are very good listeners. The only negative is that they can be boring and even send you to sleep when talking about their interests. However, if you sleep next to a Starfish, you will probably be woken up by their snoring!
Fiona, back to you.

3

- Students read the questions. Check comprehension of *snore*.
- Students predict the answers, then listen again to check.
- Check the answers with the class.

Answers

1 foetus 2 41% 3 log 4 foetus, starfish 5 soldier, starfish

4

- Students discuss the questions in small groups.
- Ask some students to report back to the class.

Optional activity

Character discussion

- Write these questions on the board:

  1 Do you agree with your classmates' descriptions of their own character?
  2 What has the most important influence on your character: your genes, your upbringing, your parents or your friends?
  3 Is it possible to change your character?
  4 Would you like to change your character? How?

- Students work in small groups and discuss the questions.
- Ask some students to report back to the class.

Revision activity

Character acting

- Students work in pairs. Give each pair a character adjective from page 13 of the Coursebook. Ask them to prepare a dialogue that demonstrates the adjective but doesn't actually use it. You could suggest a context, eg a work meeting or a social event.
- When they've had time to prepare a dialogue, they act it out for the class to guess the adjective.
- Ask the class to vote on the best dialogue.

Extra practice

Students complete the Extra practice material on page 24, either in class or for homework.

Extra practice answers

1 1 have to 2 ought to 3 should 4 must be 5 have to 6 don't need to 7 mustn't

2 1 don't have to 2 shouldn't 3 have 4 mustn't 5 ought 6 should 7 must 8 don't need

3 1 suspicious 2 confident 3 shy 4 boring 5 helpful 6 selfish 7 sensible 8 demanding 9 sensitive 10 quiet

4 1 suspicious 2 sensible 3 boring 4 confident 5 helpful 6 selfish 7 demanding 8 quiet

5 (individual answers)

References

Grammar reference Unit 3: Coursebook page 27
Wordlist Unit 3: Coursebook page 28
Communication activities: Coursebook pages 29 and 32
Photocopiable resources: Teacher's Book pages 92–93
Unit 3 test: Teacher's Book pages 125–126

CD-ROM

Unit 3 The sixth sense
Language exercise: Uncle Sid
Vocabulary activity: Characteristics
CEF-linked activity: I can describe people using character adjectives
Game: Crossword (character adjectives)

UNIT 4 What do you do?

Topic	Language study	Vocabulary	Main skills
• Any volunteers? (experiences of a volunteer working in China) • Volunteers needed	• Making promises, requests and predictions: *will*	• Work experience • Occupations	• **Reading:** identifying main information • **Listening:** identifying key information • **Speaking:** talking about jobs and career choices; making promises, requests and predictions

Learning aims

- Can make promises, requests and predictions
- Can talk about jobs and career choices
- Can understand texts about work experiences

Ideas for preparation

- pictures of people for students to guess their job (see Warmer below)

Warmer

Guess the job

- Bring in magazine photos of a variety of people – aim for a mix of sexes, races, ages and clothing styles.
- Show students the first photo. Ask: *What job do you think this person does?* Write their ideas on the board, providing any unknown vocabulary.
- Repeat with the other photos.
- Alternatively, stick the photos on the board and write suggested occupations in jumbled order. Students work in small groups and discuss which person has which job.
- Accept well-reasoned answers as correct.
- Encourage students to keep a separate page of their notebook for vocabulary relating to occupations.

Any volunteers?

Lead-in

1

- Ask students to open their books on page 14. Check comprehension of *volunteers, graduate*.
- Ask four students to read out the speech bubbles. Check comprehension of words such as *pick, au pair, children's camp, activity leader*.
- Students work in pairs and discuss the questions.
- Ask some students to report back to the class.

Background information

A year out

In the UK, many young people take a break from their studies for a year between school and university, or between finishing university and getting a permanent job. Popular choices for a 'gap year' include backpacking around the world, working abroad, particularly in Europe or Australia, and working for a charity. Many employers appreciate the skills and maturity gained in this way. Voluntary work in particular is considered to build valuable confidence and leadership skills.

Reading

1

- 11 This text is recorded on the CD. You can use it as an alternative or in addition to the teaching notes below.
- Students look at the pictures. Say: *The man in the photos is Justin Hill. Where do you think he went after graduating from university?*
- Students read the extract to check their answers. They compare his choice of job, destination, and the length of time spent there with their own choices in the Lead-in.

Answers

Justin taught as a volunteer in China for two and a half years.

2

- Students read the questions. Check comprehension of vocabulary such as *contract* /ˈkɒntrækt/, *run* (meaning *be in charge of*), *culture*.
- They read the text again and answer the questions.
- Check the answers with the class.

Answers

1 They thought he was crazy.
2 Two years.
3 He was charming.
4 That we are all more similar than we are different.

3

- Students read the definitions. Check comprehension of *ability, pleasant, achieve*.
- Students find the words and then complete the matching exercise.

- Check the answers with the class.
- Check that students can pronounce the words correctly, especially *abroad* /əˈbrɔːd/, *superficial* /suːpəˈfɪʃəl/, *developed* /dɪˈveləpt/.

Answers
1 skills 2 crazy 3 charming 4 abroad 5 superficial 6 aim 7 developed

4
- Students read the sentences. Check comprehension of vocabulary such as *rather than, refuse.*
- Students complete the sentences.
- Check the answers with the class.

Answers
1 abroad 2 skills 3 aim 4 superficial 5 crazy 6 charming 7 developed

5
- Students work individually and tick the sentences that they agree with, or that are true for them.
- Students discuss the sentences in Ex 4.
- Ask: *Is it possible to have both things: a well-paid job in which you help others?*

Occupations

Vocabulary

1
- Read out the task. Check comprehension of *create, tools, solve,* and the pronunciation of *occupation* /ɒkjuːˈpeɪʃn/.
- Students work in pairs. Encourage them to use dictionaries to check the meaning of any occupations they're unsure about.
- Check the answers with the class.

Possible answers
1 architect, engineer 2 nurse, teacher 3 agricultural worker, plumber, engineer 4 computer programmer

Optional activity

Silent pronunciation
- Students work in pairs.
- Each student takes turns to choose an occupation and mouth it at his / her partner, without saying the word aloud.
- The partner tries to guess the word by looking at the shape of the first student's mouth.

2
- Students work in pairs and brainstorm occupations for each category. Encourage them to use their dictionaries.
- Find out who thought of the most words for each category. Ask: *Do some jobs fit into more than one category?*

Possible answers
1 designer, artist, sculptor 2 doctor, policeman, social worker 3 electrician, car mechanic, builder 4 politician, management consultant, scientist

3
- Check pronunciation of *ideal* /aɪˈdɪəl/.
- Students work in pairs and discuss the question.
- Ask some students to report back to the class.

4
- Students turn to page 29 and read the test. Check comprehension of *a professional service, record* /ˈrekɔːd/, *original, energetic, observe, analyse.*
- Students ask and answer the questions in pairs, and mark their partner's answers.
- Students read their results on page 32.
- They discuss their reactions to the results.
- Ask some students to report back to the class. Ask: *Did you think the personality test was useful?*

Listening

1
- Students read the advert and answer the questions.
- Check the answers with the class.

Answers
1 Papua New Guinea 2 Eight weeks 3 Help local health workers to distribute medical supplies 4 Nothing

2
- 12 Read out the task.
- Check students understand that the first time they listen they only have to tick the things Kelly's mother mentions.
- Students listen and answer the question.
- Check the answer with the class.

Answer
Her mother mentions animals, illness, food and romance.

Listening script 12
(M = Mother, K = Kelly)
M: Kelly, what would you like to drink?
K: I'll have a cup of tea, please.
M: Come down then.
K: Thanks. Mum, what's wrong?
M: Oh, nothing. I was just thinking about you out there. There are a lot of dangerous animals …
K: Mum, don't start again, please. I'll be OK – I'll be fine, really.
M: Will they feed you properly?
K: I'm sure they will. I get all my meals included. Anyway, it's not me you should worry about. You know, more than 200 children die every week because they don't have enough food or because of malaria …
M: Malaria? You might get malaria?
K: Oh, Mum, I won't. I'm taking anti-malaria tablets and we have all the right medicines. Don't worry, Mum. I'm only going to be there for eight weeks. I'll call you every week. Honestly.
M: You might fall in love and not want to come home.
K: Mummy! Now you're just being embarrassing!

3

- Students work in groups and discuss the questions.
- Ask some students to report back to the class. Ask: *Which would you prefer, Justin's teaching job in China, or Kelly's job in Papua New Guinea? Why?*

Optional activity

Write a job advertisement

- Ask students to look again at the advertisement in Listening Ex 1 and tell you what information is included in the advert. Write their answers on the board, eg *name of employer, duties, location, what the employer provides, contact details*. Encourage them to think of extra information they could include in their own advert, eg *hours of work, salary, description of the ideal candidate's character / experience, deadline for applications*.
- Students choose a job and write an advertisement for it. Elicit useful expressions and write them on the board:
  The ideal candidate will be sociable and hardworking.
  The ideal candidate will have at least two years' experience of bar work.
  Send your application to (person / address) by (date) …
- Display the adverts for students to read. Each student chooses one job to apply for (not their own!).
- Which job had the most applicants?

Language study

Making promises, requests and predictions: *will*

1

- Ask three students to read out sentences a, b and c.
- Students complete the task.
- Check the answers with the class. If any students are unclear, give more examples to explain *promise*, *offer*, and *request*.

Answers
1 c 2 a 3 b

2

- Ask two pairs of students to read out the dialogues.
- Students decide if the statements 1–3 are true or false.
- Check the answers with the class.

Answers
1 T 2 T 3 T

3

- Read out the sentences. Check comprehension of *pipe*, *heart*, *fuel*.
- Students match the sentences to the categories.
- They compare their answers in pairs.
- Check the answers with the class.

Answers
1 a 2 b 3 c 4 b 5 c 6 a

4

- 13 Students reread the sentences in Ex 3.
- Elicit suggestions about each person's occupation.
- Students listen and check.
- Check the answers with the class.

Answers
1 politician 2 teacher 3 plumber 4 dentist 5 doctor
6 car mechanic

Listening script 13

1 I'll cut taxes and I'll introduce free health care. You have my word on that.
2 OK everybody. Will you sit in a circle, please? Sarah? Sarah! Come and sit down now, please.
3 It'll probably take about two hours to fix this pipe. Mmm, you'd better make that three hours.
4 Dentist: Will you open just a little wider, please?
Patient: Gnngnngnn.
Dentist: Yes, about 5.30, I think.
Patient: Gnnngnn … Gnngn!
5 Doctor: Your heart's fine – you'll live longer than all of us, Mrs Smith. Mrs Smith? MRS SMITH!
Mrs Smith: Mm? Oh, sorry, Doctor. I think I must have fallen asleep.
Doctor: Please, never do that to me again, Mrs Smith.
6 Fuel problem? Sure. I'll take a look right now. There's nothing wrong with your car. You've just forgotten to put petrol in it.

5

- 14 Students read the conversation on the left and complete it using *will*, *'ll* or *won't*.
- Play the CD and check the answers with the class.

Answers
1 'll 2 will 3 will 4 won't 5 'll

6

- Students work in pairs and discuss the question.
- Ask some students to report back to the class. Students vote on the most probable suggestion.

7

- Students read the sentences and discuss their answers.
- Ask some students to report back to the class, and encourage others to agree or disagree with their ideas.
- Discuss words and phrases that help them deduce the context, such as *fish, darling, coat and jacket, it won't take long*. Students can underline useful expressions for phone calls: *I'll call you back. Will you hold? The line's busy.*

Possible answers

1 a customer talking to a waiter in a restaurant
2 a priest talking to a bride in a marriage service
3 someone at work talking to his / her partner on the phone
4 someone calling to other family members from the kitchen
5 a secretary / switchboard operator / receptionist on a phone, trying to connect a caller
6 an assistant talking to a customer at a dry cleaners

Speaking

1

- Ask two students to read out the dialogue.
- Students underline examples of promises / offers, requests / orders and predictions.
- Check the answers with the class.

Answers

a I'll take you up b Will you come (and watch)?
c Will you be OK? I'll be fine.

2

- Students read through the situations.
- Elicit suggestions for the first situation.
- Students work in pairs and write a dialogue for one of situations 1–5, incorporating some target structures.

3

- Students practise their dialogues.
- Ask a few pairs to act out their dialogues.
- Discuss any recurring errors with *will.*

Find my job

4

- Demonstrate the game. If students ask any *wh-* questions, encourage them to reword the questions so you answer *yes* or *no.*
  For example: *Do you build things? Help people? Use a computer? Make things? earn a lot of money? Do you work inside? Outside? In an office? At weekends? Regular hours?*
- When they guess the job, allocate points.
- Students play the game in small groups.
- Ask each group to report back to the class. Ask: *Who scored the most points? Which was the hardest job to guess?*
- Write on the board and discuss any recurring errors.

Revision activity

Vocabulary revision and extension

- Students look through the texts on pages 29 and 32 and find all the words for character and occupations. Students add them to their notebook list of character adjectives from Unit 3, and to their occupations list from this unit.
- Ask students to write on a piece of paper five character adjectives that describe them. They can choose any words they want, not just vocabulary from this unit.
- Take in the pieces of paper.
- Students work in pairs. Give each pair two lists of adjectives (not their own). They discuss the best jobs for the people who wrote the lists, and write three suggestions for each person.
- Students reclaim their own piece of paper and look at the job suggestions. Ask: *Are these suggestions more useful than the ones from the personality test in Ex 4?* Ask some students to give examples.

Extra practice

Students complete the Extra practice material on page 25, either in class or for homework.

Extra practice answers

1 1 c, f 2 g, i 3 a, k 4 b, l 5 d, j 6 e, h

2
1 I'll phone you every day.
2 Will you make me a sandwich?
3 I'll speak to my manager.
4 Will you buy me some coffee?
5 I think it will be fantastic!
6 No, thanks. It won't rain today.
7 I'll have two coffees, please.
8 I won't tell anyone.

3 a 3 b 2 c 1 d 7 e 6 f 4 g 8 h 5

4 1 promise 2 request 3 offer / promise 4 request 5 prediction 6 prediction 7 request 8 promise

5 (possible answers)
1 I'll send you a postcard.
2 It'll be hot / sunny this afternoon.
3 Will you help me (with my homework), please?
4 I'll help you look for them.
5 I'll have a cup of coffee and a cheese sandwich.

References

Grammar reference Unit 4: Coursebook page 27
Wordlist Unit 4: Coursebook page 28
Communication activities: Coursebook pages 29 and 32
Photocopiable resources: Teacher's Book pages 94–95
Unit 4 test: Teacher's Book pages 127–128

CD-ROM

Unit 4 What do you do?
Language exercise: Perfect home
Vocabulary activity: My job
CEF-linked activity: I can understand texts about work experience
Game: Swamp disaster (career and work experiences)

Review

Ideas for preparation

- a counter for each student (see Vocabulary game on Coursebook page 19)

Warmer

- To revise character adjectives and occupations, play a version of the game Pictionary.
- Students work in two teams. Each team makes a list of six occupations and character adjectives.
- Team B shows a student from Team A one word from their list. The Team A student draws the word on the board for Team A to guess. Set a time limit of one minute.
- If Team A guesses the word, they get one point. If they don't, Team B get a point.
- Teams take turns to draw each other's words.
- The team with most points wins the game.

Lead-in

1

- Students discuss the questions in small groups.
- Ask some students to report back to the class. Ask: *Who did something interesting when they left their job / studies?*

Language study

1

- 15 Students read the task and listen for the answer.
- Check the answer with the class.

Answer

a year

Listening script 15

P = Presenter, T = Thomas

P: Good afternoon and welcome to *Moving On*. Today, I'm talking to Thomas Hunter. Last month, Thomas gave up his job as a computer programmer. He's now planning to spend the next year sailing around the world. Thomas, hello ...

T: Hello.

P: First, tell me – you enjoyed your job, didn't you?

T: Yes, I did. The people I worked with were friendly and interesting.

P: And, I think you were making quite a lot of money ...

T: That's right.

P: So, why did you decide to leave?

T: Well, I worked in an office and the truth is that I can't stand being indoors all the time. I like doing sport and other outdoor activities and, in my job, I worked so many hours, I never had any free time. I just wanted to change my life – while I'm still young.

P: I see, and when did you make the decision to go on a trip around the world?

T: It was about two months ago. I was thinking about going on holiday and I was looking on the internet when I saw an advert for a boat. It wasn't very expensive, so I bought the boat and started sailing lessons. There's a lake near my house. Then, on my first lesson, I was sailing across the lake when I had the idea – to go on a trip around the world. So, I went into work the next day and told my manager.

P: Was he shocked?

T: Yes, at first, but I think he knew I'd made the right decision.

P: Do you think you have to be a good sailor to travel so far?

T: Well, I know what I'm doing now. I'm young. I'm fit. I'm a sensible person. I think I'll be fine.

P: You certainly seem very practical, but what about money?

T: I don't need to earn any money for a while.

P: OK, but, you're going on your own. Won't you be lonely?

T: No. I don't think so. I like being on my own.

P: So, what advice would you give to people who don't like their jobs?

T: They should move on, definitely. They should change their jobs or do something else they like. They shouldn't do things they don't want to do.

P: Thank you, Thomas. Will you come and see us when you get back?

T: Of course, and I'll send you a postcard from every country I visit.

P: Thank you. Now let's move on to ...

2

- Students answer the multiple-choice questions.
- They listen again and check their answers.
- Check the answers with the class.

Answers

1 a 2 c 3 b 4 b 5 c 6 a

3

- Students read and complete the sentences, then check their answers in the Listening script on page 31.
- Discuss any queries about the verb forms.

Answers

1 being 2 doing 3 was looking 4 was sailing 5 went
6 be 7 earn 8 being 9 n't do, don't want
10 Will you come

4

- Ask three students to act out the example.
- Students underline the phrases in the dialogue that express like or dislike (*love, like, don't mind, prefer*). Ask: *What other expressions can you think of?* (can't stand, hate, enjoy).
- Ask: *What do you say when you agree with a positive statement?* (Me too.) *And with a negative statement?* (Me neither.) *And when you disagree?* (Really?)
- Students work in small groups and discuss the activities in the box.
- Ask some students to report back to the class.

Vocabulary

1

- Explain that students are going to play a game. Give each person a counter, or ask them to find a small coin or rubber to use instead.
- Students read the instructions for the game.
- Ask a pair of students to demonstrate the game for the class, until one of them gets to a life step and follows the instructions on it.
- Students play in small groups. Go around the class, giving help and adjudicating.
- When each group has a winner, ask: *Which colour was hardest?* Write on the board students' vocabulary ideas for the hardest category.

Song

1

- Students look at the photo. Ask: *Has anyone heard of Nelly Furtado? Do you know any of her songs?*
- Check comprehension of *instrument, influenced.*
- Students read the factfile and answer the questions.
- Check the answers with the class.

Answers
1 She used a tape recorder to record herself singing.
2 A drum machine 3 Three 4 September 2000

2

- 16 Students listen to the song with books closed.
- Students suggest who she is singing about.
- Play the song again. This time students can read along.
- Check the answer. Ask: *Do you like the song?*

Answer
Herself and her boyfriend / husband / partner

3

- Students read the questions and find the answers.
- They compare their answers in pairs.
- Check the answers with the class.

Answers
1 Beautiful, lovely 2 No, because she says she may change. 3 He doesn't know her very well. 4 Rare and true 5 Because she's going to leave him one day 6 Scared that it will end

4

- Students read the statements and discuss their answers.
- Check the answer with the class.

Answer
Statement 2

5

- Students work in pairs and discuss the questions.
- Ask some students to report back to the class.
- Write on the board and discuss any recurring errors.

Speaking: a TV advice show

Background information

TV advice shows are very popular in the USA and Britain. They're often shown in the mornings when the audience is largely female. Guests come on the shows to talk about problems ranging from 'I'm a shopaholic' to 'My husband is in love with my sister'. However, some shows have been criticised recently for hiring actors to play guests, rather than having real people with real problems.

1

- Ask: *Do you ever watch advice shows on TV?* Encourage students to describe popular shows in their country. Ask: *Are these programmes helpful for the guest, or for the viewer?*
- **Step 1:** Check comprehension of vocabulary such as *presenter, guest, psychologist, relative.*
- Students work in groups of four. They choose roles and plan their show. They decide on the guest's main problem together before working individually on their role card. Go around the class giving help as necessary.
- **Step 2:** Allow 15 minutes. Encourage students to improvise following an agreed structure, rather than reading out a dialogue word for word.
- Before Step 3, practise some audience participation. Make announcements for the class to react to: clapping and cheering good news and booing bad news.
- **Step 3:** The groups perform their shows. Encourage audience members with a comment to put up their hand to attract the presenter's attention.
- Have a class vote on the most entertaining show.

Reference

Module 1 test: Teacher's Book pages 129–131

Don't breathe a word!

Topic	Language study	Vocabulary	Main skills
• Gossip • You didn't hear it from me	• Talking about recent events (past simple and present perfect simple) • Phrases to talk about time and quantity	• Phrases about friendship and rumour	• **Reading:** identifying key information • **Listening:** completing details of events • **Speaking:** listening and responding to news about other people

Learning aims

- Can talk about recent events
- Can use phrases to talk about time and quantity
- Can listen and respond to news about other people

Warmer

Chinese whispers

- Organise the class so students are in a circle. Explain that they are going to play a traditional party game called Chinese whispers.
- Whisper in the ear of a student a piece of gossip, perhaps about celebrities, eg *X is getting married to her fourth husband next week.*
- Each student has to whisper this sentence into the ear of his / her neighbour, until the sentence has gone right round the circle.
- The last person in the circle says the sentence out loud. Has it changed since you whispered it at the start of the game?
- Ask two or three students to start the game with their own gossipy sentences.

Gossip

Lead-in

1

- Ask students to open their books on page 34 and look at the picture. Ask: *What are these people talking about, do you think? Are they gossiping?*
- Students read the definition and answer your question. (Yes, the people in the picture are gossiping.)
- Students work in groups and discuss the questions.
- Ask some students to report back to the class.

Reading

1

- Students read the statements. Check comprehension of vocabulary such as *communication skills.*
- Students work in pairs and discuss the statements.
- Have a quick class survey. Read out each statement, and students put their hand up if they agree with it. Discuss the results with the class.

2

- 17 This text is recorded on the CD. You can use it as an alternative or in addition to the teaching notes below.
- Students read the article and compare the opinions in it to their Ex 1 answers. They can also listen to the CD while they read.
- Check the answers with the class.

Answers

Statements 1 and 4 are true.

3

- Read out the task. Check comprehension of vocabulary such as *quarter, third.*
- Students read the text and complete the task.
- Check the answers with the class.

Answers

1 Less than a quarter 2 75% 3 number one 4 quarter
5 in different ways 6 no good

4

- Students work in pairs and discuss the survey findings. Encourage them to give reasons for their opinions.
- Ask some students to report back to the class.

Optional activity

Mobile phones debate

- Ask: *Is it a good thing that mobile phones are now the number one form of communication?* On the board, draw two columns, *Advantages of mobiles* and *Disadvantages of mobiles.*
- Students work in pairs and discuss their ideas. Encourage them to think about cost, theft, health issues, stress or dangerous driving.
- Students work in fours. One pair argues for mobiles, the other against. Write some useful language on the board, eg:

  With a mobile, you can …
  If you don't have a mobile, you / other people can't …
  Mobiles cause (car accidents / cancer).

- When they have finished, ask some students to report back to the class. Were the arguments for mobiles more convincing than the arguments against them?

Vocabulary

1

- Students match the phrases then find them in the text to check their answers.
- Check the answers with the class.

Answers
1 keep in touch 2 have a chat 3 spread rumours
4 form a bond 5 keep a secret

2

- Students find the negative phrase in Ex 1.
- Check the answers with the class.

Answers
positive: 1, 2, 4, 5 negative: 3

3

- Students work individually and complete the task.
- Check the answers with the class.

Answers
1 keep a secret 2 have a chat 3 keep in touch
4 spread rumours 5 form a bond

4

- Students discuss which questions are true for them.

5

- Students stay in pairs and discuss the questions. Encourage them to give examples.
- Ask some students to report back to the class. Find out what proportion of students think they are good at keeping in touch with friends, and at keeping secrets.

Optional activity

Vocabulary extension

- Say: *Look at the text again and underline any verbs that mean 'say' or 'talk' (or 'say' / 'talk' in a particular way).*
- Check the answers with the class and write them on the board (*gossip, speak, tell, question, admit, complain).*
- Write these gapped sentences on the board. Students complete them with the correct form of the verbs.
  1 The police ________ the man about the robbery for three hours.
  2 We ________ all afternoon about our friends from school.
  3 Please can you ________ us a story?
  4 I ________ that I sometimes make mistakes.
  5 He ________ to my boss that I made a mistake.
  6 She always ________ very quietly on the phone.
- Check the answers with the class.

Answers
1 questioned 2 gossiped 3 tell 4 admit
5 complained 6 speaks

Language study

Talking about recent events

Past simple and present perfect simple

1

- Students look at the diagram and answer the questions.
- Check the answers with the class.

Answers
1 in a finished time period: A, in an unfinished time period: B
2 the past simple: A, the present perfect simple: B

2

- Students read and answer the question. Quickly revise the formation of present perfect simple positive, negative and questions on the board if necessary.

Answer
Use the auxiliary *have / has* + past participle

3

- Students work in pairs and write the past simple and present perfect forms of the verbs in the box.
- They check their answers in the Grammar reference on page 58.
- Check the answers with the class, focusing particularly on the pronunciation of *bought* /bɔːt/ and *heard* /hɜːd/.

Answers
become, became, become break, broke, broken
buy, bought, bought eat, ate, eaten fall, fell, fallen
have, had, had hear, heard, heard see, saw, seen
speak, spoke, spoken take, took, taken

Optional activity

Irregular verbs ping pong

- Students play in two teams. Each team needs a scrunched up piece of paper to use as a ball.
- Student A 'serves' by saying a verb from Ex 3, and throwing the 'ball' to Student B on the opposing team. Student B gives the past simple and past participle forms of the verb then throws the ball to C saying another irregular verb. Teams score a point if the other team gives an incorrect verb form.
- Ask a pair of students to show the game to the class. Students then play the game in teams.
- At the end of the game, ask which verbs students found most problematic.

4

- Students work in pairs. They read out the dialogue and complete the task.
- Check the answers with the class.

Answers
2 A – because last week has finished.
3 B – because her hair is still dyed.
4 B – because she still hasn't been to class.
5 A – because Tuesday and Wednesday have finished.

5

- Students choose the correct alternative.
- Check the answers with the class. For each sentence, ask: *Which words helped you choose the correct tense?*

Answers
1 Have you done 2 Did you get 3 Have you heard
4 What did you do 5 Have you seen

6

- Ask a pair of students to read out and answer question 1 from Ex 5. Focus on the use of the past simple when giving more details in the answer, eg *Yes, I have. I went to the gym on Tuesday and I ran 5km on Thursday.*
- Students ask and answer the questions in pairs. Encourage them to give as much detail as possible.
- Ask some students to report back to the class.
- Write on the board and discuss any recurring errors.

7

- Students read the task. Check comprehension of *item.*
- Students complete the sentences with the correct verb form.
- Check the answers with the class.

Answers
2 saw 3 had 4 've bought 5 went 6 've made

8

- Read out the task. Ask: *How should you change sentence 2 if you never go to the cinema?* (I didn't see any films …).
- Students complete the task.
- Ask some students to read out their sentences.

9

- Read out the example. Focus on the change of tenses: present perfect for talking about an unfinished period of time, but past simple when giving details.
- Students work in pairs and talk about their sentences. Encourage them to give as much detail as possible.
- Ask some students to report back to the class.
- Write on the board and discuss any recurring errors.

Optional activity

Time expressions

- Students look again at the time expressions in the diagram at the top of page 36. Ask them to suggest more time expressions for each tense, eg *at ten o'clock, on Wednesday, at lunchtime* (past simple), and *this week, in the last few minutes* (present perfect).
- Students work in pairs. They take turns to say a time expression that takes either the past simple or present perfect. Their partner uses the time expression in a true sentence.
- Model a sentence, eg *At lunchtime, I had a cheese sandwich.* Then say another time expression and ask a student to make a sentence.
- Encourage students to use as wide a variety of time expressions as they can. Go around the class giving help.
- Write on the board and discuss any recurring errors.

You didn't hear it from me

Listening and speaking

1

- **18** Read out the names that students have to listen for.
- Students listen and tick the names they hear.
- Check the answers with the class.

Answers
Mika, Ben, Sara, Marco

Listening script 18

(J = Justin, N = Nick)
J: Hi, Nick.
N: Have you heard?
J: Heard what?
N: About Mika.
J: No. What?
N: According to Roger, she's gone crazy. Apparently, she left her job yesterday and now she wants to go to Thailand and live on a beach.
J: Wow! Why do you think she's done that?
N: It may be something to do with Ben. You know? Her ex-boyfriend. Well, he split up with his new girlfriend last week. I heard that he wants to go to Asia to sell jewellery.
J: Well, that's it then, isn't it? I'm sure you're right. So I guess she's still in love with him then …
(A = Ashley, L = Lisa)
A: Hi, Lisa.
L: Ash! Guess what!
A: What?
L: Sara's had her baby!
A: No! Really? When?
L: Today. This morning. She's still in the hospital with her husband and Marco.
A: Her brother Marco?
L: Yeah, and you won't believe this!
A: What? Tell me, tell me.
L: He's put on so much weight.
A: You're joking! It must have happened recently because I saw him three months ago and he looked great.
L: Yes. Oh, he's still good looking, he's just … well, bigger.

2

- Check comprehension of *split up with* and *put on weight.*
- Students try to remember the answers, then listen to the recording again.
- They compare their answers in pairs.

3

- Students listen and check their answers to Ex 2. At the same time, they match the time expressions to the news items from Ex 2.
- Check the answers with the class.

Answers
1 Sara 2 Mika 3 Ben 4 Marco
Mika – yesterday Ben – last week Sara – today
Marco – recently

4

- Students answer the questions.

Answers
a Ben is Mika's ex-boyfriend b Sara is Marco's sister

5

- Refer students to the Listening script on page 62 to help them complete the table.
- Check the answers with the class.

Answers
Introducing some news: Have you heard?, You won't believe this!
Saying it came from someone else: Apparently, I heard that …
Reacting: Wow!, You're joking!

6

- Students write their dialogues in pairs. Go around the class giving help as necessary.

7

- Students perfom their dialogues for the class.
- After a class vote on the best dialogue, ask some students why they voted as they did.
- Write on the board and discuss any recurring errors with the past simple and present perfect.

Revision activity

Present perfect memory game

- Say: *Think of a place you've visited and something you've done there.* Give a personal example, such as: *I've eaten hamburgers in New York.*
- When all the students have thought of a sentence, demonstrate the game. Going round the class, students say their sentence and try to remember their classmates' sentences in the correct order. For example:

  Katya: *I've heard Big Ben in London.*
  Noriko: *Katya's heard Big Ben in London. And I've photographed lions in South Africa.*
  Luis: *Katya's heard Big Ben in London. Noriko's photographed lions in South Africa. And I've seen the Pope in Rome …*

- Students work in groups of six to eight. If anyone thinks that a sentence is not grammatically correct, they should consult you before using it. Can they get right round the circle without forgetting anything?

Extra practice

Students complete the Extra practice material on page 54, either in class or for homework.

Extra practice answers

1 1 e 2 b 3 d 4 c 5 a

2 1 has become 2 asked 3 emailed 4 haven't seen 5 haven't sent 6 had 7 haven't spoken 8 sent

3
1 Have you spoken to your best friend lately?
2 Did you send any emails yesterday?
3 Have you used your mobile phone today?
4 Have you had a chat with your parents recently?
5 Did you buy a new computer last year?
6 Have you seen a good film this month?

4 (individual answers)

5 1 believe 2 Really 3 joking 4 According 5 Wow 6 apparently 7 heard

References

Grammar reference Unit 1: Coursebook page 58
Wordlist Unit 1: Coursebook page 60
Photocopiable resources: Teacher's Book pages 96–97
Unit 1 test: Teacher's Book page 132–133

CD-ROM

Unit 1 Don't breathe a word!
Language exercise: Has she told you what she told me?
Vocabulary activity: Gossip
CEF-linked activity: I can listen and respond to news about other people
Game: Cats in hats (present perfect / past simple)

Pass the popcorn, please

Topic	Language study	Vocabulary	Main skills
• Mad about movies • Movie mistakes message board	• Asking for and giving opinions	• Types of film • Describing elements of a film	• **Reading:** identifying main ideas • **Listening:** identifying descriptions • **Pronunciation:** emphatic stress in description phrases • **Speaking:** discussing strengths and weaknesses of a film • **Writing:** a film review

Learning aims

- Can ask for and give opinions
- Can write a film review
- Can describe different elements of a film

Ideas for preparation

- a label for each student for 'Find your film partner' (see Warmer below)
- the text of the film review on an OHT (see Revision activity p53)

Warmer

Find your film partner

- Prepare a label for each student with the name of a character from a famous film. There should be at least two characters from each film (see suggestions below).
- Attach a label to each student's back. Say: *Don't tell each other what the labels say.*
- Explain that students are going to play a game. They move around the classroom, asking *yes / no* questions to guess the name of the character on their backs and identify people from the same film.
- Model an example. Check that it's a character everyone has heard of, then ask questions to guess the character: *Am I a man? Do I live on another planet? Am I a hero? Did I live a long time ago?* until you guess who you are.
- For a weaker class, write example questions on the board.
- Students play the game. Go around the class giving help.
- When everyone has found a partner, ask some students to report back to the class.

Possible film partners

Darth Vader / Luke Skywalker / Princess Leia (*Star Wars*)
Harry Potter / Ron Weasley (*Harry Potter*)
James Bond / M (*James Bond*)
Superman / Lois Lane (*Superman*)
Frodo / Gandalf (*Lord of the Rings*)
Scarlett O'Hara / Rhett Butler (*Gone with the Wind*)
Mr Pink / Mr Blue / Mr Orange (*Reservoir Dogs*)

Mad about movies

Lead-in

1

- Ask students to open their books on page 38. Explain the task. Check pronunciation of *martial* /ˈmɑːʃəl/, *romance* /rəʊˈmæns/, *drama* /ˈdrɑːmə/.
- Students work in pairs. They describe the pictures on the left of page 38 using words from the box.
- Check the answers with the class.

Answers
1 horror 2 romance 3 western 4 comedy
5 gangster movie

2

- Students work in pairs and think of films for each genre.
- Students change pairs and compare their ideas.
- Ask some students to report back to the class.

Possible answers
animation: *Toy Story* comedy: *Notting Hill* fantasy: *The Lord of the Rings* gangster movie: *Pulp Fiction* historical drama: *Gladiator* horror: *Scream* martial arts: *Crouching Tiger, Hidden Dragon* romance: *Bridget Jones' Diary* science fiction: *Star Wars* war drama: *Saving Private Ryan* western: *High Noon*

3

- Students work in groups and discuss the questions.
- Ask some students to report back to the class.

Reading

1

- **19** This text is recorded on the CD. You can use it as an alternative or in addition to the teaching notes below.
- Explain that students are going to read a review of a film called *The Aviator*. Ask: *Do you know anything about this film? Has anyone seen it? Did you enjoy it? Why? / Why not?*
- Students read the review on page 39. Encourage them to find the answers quickly, without worrying about parts of the text that they don't understand.
- Check the answers with the class.

Answers
Five – horror, war drama, comedy, gangster movie, western

2

- Students read the text again and answer the questions.
- Check the answers with the class.

Answers
1 He directed the film *The Aviator*, which was based on Hughes's life.
2 He wrote a biography of Hughes.
3 He played the role of Hughes in *The Aviator*.
4 She was an actress who had a love affair with Hughes.

3

- Students read the statements. Check comprehension and pronunciation of vocabulary such as *government* /'gʌvnmənt/.
- Students answer the questions individually, then compare their answers in pairs. If there is any doubt about an answer, encourage them to look again carefully at the relevant part of the text.
- Check the answers with the class.

Answers
1 T 2 F (He used his money to influence governments)
3 T 4 T (Note that *produces* in this article means *made*)
5 F (He had many friends) 6 T

4

- Students look back at the text to answer the questions.
- Encourage students to underline the relevant parts of the text.
- Check the answer with the class. Also check comprehension and pronunciation of *charisma* /kə'rɪzmə/ and focus on the expression *it's a pity*.

Answers
The reviewer thinks the film is disappointing and one-sided – *Scorsese has chosen only to remember the younger Hughes' spirit of adventure as an aviator, which is a pity*. He also thinks that Leonardo DiCaprio isn't convincing as Howard Hughes – *Leonardo DiCaprio … does not have the power and charisma of the real Howard Hughes.*

5

- Read out the task. Check comprehension of vocabulary such as *leading* and *accept*.
- Students complete the questions using the words in the box. Encourage them to use the context of the words in the text to help them with meanings.
- Check the answers with the class.

Answers
1 biography 2 role 3 hesitation 4 convincingly
5 devote

6

- Students work in pairs. They ask and answer the Ex 5 questions. Encourage them to give details in their answers, and to ask follow-up questions, rather than giving one-word answers.
- Ask some students to report back to the class.

7

- Students work in groups. Read out the questions. Check comprehension of vocabulary such as *accurate*.
- Students discuss the questions in groups.
- Ask some students to report back to the class. Ask: *Is it possible to make a film about a real person that is interesting* ***and*** *accurate? Does it matter if a film about a real person isn't accurate? Why? / Why not?*

Background information

Biopics
Films which dramatise the life of historically significant people are known as 'biopics' /'baɪəʊpɪk/, a combination of 'biography' and 'picture'. Over the years, the lives of Gandhi, Elizabeth I, Johnny Cash, Cleopatra and Malcolm X have all been brought to the cinema screen.

Optional activity

Write your own film

- Explain that students are going to work in pairs to develop a pitch for a film about a real person.
- Each pair chooses a real person that they know something about, but whose life hasn't already been made into a film.
- They decide on the life events they will include, the actors for the main roles, and the locations and costumes they will need to get the right 'look' for the film.
- They plan an important scene in the film (perhaps the first or last), describing what the viewer sees and writing a few lines of dialogue.
- Ask a few pairs to give their pitch, by describing the film and actors and reading / acting out their scene.
- If you have the time and facilities available, you could record the students acting the scenes they've written. You can use it for pronunciation practice, or for other students to write a review of it.

Listening and pronunciation

1

- **20** Read out the task. Students listen and answer the question.
- Students compare their answers with a partner.
- Check the answers with the class. Ask: *What film are they talking about? (Pirates of the Caribbean).*

Answers
Jack and Chloe liked it. Ralph didn't.

Listening script 20

(J = Jack, C = Chloe, R = Ralph)

J: Well? What did you think of it?
C: I thought it was absolutely fantastic!
J: Yeah, me too.
C: Johnny Depp is so funny and so gorgeous, and he makes a great pirate.
J: How about you, Ralph? What did you think of it?
R: In my opinion, it was really childish, not very funny and it went on too long.
J: Really? What did you think about the action scenes? They were pretty impressive, weren't they?
C: Yes, I thought they were absolutely brilliant, too! And the special effects were really spectacular.
R: OK, the special effects were pretty good, but I noticed some historical mistakes. As far as I'm concerned, Hollywood doesn't care enough about historical accuracy – exploding shells didn't exist in the 1600s ...
C: Oh, come on, Ralph. Don't you think you're taking it all a bit too seriously? It's supposed to be a comedy.
R: Maybe, but I'm still going to post a message on the *Movie Mistakes* page so that other people can see the mistake too.
J: Post a message? If you ask me, the people who read those messages are worse than the people who make the mistakes.
C: Same here. Ralph, I think you need to get yourself a girlfriend.

2

- Students read the task. Check comprehension and pronunciation of vocabulary such as *gorgeous* /ˈgɔːdʒəs/. Explain that adjectives 1–7 are in the order they are spoken on the recording.
- Students listen and answer, then compare their answers with a partner. If necessary, play the recording again.
- Check the answers with the class.

Answers

1 the film 2 Johnny Depp 3 the film 4 action scenes 5 action scenes 6 special effects 7 special effects

3

- Students listen again and answer.
- Check the answers with the class.

Answers

1 absolutely 2 so 3 really, (not) very 4 pretty 5 absolutely 6 really 7 pretty

4

- 21 Students listen and repeat. Encourage them to exaggerate the intonation as they say the phrases. It may help them to mark the stressed syllables on the Listening script on page 62.

Listening script 21

1 absolutely fantastic
2 so funny
3 so gorgeous
4 really childish
5 not very funny
6 pretty impressive
7 absolutely brilliant
8 really spectacular
9 pretty good

Grammar note

Intensifiers with extreme adjectives

absolutely can only be used with extreme adjectives such as *fantastic, brilliant, terrible, exhausted.* You cannot say *absolutely good / bad / tired.*
very cannot be used with extreme adjectives. You can say *very good*, but not *very fantastic.*
If students have trouble using intensifiers correctly, they might find this table helpful:

	good, bad, tired	fantastic, terrible, exhausted
absolutely	✗	✓
so, really, pretty	✓	✓
very	✓	✗

Optional activity

Emphatic descriptions game

- Students look at Listening script 21 on page 62.
- Explain that they are going to play a game using phrases like the ones from Listening script 21.
- Give each student nine blank cards. They write a word or phrase on each card that fits the description in the Listening script. So, for example, they could write *football* on their first card if they think *football* is absolutely fantastic.
- Students work in groups of four. They put all their cards together in a pile and shuffle them. In turn, they take the top card from the pile and make a sentence using the word(s) on the card and a phrase from the Listening script, eg *football is really childish.* Encourage them to use lots of expression. They get a point for every person in their group who agrees with their sentence.
- At the end of the game, each group works out the winner. Students report back to the class about their group's most interesting sentences.

Language study

Asking for and giving opinions

1

- Students match phrases a–i with functions 1–4.
- They check their answers in the Grammar reference on page 58.
- Check the answers with the class.

Answers

1 a 2 b, d, e, h 3 c, f 4 g, i

2

- **22** Students read through the dialogue then complete the gaps with the anagrammed phrases.
- Play the recording so they can check their answers.
- Check the answers with the class.
- Play the recording again, pausing after each sentence for students to repeat.

Answers
1 What do you think of 2 think 3 Me too
4 Really? If you ask me 5 same here 6 Oh, come on
7 As far as I'm concerned

Listening script 22

A: What do you think of Leonardo DiCaprio?
B: I think he's gorgeous.
C: Me too.
A: Really? If you ask me, Johnny Depp is more interesting.
C: Ooh, same here. I prefer him, actually.
B: Oh, come on! Johnny Depp's too old now.
A: As far as I'm concerned, they both are.

3

- **23** Students complete the dialogue using phrases from Ex 1.
- Play the recording so they can check their answers.
- Check the answers with the class.

Answers
1 think of 2 In my 3 Really 4 think
5 you ask 6 come

4

- Students work in pairs. They write and practise a dialogue. Go around the class giving help as necessary.
- Ask some pairs to act out their dialogue for the class. Encourage other students to correct any errors in the use of the phrases from this unit.

5

- Students read through the task in part 1 on page 61. Check comprehension and pronunciation of problematic vocabulary such as *generally* /ˈdʒenrəli/ *maximum* /ˈmæksɪməm/, *weapons* /ˈwepənz/, *relevant* /ˈreləvənt/, *maturing* /məˈtʃʊərɪŋ/, *lowered* /ˈləʊəd/, *banned* /bænd/ and *punished* /ˈpʌnɪʃt/.
- Students work individually and give each statement a score from 1–5, following the key.
- In part 2, students work in groups. Discuss the first statement as an example, using some of the phrases from the box. Go around the class giving help as necessary and noting any errors.
- Write on the board and discuss any recurring errors.

Vocabulary

1

- Students refer to Listening script 20 on page 62 to remind themselves of the conversation they heard earlier in this unit.
- They read the message board to find Ralph's message. Encourage them to complete the task as quickly as possible, without worrying about parts of the text that they don't understand. If students have already talked about which film was discussed, go straight on to Ex 2.

Answer
The message is about *Pirates of the Caribbean*

2

- Students read the text again more carefully. They work in pairs and discuss the question.
- Students report back to the class. Do they agree on the worst mistake?

3

- Students read the words in the box. Check comprehension of vocabulary such as *reveal*.
- Students complete the questions with the words in bold in the text. Encourage them to use the context to help them work out the meanings.
- Check the answers with the class. Check pronunciation of *character* /ˈkærɪktə/, *close-up* /ˈkləʊsʌp/ and *scene* /siːn/.

Answers
1 close-up, character 2 set 3 played by 4 scene
5 in the background

4

- Students look again at the message board and answer the questions in Ex 3.
- Check the answers with the class.

Answers
1 *Lord of the Rings* and *Minority Report* 2 *Pirates of the Caribbean* and *Gladiator* 3 Mr Pink, *Reservoir Dogs*
4 *Spiderman* 5 Because radios weren't around in 180 AD

Optional activity

Class Oscars

- Students work in small groups. Say: *You're going to give Oscars for your favourite films of all time.*
- Students discuss the categories that they want to give awards in, and agree on nominations. They can have unusual categories, eg worst haircut, best animal actor or best / worst mistake.
- Ask students to report back to the class. Do their classmates agree with them?

Speaking and writing

1

- Read out the task. Check comprehension and pronunciation of vocabulary such as *recommend* /rekə'mend/.
- Students prepare their questions and answers, then interview each other in pairs.

2

- Students work individually to write a film review. Suggest that they structure their writing by following the order of the questions in Ex 1. You could set this activity for homework.

3

- Display students' reviews around the class, labelled with the writer's name.
- Students read the reviews. They talk to people who have written about films they know, agreeing or disagreeing with their opinions.
- Students report back to the class.
- Write on the board and discuss any recurring errors.

Revision activity

Film review dictogloss

- Explain to students that you are going to read them a film review. They have to make notes then work in pairs to reconstruct the text.
- Read this text twice. The first time, read it quite slowly. Students listen carefully without taking notes. The second time, read it slightly faster. Students listen and take notes.

Kingdom of Heaven
The film is a historical drama set in the 12th century. The main character, played by Orlando Bloom, has to leave his home in France. Soon he is fighting a war in Jerusalem. There's romance when Bloom meets the sister of the King of Jerusalem. But as far as I'm concerned, people should watch this film for its convincing battle scenes. The special effects are really spectacular.

- Students compare their notes in pairs and work together to reconstruct the text.
- Put pairs together into groups of four. They write a shared version of the text, editing for content, punctuation and spelling.
- Ask each group to read out their version of the text. Read your own version again and discuss the differences.
- Alternatively, show students the original written version on an OHP so they can compare their work with it.

Extra practice

Students complete the Extra practice material on page 55, either in class or for homework.

Extra practice answers

1 1 science fiction 2 comedy 3 western 4 martial arts 5 animation 6 historical drama

2 1 absolutely 2 really 3 childish 4 impressive 5 pretty 6 so

3 1 What do you think of 2 As far as I'm concerned 3 If you ask me 4 Oh, come on 5 in my opinion

4 1 set 2 character 3 played 4 close-ups 5 scenes 6 background

5 (individual answers)

References

Grammar reference Unit 2: Coursebook page 58
Wordlist Unit 2: Coursebook page 60
Communication activities: Coursebook page 61
Photocopiable resources: Teacher's Book pages 98–99
Unit 2 test: Teacher's Book pages 134–135

CD-ROM

Unit 2 Pass the popcorn, please
Language exercise: What did you think?
Vocabulary activity: Films
CEF-linked activity : I can write a film review
Game: Witch's pot (words connected with films)

UNIT 3

You must try it

Module 2

Topic	Language study	Vocabulary	Main skills
• A question of taste (response to blue food) • Good manners cost nothing (politeness in restaurant conversations) • Doing the right thing (cultural expectations)	• Quantifiers with countable and uncountable nouns	• Food • Ordering food in restaurants	• **Reading:** understanding main ideas • **Speaking:** role-play between customer and waiter; discussing good and bad manners • **Listening:** identifying correct information

Learning aims

- Can use quantifiers to talk about food
- Can order food in restaurants
- Can discuss good and bad manners

Ideas for preparation

- real or toy food items, or pictures of food (see Warmer below)

Warmer

Food bingo

- Bring in a selection of real or toy food items, or pictures of food. Try to include some vocabulary from the communication activity on pages 61 and 64.
- Hold them up one by one to revise the vocabulary. Write the words on the board. Encourage students to keep a separate page of their notebooks for food words.
- Ask students to write down six food words from the list on the board, in random order.
- Hold up your food items one by one. Students cross out the word if they have it. The first person with all six words crossed out and who shouts 'Bingo!', is the winner.

A question of taste

Lead-in

1

- Ask students to open their books on page 42. Students work in small groups and discuss the questions.
- Ask some students to report back to the class.
- Ask: *How many people ate something red? Green? Yellow? Blue? Brown?*

Reading

1

- 24 This text is recorded on the CD. You can use it as an alternative or in addition to the teaching notes below.
- Quickly revise the vocabulary in the pictures, focusing on the pronunciation of difficult words, eg *margarine* /mɑːdʒəˈriːn/, *biscuits* /ˈbɪskɪts/, *vegetables* /ˈvedʒtəblz/, *knife* /naɪf/.
- Students read the report and answer the question.
- Check the answer with the class.

Answer
The glass

2

- Students read the statements. Check comprehension of vocabulary such as *mask*.
- Students read the text more carefully and complete the statements.
- They compare their answers in pairs.
- Check the answer with the class.

Answers
1 to eat it 2 more natural / delicious 3 poisonous / dangerous to eat 4 lose weight / with weight problems 5 blue food than the group without masks

3

- Students work in groups. Read out the questions. Check comprehension of vocabulary such as *put off* and *refuse*.
- Students discuss the questions.
- Ask some students to report back to the class.

Optional activity

Interview the tester

- Students work in two groups. One group are journalists, the other the scientists who carried out the tests on blue food.
- Journalists work together to make a list of questions to ask the testers, based on information in the text.
- Testers work together and reread the article so they can talk about their experiment and its results. They can invent more details to make their accounts more interesting.
- Each journalist finds a tester and interviews him / her. Make sure they take notes.
- Journalists write a report of their interview while testers can write up the experiment in their own words. This activity can be set for homework.

Language study

Quantifiers with countable and uncountable nouns

1

- Students answer the questions.
- Check the answers with the class. If necessary, explain that countable nouns are things you can count, eg *1 apple, 2 apples, 3 apples,* whereas uncountable things cannot be counted – you have to count meat by saying *1 slice of meat, 2 slices,* etc.

Answers
1 countable 2 uncountable

2

- Students look back at the text on page 43 and underline the quantifiers.
- Check the answers with the class.

Answers
countable: a few (biscuits)
uncountable: a little (pasta)
both: a lot of (people, food), any (blue vegetables, meat)
some: (biscuits, spaghetti, rice)

3

- Students complete the Phrases column.
- They check their answers in the Grammar reference on pages 58–59.
- Check the answers with the class, in particular the correct use of *of.*

Answers

Countable	?	How many?
	–	There aren't any
	+	There are some / a few / a lot of
Uncountable	?	How much?
	–	There isn't any
	+	There is some / a little / a lot of

4

- Students add more nouns to the table in Ex 3.
- Check the answers with the class.

Answers
Countable: vegetables, biscuits, knife, fork, spoon, bowl, glass, plate
Uncountable: butter, margarine, meat, colouring, rice, spaghetti

5

- Students read the sentences. Check comprehension of *could you live on.*
- Students complete the sentences.
- Check the answers with the class.

Answers
1 many 2 much 3 much 4 many 5 many

6

- Students work individually and plan their four truthful and one untruthful answers to the questions in Ex 5.
- They find a partner, and ask and answer the questions. Encourage them to ask for more details to help them guess which answer is untrue.
- Ask: *How many people guessed their partner's untruthful answer correctly?*

7

- Briefly revise the food vocabulary required for the communication activity on pages 61 and 64.
- Students work in pairs and complete the task. Go around the class giving help and noting errors.
- Students report back to the class. Ask: *Did all Student As write the correct shopping list?*
- Write on the board and discuss any recurring errors in the use of countable and uncountable nouns and quantifiers.

8

- Students work individually and personalise the sentences.
- Students report back to the class.

Answers
1 a few / a lot of 2 a little / a lot of 3 a few / a lot of
4 a few / a lot of 5 a little / a lot of

9

- Ask two students to read out the dialogue. Explain that they are going to hear each other's sentences from Ex 8 and find out at least one extra piece of information about each sentence.
- Students work in groups and talk about their sentences.
- Students report back to the class.

Optional activity

Healthy living

- Write on the board:

In my family / household, we eat:
a lot of a few a little
we don't eat:
much many
we drink:
a lot of a little

Chinese food / takeaways / fruit / vegetables / tea / bread / salad / steak / rice / Italian food / cola

- Adapt the list to suit the age / nationalities of your students.
- Students work individually and make sentences using the prompts on the board.
- Students find a partner and compare their sentences.
- Ask: *How are you similar to your partner?*

Good manners cost nothing

Background information

Table manners

In British culture, the following are considered good table manners:

- waiting for everyone on the table to be served before you start eating
- leaving your knife and fork together across the middle of the plate when you've finished
- saying *please* and *thank you* a lot
- offering to split a restaurant bill
- attracting a waiter's attention discreetly

The following are considered bad table manners:

- talking with your mouth full
- putting your elbows on the table
- attracting a waiter's attention by calling 'Waiter!'

Vocabulary

1

- **25** With books closed, ask students for examples of good manners in their culture.
- Students open their books at page 44 and read the quote at the top. Check comprehension and discuss whether students agree.
- Explain that students are going to listen to a conversation in a restaurant. Ask them to predict some of the words they might hear, and pre-teach if necessary the words *starter, main course, dessert* /dɪˈzɜːt/.
- Students read and listen to the conversation, then answer the question.
- Check the answer with the class.

Answers

The waiter thinks the customer's horrible.

2

- Students work in pairs and replace comments 1–9 in the Ex 1 dialogue with the comments in the box.

3

- **26** Students listen and check their answers to Ex 2.
- Check the Ex 2 answers with the class, then discuss the questions in Ex 3.
- Students count how many times *please* and *thanks / thank you* are used in the polite version of the dialogue. Ask: *Are these words used more or less in English than in your own language?*

Answers

1 I'd like a table for one, please.
2 No, I haven't.
3 Could I see the menu, please?
4 Yes, please.
5 I'll just have the spaghetti, please.
6 No, thanks.
7 Oh, excuse me, could I have some more water, please?
8 Just the bill, please.
9 Here you are. Thanks.

The waiter thought the customer was lovely. A tip is the extra money you leave for the waiter at the end of a meal, to thank him for his service.

Listening script 26

A: I'd like a table for one, please.
B: Certainly, sir. Have you booked?
A: No, I haven't.
B: No problem. Would you come this way, please?
A: Could I see the menu, please?
B: Of course, sir. I'll get you one immediately.
B: Are you ready to order?
A: Yes, please.
B: Any starters?
A: I'll just have the spaghetti, please.
B: Main course. Certainly. Anything else?
A: No, thanks. Oh, excuse me, could I have some more water, please?

B: I'll bring you another bottle, sir.
B: Would you like any dessert, or coffee?
A: Just the bill, please.
B: Certainly. That'll be £12.50, please.
A: Here you are. Thanks.
B: Thank you very much, sir. See you again, I hope. What a lovely man and what a generous tip.

Optional activity

Disappearing text

- Write part of the polite version of the dialogue on the board, from *Anything else?* to *Here you are* (see Listening script 26 on page 62).
- Play the relevant part of the recording line by line. With books closed, students listen and repeat.
- Rub off small parts of the dialogue on the board. Students have to read out the whole dialogue, saying the missing words from memory.
- Repeat the process several times, each time rubbing off more of the dialogue. Eventually, students will be saying most of the dialogue from memory.

4

- Students read the sentence halves. Check comprehension and pronunciation of problematic vocabulary such as *avocado* /ævəˈkɑːdəʊ/.
- Students complete the task in pairs.
- Check the answers with the class.

Answers

1 c customer)
2 e (customer)
3 a (waiter)
4 h (customer)
5 b (waiter)
6 g (waiter)
7 d (customer)
8 f (waiter)

5

- Students work in pairs. They practise their own restaurant dialogue. Go around the class giving help as necessary.
- Each pair acts out their dialogue, either for the whole class or for a group of students. Note errors in the new language they have learnt.
- Discuss which was the funniest / politest / rudest dialogue with the class.
- Write on the board and discuss any recurring errors.
- Ask: *Has anyone worked as a waiter or waitress? Did you like it? What are the advantages and disadvantages of this type of job?*

Doing the right thing

Listening and speaking

1

- Ask: *What can you see in the pictures?* Elicit or teach the words *formal, chopsticks, barbecue.*
- Students read the questions quickly. Check comprehension of problematic vocabulary such as *offend, host, casually.*
- Students answer the questions.
- Students compare their answers with a partner.

2

- **27** Students listen and check their answers to Ex 1.
- They compare their answers with their partner. If necessary, play the recording again.
- Check the Ex 1 answers with the class. Ask: *Did any of the answers surprise you?*

Answers

1 a 2 b 3 a 4 c 5 b 6 a 7 b

Listening script 27

A lot of people worry about doing the wrong thing when they eat in another country. My advice is: don't worry. Most of the time, the rules are the same around the world: don't put your elbows on the table, don't speak with your mouth full. That sort of thing. But sometimes it helps if you know one or two things about the place where you are eating. I was at a formal dinner in Canada with a friend who saw all the knives and forks and said, 'What do I do? How do I know which ones to use?' She was so worried, but I told her, 'Just start on the outside and work in.' Easy. It's the same all over the world, where people use a knife and fork.

But you have to be careful if you're in a country where they use chopsticks. I was enjoying a delicious meal in China and I wanted to put my chopsticks down for a moment. I didn't want to put them on the table – it seemed dirty – so I stuck them into my bowl of rice. Two or three people quickly told me that this was bad manners and so I rested them across my plate, and that was OK. That was a cultural mistake, but sometimes the mistake may offend someone's religious beliefs. In Tunisia, which is a Muslim country, I picked up a piece of bread in my left hand. My Tunisian friend told me that I should use my right hand to pick up food. It is bad manners to use the left hand to pick up food or shake someone's hand. I think that is important to know.

Traditions, though, are not always so important. In Britain people argue about how to make tea properly – do you put the milk in first or the tea in first? The truth is, it's not really important. You won't offend anyone if you get the order wrong. You might offend a lot of people, though, if you drink your tea loudly. Slurping your food or drink is not generally regarded as polite behaviour. It's the same in Asia, but there is an exception. It's perfectly acceptable to make a noise when eating noodles, particularly if you are a man. I was at a noodle restaurant in Japan, with a friend, a young Japanese man, and he told me that if I make a lot of noise eating my noodles, the chef will be happy. Of course I tried, but I have to say it felt strange.

If you're invited to someone's house for a meal, it's common across Europe to take a bottle of wine, or flowers. It's the same in Australia, where I'm from, but if you are invited to a barbecue at someone's house, it's really important to relax and show that you are enjoying yourself. We usually dress casually for a barbecue and treat it as a very informal occasion. You shouldn't be too formal – don't wait for service, serve yourself. It shows the host that you really feel at home. They will feel relaxed if they see that you are relaxed.

Optional activity

Listening extension: true or false?

- Write these statements on the board:

  1 In most countries it's rude to put your elbows on the table.
  2 In Tunisia, you should shake someone's hand with your left hand.
  3 In Britain, you shouldn't slurp your tea.
  4 The speaker likes making a noise when he eats.
  5 The speaker comes from Asia.

- Students read the sentences. Check comprehension of problematic vocabulary such as *elbows*, *slurp*.
- Students listen to the recording again and decide if the sentences are true or false.
- They compare their answers in pairs.
- Check the answers with the class.

Answers

1 T 2 F (Use your right hand) 3 T 4 F (He did it once in Japan, but it felt strange) 5 F (Australia)

3

- Students work in groups and discuss the questions. Go around the class giving help as necessary.
- Students report back to the class.
- Ask: *How can you find out about manners in a country you are going to visit?* (Look on the internet, read a guidebook or ask someone who knows the country well.)

Revision activity

Ask your partner

- Students work individually and prepare questions to ask their partner about their last restaurant visit.
- Elicit examples, like *Was it your first visit? What did you have for dessert? Is it an expensive restaurant?*
- Students take turns to ask and answer questions.
- They write their partner's answers as an email to a third friend, telling him / her about the classmate's visit.

Extra practice

Students complete the Extra practice material on page 56, either in class or for homework.

Extra practice answers

1 1 aren't 2 is 3 a few 4 any 5 is 6 isn't

2 1 few 2 much 3 lot 4 many 5 are 6 little 7 isn't

3 1 How many 2 How much 3 How many 4 How much 5 How many 6 How much

4 (individual answers)

5 1 Can I have a table for one, please?
2 Could I see the menu, please?
3 Are you ready to order?
4 Could I have some more water, please?
5 Would you like any coffee?
6 Can I recommend avocado as a starter?

6 a 2 b 5 c 4 d 6 e 3 f 1

References

Grammar reference Unit 3: Coursebook pages 58–59
Wordlist Unit 3: Coursebook page 60
Communication activities: Coursebook pages 61 and 64
Photocopiable resources: Teacher's Book pages 100–101
Unit 3 test: Teacher's Book pages 136–137

CD-ROM

Unit 3 You must try it
Language exercise: Everyone is different
Vocabulary activity: Eating out
CEF-linked activity: I can order food in restaurants
Game: Neighbourhood (eating in restaurants)

Followers of fashion

Topic	Language study	Vocabulary	Main skills
• Looking good (beauty contest) • Body art	• Recognising and using phrasal verbs	• Describing appearance and things you wear	• **Reading:** identifying main ideas • **Speaking:** discussing beauty and body decoration • **Listening:** understanding descriptions of body art • **Writing:** an email explaining a decision

Learning aims

- Can recognise and use phrasal verbs
- Can discuss beauty and body decoration
- Can write a short email explaining a decision

Ideas for preparation

- flashcards with clothes words, pictures from a fashion magazine (see Warmer below)

Warmer

Fashion pictures

- Bring in some pictures from a fashion magazine. They should reflect a variety of clothing styles and show shoes, jacket, T-shirt, dress, jumper, boots, coat, hat, etc.
- Students look at the pictures – in groups if you have a large class – and discuss what they think of the clothes, to revise the vocabulary and structures connected with clothes.
- Elicit the English words for the clothes they see. Write their ideas on the board.

Looking good

Lead-in

1

- Ask students to open their books on page 46. Students look at the title *Looking good* and the photo of the man at the top of the page. Ask: *Do you think the man in the photo looks good?*
- Students read the statements. Check comprehension *beauty contest, seriously, old-fashioned, sexist.*
- Students work in groups and discuss the statements. Go around the class giving help as necessary.
- Students report back to the class on their discussions. Have a show of hands to see how many people agree with each statement.

Reading

Background information

Miss World

The *Miss World* beauty contest began in the UK in 1951 and it was a huge international event for many years.

Under pressure from feminism in the 1980s, Miss World repositioned itself by adopting the slogan *Beauty With a Purpose.* The contest now tests intelligence and personality, as well as beauty. Nevertheless, beauty contests are considered not to be politically correct, as they can be offensive to women.

1

- **28** This text is recorded on the CD. You can use it as an alternative or in addition to the teaching notes below.
- Ask: *What does the photo at the bottom of the page show?* Elicit or teach *tribe.*
- Read out the task. Check comprehension and pronunciation of *contestant* /kənˈtestənt/, *judge* /dʒʌdʒ/.
- Students read the extract to answer the questions.
- Check the answers with the class.

Answers

a Beautiful young men of the Wodaabe tribe
b Three beautiful young Wodaabe women from different tribes

2

- Students read the text again and answer the questions.
- They compare their answers with a partner.
- Check the answers with the class. Check comprehension of *powder* /ˈpaʊdə/ and *honour* /ˈɒnə/. Ask someone to demonstrate *cross their eyes,* and *roll their eyes.* Ask: *What do you think 'charm' means here?* (A small object that is believed to bring good luck.)

Answers

1 Seven days 2 The women of their tribe 3 Yellow powder 4 Charms; watches hanging from necklaces 5 Roll their eyes and smile 6 Honour, fame and many wives 7 Looks

3

- Students work in pairs and discuss the questions.
- Ask some students to report back to the class. Ask: *Would you like to see a Gerewol-style beauty contest in your own country? Why? / Why not?*

Vocabulary and speaking

1

- Students categorise the words in the box. Encourage them to find the words in the text and use the context to help them with meanings.
- Check the answers with the class.

Answers

Things you wear: necklace, watch
Describing appearance: attractive, beautiful, traditional, trendy, up-to-date

2

- Students read the words in the box. Check comprehension of *fashionable* /ˈfæʃnəbl/, *neutral* /ˈnjuːtrəl/. Check they know to answer questions 1–3 with the words from Ex 1 as well as Ex 2.
- Students complete the task in pairs, using their dictionary where necessary.
- Check the answers with the class. Discuss differences of opinion, eg are earrings for men and women, or just women?

Answers

Things you wear: earrings, glasses, skirt, socks, tie, trousers
Describing appearance: casual, conservative, old-fashioned, scruffy, smart

Suggested answers

1 a tie b necklace, skirt, earrings
c watch, glasses, socks, trousers
2 a trendy, up-to-date b attractive, beautiful
3 a attractive, beautiful, trendy, up-to-date, smart
b conservative, old-fashioned, scruffy c traditional, casual

Optional activity

Picture dictation

- Explain that you are going to describe a picture. Students should listen carefully, as they will have to draw it later.
- Read the following description quite quickly. Make sure students don't start drawing at this stage.

The woman has long dark hair and she's wearing some big, square glasses. She also has earrings on. They're very long – they almost touch the jacket that she's wearing. It's a smart jacket, and she's wearing a tie as well. Then she's got a short skirt, and long socks. The socks are very scruffy, with lots of holes in them. And she isn't wearing any shoes. She looks a bit strange.

- Read the text again, more slowly. This time students draw as you speak.
- Students compare their pictures and choose their favourite to show to the class.

3

- Students work in groups. Check pronunciation of *jewellery* /ˈdʒuːəlri/.
- Students discuss the questions. Go around the class giving help as necessary.
- Students report back to the class.

Language study

Recognising and using phrasal verbs

1

- Tell students that they will be learning about phrasal verbs (some students may have come across them as *multi-word verbs*). Elicit examples of common phrasal verbs such as *pick up, go out with, get on with.* Explain that phrasal verbs usually consist of a verb and one or more prepositions.
- Students find the phrasal verbs in the sentences.
- Check the answers with the class.

Answers

1 get up 2 dress up 3 try on

2

- Students work in pairs and discuss the meaning of the phrasal verbs from Ex 1.
- Listen to suggestions, but don't give the answer.

3

- Students read the dictionary entries. Check comprehension of vocabulary such as *formal, effort, occasion.*
- Students work in pairs and complete the sentences with the verbs from Ex 1.
- Check the answers with the class.

Answers

1 dress up 2 try, on 3 gets up

4

- Write on the board: *I love chocolate.* Ask: *Which word is the object? Which word is a pronoun?* Explain the terms if students are unsure.
- Students follow the diagram and answer the question.
- Check the answer with the class.

Answer

Steps 1 and 2

5

- Students find the verbs in the diagram and match the verbs to their grammar.
- Students compare their answers with a partner.
- Check the answers with the class.

Answers

1 b 2 c 3 a

6

- Students find the verbs in the text on page 46 and discuss their meaning in pairs.
- They look up the words in their dictionaries to check.
- Check the answers with the class. They mime the actions to each other to make sure they understand. Ask: *Were your ideas correct?*

Answers
show off: [intransitive] to behave in a way that is intended to attract people's attention and make them admire you
make up: [transitive] to put make-up on someone's face
put on: [transitive] to cover a part of your body with a piece of clothing or jewellery so that you are wearing it

7

- Students work in pairs and discuss the meaning of the verbs, then check their answers in a dictionary.
- Alternatively, if time is limited, check their answers yourself.

Answers
1 meet by chance 2 give something to someone else for free 3 cancel 4 take care of 5 arrive 6 make a noise / ring

8

- Students answer the questions by looking at the way the phrasal verbs are used in Ex 7, and by looking again at steps 3 and 4 of the diagram.
- Check the answers with the class.

Answers
a turn up, go off b give away, call off
c come across, look after

9

- Check students understand that they only need to insert the pronouns where necessary; some sentences are correct as they are.
- Students work individually to complete the task.
- Check the answers with the class.

Answers
1 gave them away 2 No pronoun necessary 3 came across it 4 No pronoun necessary 5 call it off 6 look after her

Optional activity

Free practice of phrasal verbs

- Write on the board:

1 You win €10 million on the lottery. How much of your money do you give away? Who to?
2 On holiday, have you ever come across someone you know from home?
3 How often do you turn up late for class / work?
4 Have you ever had tickets for an event that was called off at the last minute?
5 Do you like dressing up for parties?
6 Have you ever looked after anyone else's pet?

- Students work in small groups and ask each other the questions. Encourage them to use the phrasal verbs in their answers.
- Students report back to the class.
- Write on the board and discuss any recurring errors.

Body art

Listening and speaking

1

- Explain the task. Check comprehension of vocabulary such as *consider*. Check pronunciation of *piercing* /ˈpɪəsɪŋ/ and *mohican* /məʊˈhiːkən/.
- Students work in groups and discuss the questions and the pictures at the top of the page.

2

- **29** Students look at pictures a–d and discuss who has this style of tattoo.
- Students report back to the class.
- Students listen to the recording and decide which tattoo isn't mentioned.
- Check the answer with the class.

Answer
Tattoo c (Harley Davidson) is not mentioned.

Listening script 29

(E = Ellen, F = Frank)

E: Is tattooing an old custom?

F: Oh yeah, tattoos have been around for a long time. The Greeks and the Egyptians had tattoos, and that was in about 2000 BC. Some people have found examples of tattoos from as far back as 3500 BC.

E: Wow! That's over 5,000 years ago. So, where does the word tattoo come from?

F: It comes from the Tahitian word 'tatau', which means 'to mark'. When the explorer Captain Cook sailed to the South Pacific – you know Captain Cook?

E: Sure. The man that discovered Australia in the 1800s.

F: It was in 1770, actually, but that's not really important. Anyway, he saw lots of people in the Pacific islands wearing tattoos, and when he saw the Maoris ...

E: In New Zealand? The Maoris of New Zealand?

F: Exactly. When he saw the Maoris, he was really impressed. The old men's faces and bodies were covered in tattoos. Now, of course, the Maori-style tattoo is famous, and fashionable, all over the world. By the way, is that OK? Does it hurt?

E: No, it's fine, thanks. So, have people always tattooed themselves just to look good?

F: Most of the time, yeah, but in some cultures tattoos tell us about the person's position in society. For example, the early Romans tattooed criminals. In Tahiti, your tattoos tell the story of your life. And a long time ago, sailors travelling to exotic countries collected tattoos as souvenirs – a famous symbol of China is the dragon, so when sailors went to China they usually had a tattoo of a dragon to show where they had been. People still like having dragon tattoos because they're so beautiful, not because they've been to China.

E: These days I guess people get tattooed because it's trendy, don't they?

F: In this country, yes. Young people who want to stay up-to-date have a tattoo, but it's not the same in every country. In Japan, having a lot of tattoos is often a sign that you are a member of the yakuza, the Japanese mafia.

E: Really? So, I shouldn't go to Japan with this, then?

F: This is a small tattoo – not a big problem. These days, more and more fashionable young Japanese are getting a small tattoo. The yakuza are covered in beautiful tattoos, on their back and their front, so don't worry, you need a lot more work than this. Out of interest, why did you choose to have this particular tattoo?

E: Oh, because everyone in the world understands what it is – it's not a pretty picture, it's a code. You see it on everything that you buy. I think it's really modern, and my favourite singer has one exactly the same.

3

- Read out the task. Check comprehension of problematic vocabulary such as *be around, mafia.*
- Explain that question 6 refers to the pictures at the bottom left. Ask students to describe the tattoos in the pictures. Elicit or pre-teach *bar code, tiger, cross, wings.*
- Students listen and choose their answers.
- They compare their answers with a partner.
- Check the answers with the class.

Answers

1 5,500 2 tatau 3 1770 4 criminals 5 trendy 6 2

4

- **30** Students work in pairs and match the tattoos to the celebrities.
- They listen and check, then compare their answers with their partner.
- Check the answers with the class. Say: *Look at the photos on page 64 to check.*

Answers

a Pink 2 b David Beckham 3 c Angelina Jolie 1
d Robbie Williams 5 e Johnny Depp 4

Listening script 30

F: Your favourite singer? Which singer has a tattoo of a bar code?

E: Pink. She's got it on the back of her neck.

F: On her neck, eh? I suppose it's better than the one David Beckham's got on his neck – it's a cross, with wings.

E: Mm, it's too big. I prefer the smaller ones like the little bird Johnny Depp's got on his arm ...

F: Mm, I must say, I like the bigger tattoos. The singer Robbie Williams has got a large Maori design on his arm and Angelina Jolie has got a really large, beautiful tiger on her back. That must have taken a long time to do ...

5

- Focus on *be in fashion* and *go out of fashion* and check comprehension. Check pronunciation of *design* /dɪˈzaɪn/.
- Students work in groups and discuss the questions. Go around the class giving help as necessary.
- Students report back to the class. Ask: *Who thinks tattoos are in? Who thinks they are out?*

Writing

1

- Read out the task. Check comprehension of vocabulary such as *cosmetic surgery, style makeover.*
- Students decide on the topic of their email. They need to think about the details, eg if they're going to have a piercing, they need to decide where on their body.

2

- Students read the task. With a weaker class, elicit useful language, and write it on the board.
- Students write their email, using the ideas in the Coursebook in the correct order. You could set this activity for homework.
- When they have finished writing, encourage them to check it for grammar, spelling and punctuation.

Revision activity

Find someone who …

- Write on the board:

  Find someone who …
  1 has purple trousers.
  2 has a necklace that was bought in a foreign country.
  3 prefers old-fashioned clothes.
  4 wore a tie at school.
  5 wore glasses as a child.
  6 has a tattoo.
  7 never wears a watch.
  8 spent more than €40 last year on accessories.
  9 is wearing odd socks.
  10 refuses to dress up for special occasions.

- Adapt the prompts to fit your students' backgrounds.
- Check comprehension of *odd socks, refuse, special occasions.*
- Students work individually to prepare questions using the prompts on the board.
- They have to find out which of their classmates can answer *yes* to their questions.
- Students complete the task. Go around the class giving help and encouraging them to ask for extra information.
- After about ten minutes, ask: *Did you manage to find someone for each sentence?*

Extra practice

Students complete the Extra practice material on page 57, either in class or for homework.

Extra practice answers

1 1 scruffy 2 traditional 3 conservative 4 watch 5 skirt 6 socks 7 trendy 8 glasses 9 beautiful 10 necklace 11 tie

2 Possible answers:
1 The man is smart. He's wearing smart trousers, a tie and a big, expensive watch.
2 The woman's clothes are traditional. She's wearing a beautiful necklace and earrings.
3 The man's clothes are up-to-date. He's wearing trendy, casual trousers and a necklace.

3 1 I gave ~~away them~~ them away 2 went ~~it~~ off 3 came across ~~them~~ some 4 made ~~it~~ up 5 look ~~her~~ after

4 1 dress up 2 put on 3 show off 4 got up 5 tried on 6 take after 7 came across 8 turn up

References

Grammar reference Unit 4: Coursebook page 59
Wordlist Unit 4: Coursebook page 60
Communication activities: Coursebook page 64
Photocopiable resources: Teacher's Book pages 102–103
Unit 4 test: Teacher's Book pages 138–139

CD-ROM

Unit 4 Followers of fashion
Language exercise: What they look like
Vocabulary activity: Clothing and style
CEF-linked activity: I can understand a text about beauty and decoration
Game: Swamp disaster (beauty, clothes and accessories)

Review

Ideas for preparation
- a counter per student and a dice for each group (see Language study game on Coursebook page 51)

Warmer
- Students work individually. They write the names of their three favourite and least favourite actors, vegetables and songs randomly on a piece of paper.
- They find a partner who has to guess which items belong in the 'favourites' list, and which in the 'least favourite'. Ask: *How well do you know each other?*

Lead-in

1
- Students work in pairs and discuss the questions.
- Ask: *Is it important that your friends have similar tastes to you?*

Vocabulary

1
- 31 Students tick the subjects they hear.
- They compare their answers with a partner.
- Check the answers with the class.

Answers
fashion, film, food, gossip, sport

Listening script 31

(M = Maya, H = Hannah, J = Josh)

M: I read an interesting article about taste this morning.

H: Oh, yeah?

M: Yeah. It talked about how people like each other because they have the same tastes. What do you think of that, Josh?

J: I disagree. I think some people like each other and they've got completely different tastes. Take this old friend of mine, Miguel. We're completely different. He's noisy and likes football and martial arts. I'm quiet and I prefer reading and going to the cinema. My idea of a good night out is watching a good comedy film. Miguel would hate that.

M: So why do you like him, then?

J: I think, well, when we met, we didn't know anybody at college and, you know, I think we just formed a strong bond early on. It didn't matter that we didn't have the same tastes, in anything.

H: Did you study the same subjects?

J: No. He did computer studies and I did film studies.

M: Do you keep in touch?

J: Yeah. I saw him last week and we usually have a chat on the phone about two or three times a week.

M: What about you, Hannah?

H: I agree with Josh. I like Grace, my manager at work, but we've got completely different tastes. For a start, Grace wears up-to-date clothes and I mean really up-to-date. She spends loads of money on fashion and she looks absolutely fantastic.

M: You look good too, Hannah.

H: Oh, come on! I wear scruffy jeans all the time. But, thanks. Oh, and we've got different ideas about food, too.

M: Food?

H: Yeah, Grace is really healthy. At lunchtime, she eats lots of fruit and vegetables. She never eats fast food. She hates the stuff.

M: Really? She sounds great. I think good food is important too.

H: Yes, well, I agree with you, Maya, but I also love hamburgers and chips. Anyway, it doesn't matter that we don't have the same taste in fashion, or in food, she's a great manager and I like her.

J: Hmm. What about you, Maya? What do you think?

M: As far as I'm concerned, the most important quality in a person is that you can trust them. I mean, I phone my best friend almost every day and tell her my news – you know, personal stuff, and it's really important for me to feel that she can keep a secret.

J: Yeah, I suppose so. But sometimes I like talking to people who can't keep a secret! A little bit of gossip can be really interesting.

H: Well, if you like gossip – only the other day, I saw Howard and he told me ...

2
- Ask: *Which of the speakers is a boy?* (Josh). *Which girl talked about someone she works with?* (Hannah).
- Students predict the answers, then listen and check.
- Check the answers with the class.

Answers
1 Josh 2 Josh, Maya 3 Hannah 4 Maya, Hannah 5 Hannah 6 Josh, Hannah

3
- Students choose the correct alternatives.
- Check the answers with the class, and quickly revise any areas of vocabulary that caused problems.

Answers
1 formed 2 in 3 chat 4 up- 5 absolutely 6 scruffy 7 keep

4
- Students complete the task individually.
- Check the answers with the class.

Answers
Film words: character, comedy, played by, romance, scene, set
Adjectives: attractive, brilliant, casual, funny, gorgeous, impressive, smart, trendy
Adverbs: absolutely, really, so, very

5
- Read out the task.
- Students complete the table individually, then compare their answers in pairs.
- Ask some students to report back to the class.

Language study

1

- Give each person a counter. Organise them into groups of four or five, and give each group a dice.
- Read through the instructions with the class.
- Ask a pair of students to demonstrate the game until one lands on a person and has to correct a sentence. The rest of the class judges whether the sentence has been corrected properly. If it has, the player wins a 'friend'.
- Students play the game in their groups.
- Check each sentence has been properly corrected.

Answers

1 **haven't seen** 2 **I'm** concerned 3 **I** met 4 **little** time 5 dressed **up** 6 **went** to 7 Me **too.** 8 How **many** 9 think **of the** film 10 takes **after** 11 shows **off** in front of 12 **isn't** any 13 try **on** 14 **Are** there 15 In **my** opinion 16 turn **up** at 17 you **ask me** 18 **Have** you **bought** 19 a **few** 20 **I've** made

Song

Background information

Carnaby Street

In the 1950s, Carnaby Street was an unimportant side-street in central London. Then a few tailors moved there, offering cheap made-to-measure clothes for men. This was the first time that there had been real fashion for men. Soon there were lots of little clothes shops (*boutiques*) for men and women, and Carnaby Street was the fashion centre of the world. *Carnabetian army* in the song refers to the fashion-conscious people who used to hang out in Carnaby Street.

These days, Carnaby Street is a popular destination for tourists, but the shops mostly sell kitsch souvenirs and reproduction memorabilia.

1

- Students look at the picture of the band. Ask: *Does anyone know anything about the Kinks? Do you know any of their songs?*
- Check comprehension of *original, record contract.*
- Students read the factfile and answer the questions.
- Check the answers with the class.

Answers

1 a mix of traditional pop, country, folk and blues
2 Ray and Dave Davies, Peter Quaife and Micky Willet
3 the Ravens
4 Mick Avory
5 *You really got me*

Optional activity

Introduce the song

- Write these words on the board:
  clothes fashion London New York concerts parties butterfly spider shoes handsome
- Students listen to the song with their books closed and note down the words that they hear.
- Ask: *Do you like the song?* Then check their answers and ask: *Which of these things is the man in the song most interested in?* (Clothes, fashion and parties.)

Answers

clothes, fashion, London, parties, butterfly

2

- 32 Check comprehension of problematic vocabulary such as *material, pattern, weak, fragile.*
- Play the song again. Students can read along.
- Students complete their answers.
- Check the answers with the class.
- Show students the road sign *Carnaby St* at the bottom of the page. Ask: *What is its connection to the song?* Students find the reference to *Carnabetian army* in the song. Ask: *What do you know about Regent Street* (lots of shops, similar to Oxford Street), *Leicester Square* (lots of cinemas) and *Carnaby Street?* (see Background information).

Answers

1 c 2 a 3 b 4 c 5 b

3

- Students work in pairs and discuss the questions.
- Ask some students to report back to the class.

Speaking: exchanging information

1

- **Step 1:** Students work in groups of three and prepare their new identities.
- **Step 2:** Students prepare questions to ask at the party.
- **Step 3:** Students practise their conversations.
- **Step 4:** Students perform their conversations for the class.

2

- Students vote on their favourite conversation.
- Write on the board and discuss any recurring errors.

Reference

Module 2 test: Teacher's Book pages 140–142

UNIT 1

Get down to the rhythm

Module 3

Topic	Language study	Vocabulary	Main skills
• Shake that thing (types and origins of music) • It's party time (festivals)	• *for* and *since* with the present perfect	• Types of music • Musical instruments	• **Reading:** ordering a text summary • **Speaking:** talking about music and festivals • **Pronunciation:** recognising strong and weak forms in sentences • **Listening:** identifying main information

Learning aims

- Can use *for* and *since* with the present perfect
- Can recognise strong and weak forms in sentences
- Can talk about music and festivals

Ideas for preparation

- your favourite music album (see Warmer below)

Warmer

Favourite album

- Bring in one of your favourite music albums and show it to the class. Briefly describe the band and the music, and say why you like it.
- Students work in groups and talk about their own favourite albums and why they like them.
- Students report back to the class.

Shake that thing

Lead-in

Background information

World music

The styles of traditional music mentioned in this unit are sometimes grouped under the label 'world music', which describes musical genres and styles usually outside a European tradition.

Like everything else, music changes; for example, calypso fused with rhythms from Indian music to produce soca, a style which has grown into its own genre.

1

- Write the word *music* on the board. Ask: *When do you listen to music?*
- Ask students to open their books on page 66. Read out the task.
- Students work in groups and discuss the questions.
- Ask some students to report back to the class.

2

- **01** Students read the styles of music in the box. Ask: *Where have you heard any music in these styles?*
- Students listen and match the music with the styles.
- They compare their answers with a partner.
- Check the answers with the class. Ask: *Which style of music do you like / dislike?*

Answers

1 Classical 2 Fado 3 Blues 4 Han 5 Bhangra 6 Jazz 7 Zulu (Mbube) 8 Samba 9 Calypso

3

- Students work in pairs and discuss the question.
- Ask students to look at the map on page 93 to check their answers.
- Check the answers with the class.

Answers

Bhangra: (traditional music from the Punjab, in Northern India / North-Eastern Pakistan) Blues: (Mississippi, or Chicago Blues) Calypso: (originally from Trinidad in the Caribbean) Classical: (Central) Europe Fado: (traditional music from Portugal) Han: (traditional music from China) Jazz: (New Orleans) Samba: (Brazil) Zulu (Mbube): (from the Zulu region of South Africa)

4

- Students read the task. Check comprehension of vocabulary such as *middle-aged, elderly, festival.*
- Students work in pairs and discuss the questions.
- Ask some students to report back to the class.

Reading

1

- **02** This text is recorded on the CD. You can use it as an alternative or in addition to the teaching notes below.
- Students look at the photos on page 67. Ask: *Where do you think these photos were taken?*
- Read out the task. Check comprehension of problematic vocabulary such as *connection, slave* and *Easter.* Ask: *What do many Christians do in the weeks before Easter?* (eat very little food). Pre-teach the word *fast.* You could explain that *breakfast* is the meal when

we break the 'fast' of night-time.
- Students read the text and answer the questions. Encourage them to find the answers as quickly as possible, without worrying about parts of the text that they don't understand.
- Check the answers with the class.

Answers
1 Straight after carnival, there were six weeks of fasting leading up to Easter.
2 Jazz was invented in New Orleans.
3 Samba originated in West Africa.
4 Steel drums are played at every carnival in Trinidad.

2
- Students read the task. Check comprehension of vocabulary such as *mixture, take place in, expect.*
- Students read the text again and answer the questions.
- Check the answers with the class.

Answers
1 France, Spain and Portugal 2 Mardi Gras
3 Portugal and Africa 4 Hip hop, house, salsa and calypso

Optional activity

Written conversation
- Students work individually and write about eight questions to another student about the music at a festival in their country.
- If students have difficulty thinking of questions, elicit ideas and write them on the board.
- Check questions are grammatically accurate.
- Students exchange questions with a partner, and answer those they are given, in writing.
- Check answers orally with the class.

3
- Students match the word combinations and find them in the text to check their answers.
- Check the answers with the class.

Answers
1 in (para 4) 2 from (para 5) 3 for (para 3)
4 with (para 4) 5 of (para 4)

4
- Read out the task. Find the second sentence with the class.
- Check the answers with the class by asking individual students to read out the text sentence by sentence, breaking with the full stops rather than the ends of lines.

Answers
1 c 2 d 3 a 4 f 5 e 6 b 7 g

Vocabulary and speaking

1
- Students work in pairs and answer the questions.
- Check the answers with the class and write all their extra musical instruments on the board.

Answers
Mentioned in text: 1 guitar 3 violin 7 steel drums 8 trombone 9 accordion 10 trumpet
Not mentioned in text: 2 piano 4 tambourine 5 saxophone 6 flute

2
- Students work in groups and discuss the questions. Go around the class giving help as necessary.
- Ask some students to report back to the class.
- Write on the board and discuss any recurring errors.

Optional activity

Role-play: forming a band
- Explain that students are going to work in groups to form a band. There will be a class vote on the most interesting band, and only the winner will get a record contract.
- Ask: *What does a band need to decide on when it starts out?* Write ideas in note form on the board, eg: *name? style of music? instruments? when and where practise? when and where perform?* (eg pubs, clubs, weddings, festivals) *clothes?*
- Students work individually and plan *going to* questions to ask their group, eg *What name are we going to have?* They also think about their own character for the role-play. What instruments does he / she play? What music does he / she like? Does he / she have to fit in the band around work or family commitments?
- Students work in groups of four or five and discuss their band, trying to agree on the points on the board. Go around the class giving help as necessary.
- Each group presents their ideas to the class.
- Students vote for the band that most deserves a record contract.

Language study

for and *since* with the present perfect

1
- Students read the sentences and answer the questions.
- Check the answers with the class.

Answers
a since b for

2

- Students answer the questions and check their answers in the Grammar reference on page 90.
- Check the answers with the class.
- Briefly revise the forms and uses of the present perfect simple and present perfect continuous.

Answers

have celebrated: present perfect simple
have been playing: present perfect continuous

Optional activity

Present perfect continuous

- If students are meeting this tense for the first time, look at it in more detail. Firstly write the forms on the board:

I have been playing	he / she has been playing
I haven't been playing	he / she hasn't been playing
have you been playing?	has he / she been playing?

- Write on the board:
  1 I've come / I've been coming to this swimming pool every week recently.
  2 He's stayed / He's been staying with his mother this week.
  3 I've played / I've been playing basketball. I'm really tired.
  4 She hasn't moved / She hasn't been moving house before.
  5 Has she lived / Has she been living in the same town all her life?
- Students choose the correct verb form for each sentence, using the Grammar reference to help them.
- Check the answers with the class.
- Leave sentences 1–5 on the board. Under them, add:
  a completed action b repeated action
  c permanent state d temporary state e activity
- Students match uses a–e with sentences 1–5.
- Check the answers with the class.
- Finally, ask: *Which verbs are usually only used in the present perfect simple?* (*know* and *like*).

Answers

1 I've been coming (b) 4 She hasn't moved (a)
2 He's been staying (d) 5 Has she lived (c)
3 I've been playing (e)

3

- Students complete the task.
- They look at the Grammar reference to check their answers.
- Check the answers with the class.

Answers

for: ages, a long time, 25 years, two months
since: I was young, last week, three o'clock, 2005

4

- Students complete the sentences.
- Check the answers with the class.

Answers

1 since 2 since 3 for 4 since 5 for

5

- Students look at the picture of Howlin' Hopkins. Go through the first two signs on the path and elicit how long ago they happened, before students read the text.
- They complete the text with points or periods of time.
- Check the answers with the class.

Answers

Assuming the year is 2006:
1 16 2 1991 3 1975 4 1 5 7

6

- Read out the task. Check comprehension and pronunciation of vocabulary such as *possession* /pəˈzeʃn/.
- Students personalise the sentences.

7

- Students write the questions. Refer them to Ex 6 if they have difficulty with the different tenses in the questions.
- Check the answers with the class.

Answers

2 What's your favourite possession? How long have you had it?
3 What's your best friend's name? How long have you known each other?
4 What's your favourite hobby? How long have you been doing it?

8

- Students work in pairs. They ask and answer the questions. Go around the class and note any errors.
- Students report back to the class.
- Write on the board and discuss any recurring errors.

Optional activity

Interview a famous musician

- Students work in pairs. They choose a famous musician that they know quite a lot about. Alternatively, they can invent a musician, or use Howlin' Hopkins from the text.
- They write an interview between a journalist and their musician. Encourage them to use lots of questions with *How long* + present perfect simple and continuous, and to make it as interesting and funny as possible. Go around the class checking the correct use of tenses.
- They practise their interview then perform it for the class. Note any errors in the target language.
- Alternatively, choose four or five students to be a band. The rest of the class are journalists who interview them. Give each group time to prepare questions and answers.
- Write on the board and discuss any recurring errors.

Pronunciation

Weak forms

1

- Students read and match the questions and answers.
- Check the answers with the class.

Answers

1 Bangkok. It's the capital of Thailand.
2 For six years.
3 None. I prefer listening to music.

2

- **03** Students listen and answer the question.
- Check the answer with the class and explain that the vowel sound in the underlined words is a *schwa* /ə/.
- Play the recording again and pause after each sentence for students to repeat.

Answer

Not stressed

Pronunciation note

The schwa is a very common sound in English, and unstressed *a*, *e*, *o* and *u* (but not *i*) are often pronounced in this way. Many common words have both a 'strong form' when the word is stressed, and a 'weak form' when it isn't. The vowel sound shifts to a schwa in the weak form, eg *do* /duː/ becomes /də/.

3

- Students work in pairs and complete the task.
- Ask some students to repeat their questions and answers for the class.

It's party time!

Listening

1

- **04** Students work in pairs and discuss their ideas about the photos.
- Ask some students to report back to the class. Elicit or pre-teach *parade* /pəˈreɪd/ and *costume* /ˈkɒstjuːm/.
- Students listen to the recording and check their ideas.
- Check the answers with the class.

Answers

1 Ivrea, Italy 2 Chiang Mai, Thailand 3 London, UK

Listening script 04

1

Every February we have a fantastic carnival. It's called the Carnevale d'Ivrea. Ivrea is my town. It's in the north of Italy, not far from the Swiss border. The carnival lasts for five days. This carnival has taken place every year since 1808, so it's been held for about 200 years. We have different teams, like armies. Everybody wears different costumes. There are the Devils, the Mercenaries, the Panthers, and many more. When the soldiers come into the city on their horses, we throw oranges at them, thousands of oranges. You have to take care – with more than 10,000 people throwing oranges, it's easy to get hit. Like in the French revolution, a red hat is the symbol of liberty, and everyone should wear one. If you don't, be careful because everyone will throw oranges at you. On the very last day of the carnival, we eat fish and fried polenta – oh, it's so delicious, and on the final evening we light huge bonfires in the town square. I recommend you go there if you are in Italy in February. You won't regret it.

2

We have Mardi Gras and the Music Festival in December, but my favourite festival is actually the Flower Festival. It takes place every February and it lasts for three days. Chiang Mai is Thailand's second city; it's called the Rose of the North because it's a beautiful place and in January and February, when the flowers blossom, it smells so good. The best part of the festival is the parade. Each float is decorated with flowers and on the top of each one is a contestant in the beauty contest, wearing traditional Thai clothes. The winner of the beauty contest is crowned the Flower Festival Queen. The first flower festival was held in 1977. We have held one every year since then. I usually go with my sister. We stand at the side of the road as the parade passes in front of us. The people in the parade hand out roses, orchids and lilies to the spectators, so we all go home with handfuls of sweet-smelling flowers.

3
When the Carnival first started in Notting Hill in 1964, it was a place where a lot of people from Trinidad lived. Now there are a lot of rich people living in Notting Hill, but for two days every August it becomes a little part of the Caribbean again. The festival is famous for its parade. There is an eight-kilometre route which goes all round west London. Hundreds of thousands of people come to watch the floats – you know, the decorated vehicles in the parade – with the people in their carnival costumes. Everybody loves the music, too. The music of the festival is calypso, the music of Trinidad. There are more than ten steel drum bands and they make sure the calypso never stops. It's great to see so many people dancing in the street. When you come to the Notting Hill Festival, you have to try Jerk chicken – it's a spicy Caribbean speciality and it's delicious. See you next August.

2

- Students read the task and look at the table. Check comprehension of vocabulary such as *polenta* (a thick maize porridge), *beauty contest* /'bju:ti 'kɒntest/, *main event*.
- Students listen and complete the table.
- They compare their answers with a partner. If necessary, play the recording again.
- Check the answers with the class.

Answers

What's it called?
1 Carnevale d'Ivrea 2 Chiang Mai Flower Festival
3 Notting Hill Carnival
When does it take place?
1 February 2 February 3 August
How long does it last?
1 five days 2 three days 3 two days
When did it first take place?
1 1808 2 1977 3 1964
What is the main event?
1 throwing oranges 2 parade and beauty contest 3 parade
Is there any special food connected with it?
1 fish and polenta 3 Jerk chicken
Is there any special music connected with it?
3 Calypso

Speaking

1

- Students work individually and make notes about a festival in their country. Encourage them to use their dictionaries for unknown vocabulary.

2

- Students work in groups and describe their festivals. They decide on the most interesting fact about each one.
- Ask each group to report back to the class with their most interesting facts.

Revision activity

Festival dictogloss

- Explain to students that you are going to read them a description of a festival called *San Marcial* /sæn mɑ:θi'al/ in Irun /ɪ'ru:n/, Spain (write the name of the festival and the town on the board). They have to make notes then work in pairs to reconstruct the text.
- Read this text twice. The first time, read it quite slowly. Students listen carefully without taking notes. The second time, read it slightly faster. Students listen and take brief notes.
  Spain is famous for its traditional festivals. The people of Irun have been celebrating San Marcial on 30th June since the 16th century. The men wear red hats and play flutes and drums in a parade to a hill outside the town. A beautiful girl from each part of the town parades with all the men. For ten years a second parade has taken place, too. Women mix with men to play the music in a non-sexist parade.
- Students compare their notes in pairs and work together to reconstruct the text.
- Put pairs together into groups of four. They write a shared version of the text, editing for content, punctuation and spelling.
- Ask each group to read out their version of the text. Read your own version again and discuss the differences.

Extra practice

Students complete the Extra practice material on page 86, either in class or for homework.

Extra practice answers

1 1 with 2 in 3 of 4 from 5 for
2 1 b 2 d 3 a 4 c
3 1 trumpet, c 2 violin, d 3 steel drums, b 4 guitar, a 5 trombone, f 6 accordion, e
4 1 have performed 2 has been 3 have enjoyed 4 have changed 5 have been
5 (individual answers)

References

Grammar reference Unit 1: Coursebook page 90
Wordlist Unit 1: Coursebook page 92
Communication activities: Coursebook page 93
Photocopiable resources: Teacher's Book pages 104–105
Unit 1 test: Teacher's Book pages 143–144

CD-ROM

Unit 1 Get down to the rhythm
Language exercise: Fun time
Vocabulary activity: Musical instruments
CEF-linked activity: I can recognise strong and weak forms in sentences
Game: The big squeeze (*for* or *since*)

UNIT 2
Just do it

Module 3

Topic	Language study	Vocabulary	Main skills
• Hit the streets (an unusual new sport: parkour) • Get moving (skating into work)	• Comparatives and superlatives	• *play, do, go* with sports and activities • Phrases with *get*	• **Listening:** understanding gist and identifying key information • **Speaking:** discussing sport and exercise • **Reading:** selecting an appropriate title • **Writing:** a short story with sequencers

Learning aims

- Can make comparative and superlative statements
- Can use phrases with *get*
- Can write a short story using sequencers

Ideas for preparation

- letter cards (see Warmer below)
- a large picture, or set of pictures, of three or more people that are easy to compare (for Language study, Coursebook page 71)
- superlative questions on cards (for Optional activity, page 73)

Warmer

- With one letter on each card, spell out some sports words of a similar length, eg *running, cycling, football.* You need one card for each student in the class.
- Explain that students are going to play a team game. They will have to organise themselves in the right order to spell a word to do with the unit topic.
- Hand out the letter cards in jumbled order to teams of students, so each student in the team has one letter and each team has a complete word. Make sure they don't look at the cards until you say *Go.*
- When everyone has a card, say *Go.* Teams work out the anagrams and stand in a row, holding their letter cards in the right order.
- Alternatively, students can remain seated and rearrange the letters on their table.
- The first team to finish is the winner. Ask: *What's the topic of the unit?* (sport).

Hit the streets

Lead-in

1

- Ask students to open their books on page 70. Students look at the pictures. Ask: *Have you heard of all these sports?* If people are unsure about free-running, explain that people run and jump around on top of city buildings.
- Students discuss the questions in groups.
- Ask some students to report back to the class.

Listening

1

- 05 Students listen and answer the questions.
- Check the answers with the class.

Answers

1 They are talking about picture a – they call it *parkour.*
2 Three

Listening script 05

(I = Interviewer, S = Sam, Sp = Spider, M = Monkey)

I: I'm here on the streets of London with a group of young athletes. Are they here to play basketball? No, nothing so obvious. They are going to tell me about parkour. It's the fastest growing urban sport in the world. Sam, let me speak to you first. What is parkour?

S: Parkour is the art of free-running. We move through a part of the city without stopping. Like a river. You run, you jump, but you don't stop. You always move forwards, in harmony with everything around you. It's total freedom – it's the most beautiful feeling.

I: And have you played parkour for a long time, Sam?

S: Well, you don't play parkour – you play a game. Parkour is not a game, it's an art. You do parkour. I've done it for three years, but it started in Paris years ago. It's not new.

I: Spider, how long have you been doing parkour?

Sp: It all started when I was about ten. A friend dared me to jump off a balcony. I was like 'No way!' But this kid who was younger than me did it. So, because I was bigger than him, I did a more dangerous jump.

S: A lot of people think that parkour is all gymnastics and jumping off tall buildings. But that's only a small part of it.

I: I see. Monkey, what do you call someone who does parkour?

M: We call ourselves traceurs or free runners.

I: Free runners? Right. Is parkour good for you?

M: Is it good for your health? Yeah, absolutely. I've never really been into sport – I prefer PlayStation to playing football – I was the fattest boy in my class. But since I started parkour, I've got really fit. I would say to anyone: If you want to do a sport, do parkour. It's better than any other sport.

I: But is it scarier than any other sport? Have you ever hurt yourself?

M: Not really. I hurt my foot once. Nothing special – that was the worst thing that's happened to me. Anyway, it's not as scary as going skiing or going scuba diving.

I: Last question, Sam. Why do you do it?

S: Because it's cool. Most of us do other sports as well, but parkour is more than just a sport, it's a way of life. And it's the easiest way for us to do exercise, get fit and feel totally free all at the same time. We're not stuck in a gym, we're out in the heart of the city.

2

- Students read the words in the box and complete the questions.
- Check the answers with the class.
- Students listen to the interview again and answer the questions.
- Check the answers with the class.

Answers
1 What, Running and jumping through a city without stopping 2 long, Since he was ten 3 call, Traceurs or free-runners 4 good, Yes 5 hurt, He hurt his foot once, but it wasn't serious 6 Why, Because it's cool, and it's the easiest way to do exercise

3

- Students work in pairs and discuss the questions.
- Ask some students to report back to the class. Ask: *In the interview, they say the sport's popularity is growing fast. Do you think people will be doing it in every street soon?*

Optional activity

Personalisation

- Write these questions from the interview on the board:
  1 What is _______?
  2 Have you played / done _______ for a long time?
  3 What do you call someone who does _______?
  4 Is _______ good for you?
  5 Have you ever hurt yourself?
  6 Why do you do it?
- Students tell a partner which sport they'd like to answer questions on.
- The partner asks questions and makes notes on the answers. Then they swap roles.
- Ask students to report back to the class about their partner.

Vocabulary and speaking

1

- Check pronunciation of vocabulary such as *exercise* /ˈeksəsaɪz/, *scuba diving* /ˈskuːbə ˈdaɪvɪŋ/, *skiing* /ˈskiːɪŋ/.
- Students complete the task, then compare their answers with a partner.
- Check the answers with the class.

Answers
You play: basketball, football, a game
You do: exercise, a sport
You go: scuba diving, skiing

2

- Check comprehension and pronunciation of vocabulary such as *athletics* /æθˈletɪks/, *gymnastics* /dʒɪmˈnæstɪks/, *judo* /ˈdʒuːdəʊ/, *squash* /skwɒʃ/.
- Students work in pairs and add the sports to their lists from Ex 1.
- Check the answers with the class.

Answers
You play: ice hockey, squash, tennis
You do: athletics, gymnastics, judo, karate
You go: cycling, in-line skating, skateboarding, swimming

3

- Read out the task.
- Students complete the sentences.
- Check the answers with the class.

Answers
1 do 2 do 3 go 4 play 5 go, go

Background information

Dangerous sports
Here is one list of the top 10 most dangerous sports:
1 BASE jumping (skydiving from a high building or cliff)
2 heli-skiing
3 diving
4 cave diving
5 bull riding
6 big-wave surfing
7 street luging
8 mountain climbing
9 BMX biking
10 white-water rafting

4

- Students work in pairs and discuss the statements in Ex 3. Encourage them to justify their opinions.
- Ask some students to report back to the class.

Language study

Comparatives and superlatives

1

- Bring in a picture of a group of three or more people that are easy to compare. Say: *Tell me about these people's age / height / hair. Can you compare them?*
- On the board, write one simple sentence about your picture that uses a comparative, and another that uses a superlative. Elicit the names of these adjective forms.
- Students refer to Listening script 5 and complete the table.
- Check the answers with the class.

Answers
1 younger, the fastest 2 bigger, the fattest
3 more dangerous, the most / least beautiful
4 better, the worst 5 scary, scarier, the easiest

2

- Students complete the task.
- Check the answers with the class. Check comprehension of *less* and *least*.

Answers
a 5 b 4 c 2 d 3 e 1

3

- Students look at the picture and complete the task.
- Check the answers with the class.

Answers
1 comparative 2 adjective 3 superlative

4

- **06** Students complete the text.
- Students listen and check their answers, and identify Tanya in the photo.
- Check the answers with the class.

Answers
1 fatter 2 better 3 easier 4 tall 5 more beautiful
Person a is Tanya

5

- **07** Students read the words in the box and predict which sentence they refer to. Check comprehension of problematic vocabulary such as *quad bike* /kwɒd baɪk/.
- Students listen and work out what the sports people are famous for.
- They complete the sentences with the correct superlative form.
- Check the answers with the class.

Answers
1 longest 2 shortest 3 heaviest 4 most successful
5 worst

Listening script 07

1 On April 17, 2000 Australian Matt 'The Kangaroo Kid' Coulter jumped a distance of 40.9m on his quad bike in Suffolk, England, earning him a place in the Guinness Book of Records.
2 Former NBA player Tyrone 'Muggsy' Bogues, is just 1.60m tall. Despite his height, he was one of the fastest and most popular players on the NBA circuit.
3 Hawaiian-born Akebono became the first non-Japanese wrestler to reach the level of yokozuna, the highest rank in sumo wrestling. He is 2.40m tall and weighs 235kg. He retired in 2001.
4 French snowboarder Karine Ruby won six World Cup titles between 1996 and 2003 and has nearly 120 World Cup medals, 65 of them gold. No other snowboarder has achieved as much.
5 Eddie 'The Eagle' Edwards was Britain's first (and only) Olympic ski jumper. He jumped in the 1988 Winter Olympics in Calgary. He never won a medal. The only thing he came away with was bruises.

Optional activity

Listening extension: numbers

- Write on the board:

1 *40.9m*	4 *1.60m*
2 *235kg*	5 *1988*
3 *nearly 120*	

- Students look at the numbers. Ask: *Can you remember what the numbers refer to?*
- Students listen again and note what the numbers refer to.
- Check the answers with the class.

Answers
1 The distance Matt Coulter jumped.
2 The weight of Akebono.
3 The number of medals Karine Ruby won.
4 The height of Muggsy Bogues.
5 The year Eddie Edwards went to the Olympics.

Optional activity

Superlative questions

- Write on individual cards questions that use the superlative form. You can use these questions or others that better reflect the interests of your students.
- Give students cards with three–five of these questions on them.
  Who's the greatest sports person of all time?
  What's the world's silliest / most boring sport?
  What's the most exciting sports event you've ever seen?
  What school subject were you best / worst at?
  What's the healthiest / most unhealthy habit you have?
  Where's the scariest / most interesting / most expensive place you've been?
  Who's the craziest / most annoying person you know?
  What's the biggest problem for young people in your country at the moment?
- Students ask each other their questions. Encourage them to give information in their answers.
- Students find new partners and ask their questions again. Can they remember the questions exactly?
- Each student tells the class one interesting thing they found out about a classmate.

Get moving

Reading

1

- **08** This text is recorded on the CD. You can use it as an alternative or in addition to the teaching notes below.
- Students look at the picture and guess the answer.
- They read the text. Encourage them to find the answer as quickly as possible.
- Check the answer with the class.

Answer
c

2

- Read out the task. Check comprehension and pronunciation of problematic vocabulary such as *annoyed* /əˈnɔɪd/, *inspired* /ɪnˈspaɪəd/, *mystery man* /ˈmɪstri mæn/.
- Students read the text again and choose the correct answers.
- Check the answers with the class.

Answers
1 a 2 a 3 c 4 b 5 a 6 b 7 b

3

- Students work in groups and discuss the questions.
- Ask some students to report back to the class.

Optional activity

Transport debate

- Explain that students are going to role-play local councillors at a debate in a town planning meeting. One group are members of the Fitness Party who want to have a town in which most people travel on foot, by bike or on skates. One group are members of the Public Transport Party who want everyone to travel on public transport. The final group are members of the Car Party who think the town should be designed for car users.
- Students plan what they are going to say in the debate. Set a time limit of five minutes. They need to think about the changes they want for the town, and their reasons for these changes. Go around the class giving help.
- Alternatively, all students from the same party can plan their arguments together.
- Put a pair from each party together, so students are working in groups of six. They have ten minutes for their debate. Refer them to the language for giving opinions on Coursebook page 40.
- Ask groups to report back to the class. Have a class vote on the party that put forward the most convincing arguments.
- Write on the board and discuss any recurring errors.

Phrases with *get*

Vocabulary

1

- Ask: *Which English word has the longest dictionary entry, do you think?* (get). Explain that *get* has a long entry because it has many different meanings.
- Students underline phrases with *get* in the text.
- Check the answers with the class.

Answers
(Get moving), getting angry, get fit, got lost, got better, got into

2

- Students complete the matching activity.
- Check the answers with the class.

Answers
2 got lost 3 get fit 4 getting angry 5 got better
6 got into

3

- Students discuss the questions. Go around the class and note errors.

4

- Ask students to report the most interesting thing their partner told them.
- Discuss any recurring errors from Ex 3.

Writing

1

- Read out the task. Check comprehension of *contrast* and *sequence*.
- Check the answers with the class.

Answers
Time sequence: the next day, after that, after a while
Contrast: however, but

2

- Students add the words in the box to the lists from Ex 1.
- Check the answers with the class.
- Ask: *Which time expression is used near the start of a story?* (to begin with). *Which is used near the end?* (finally).

Answers
Time sequence: finally, to begin with
Contrast: although, on the other hand

Optional activity

Contrast words

- Write on the board:

  1 I love watching football. ________ , I hate playing it.
  2 ________ I love watching football, I hate playing it.
  3 I love watching football, ________ I hate playing it.

- Ask: *Which contrast words can we use in sentence 1?* (However / On the other hand). *Which can we use in sentence 2?* (Although). *And in sentence 3?* (although).
- Explain that *although* is used to contrast two clauses in a sentence and it can introduce either the first or the second clause. *However* and *On the other hand* contrast two separate sentences and are used at the start of the second sentence.

3

- Students read the task and choose a topic.

4

- Students plan their story. Encourage them to think through the beginning, the main part of the story and the ending before they start writing.
- Students write the story. You could set this activity for homework.

Revision activity

Comparisons game

- Give each student a blank sheet of paper.
- Students cut their paper into eight pieces, and write an object, person or place on each piece.
- Explain that students are going to play a game in groups of four. They should mix up all their pieces of paper and put them face down on the table. In turns, students pick up three pieces of paper and make one comparative and one superlative sentence about them, each with a different adjective. As an example, write on the board:

  carrot skateboard Gwyneth Paltrow

- Ask students for sentence ideas. They can be as imaginative or as silly as they like! You could suggest:

  A skateboard is the fastest. Gwyneth Paltrow is taller than a carrot.

- Students play the game. After each turn, they put the words back face down on the table and mix them again.
- Students get a point for every grammatically correct sentence with an adjective that hasn't already been used, and an extra point for making the group laugh.

Extra practice

Students complete the Extra practice material on page 87, either in class or for homework.

Extra practice answers

1 1 ~~goes~~ does 2 ✔ 3 ~~does~~ plays 4 ~~go~~ do 5 ~~go~~ play 6 ✔ 7 ~~play~~ do 8 ✔

2 1 older 2 bigger 3 longer 4 faster 5 the best 6 the most dangerous 7 heavy 8 more successful

3 Possible answers:
1 Tennis is more interesting than golf.
Basketball is the most interesting sport.
2 Leonardo DiCaprio is more handsome than Tom Cruise.
Brad Pitt is the most handsome actor.
3 Nicole Kidman is prettier than Angelina Jolie.
Halle Berry is the prettiest actress.

4 1 The next day 2 Although 3 After that 4 Finally 5 but 6 However

5 a get fit b get in shape c get lost d get angry e get into

References

Grammar reference Unit 2: Coursebook pages 90–91
Wordlist Unit 2: Coursebook page 92
Photocopiable resources: Teacher's Book pages 106–107
Unit 2 test: Teacher's Book pages 145–146

CD-ROM

Unit 2 Just do it
Language exercise: Better or best?
Vocabulary activity: Sports participation
CEF-linked activity: I can use *play* / *do* / *go* + sports
Game: Crossword (sport and vocabulary from the unit)

UNIT 3
On the road again

Module 3

Topic	Language study	Vocabulary	Main skills
• Save our soles (three pilgrimage experiences) • Take a break (holidays)	• *say* and *tell* • Direct and indirect speech	• Prepositions of place • Words to describe location, accommodation and holiday activities	• **Reading:** understanding key details and summarising a story • **Listening:** identifying main information • **Speaking:** discussing travel and holiday preferences

Learning aims

- Can make phrases *say* and *tell*
- Can summarise a story
- Can discuss travel and holiday preferences

Ideas for preparation

- brochures for contrasting holiday types (see Warmer below)
- a backpack of useful things to take on a walking holiday (see Optional activity, page 77)

Warmer

Which holiday?

- Show students brochures for different types of holiday, eg a sightseeing tour, a beach holiday, a cruise, a walking holiday, a safari.
- Elicit the names of these holiday types and write them on the board. Check pronunciation of words such as *cruise* /kruːz/, *safari* /səˈfɑːri/.
- Students brainstorm words connected with each type of holiday.
- Students work in pairs and discuss which of the holidays they'd like to go on.

Save our soles

Lead-in

1

- Ask students to open their books on page 74. Students work in pairs and discuss the questions.
- Ask some students to report back to the class.

Reading

1

- **09** This text is recorded on the CD. You can use it as an alternative or in addition to the teaching notes below.
- Ask: *Where are these places?* Elicit or teach *pilgrimage* /ˈpɪlgrɪmɪdʒ/ and *religious* /rɪˈlɪdʒəs/.
- Students read the stories to match them with the maps.
- Check the answers with the class.

Answers

Map a with story 2, Map b with story 3, Map c with story 1

2

- Allocate a letter, A, B or C, to each student.
- They read one story each and complete the map.
- Check the answers with the class.

Answers

1 Finisterre 2 Sarria 3 Matsuyama 4 Kochi 5 Mina
6 Plain of Arafat

3

- Students work in groups of three; an A, a B and a C.
- They describe their story to the rest of their group.
- Ask one student to summarise each story for the class.

4

- Read out the task. Check comprehension and pronunciation of vocabulary such as *nervous* /ˈnɜːvəs/, *physically* /ˈfɪzɪkli/, *spiritually* /ˈspɪrɪtʃʊəli/.
- Students read the texts again and complete the task.
- Check the answers with the class.

Answers

a 1 b 2 c 1, 3 d 3 e 3 f 2 g 1, 3

Optional activity

Vocabulary extension

- Write these phrases from the text on the board:
  1 I was surprised to discover …
  2 I honestly feel that …
  3 I had a wonderful holiday.
  4 It was a life-changing experience for me.
  5 It's good for the soul.
- Students think of a trip / holiday / experience, and prepare to talk about it using these expressions.
- Students tell a partner about their experience.
- Ask some students to report back to the class.

5

- Students discuss the questions in groups.
- Ask some students to report back to the class. Find out if anyone has done a walk that lasted more than a day, and ask for details of the journey.
- Ask: *Who can explain the joke in the title 'Save our soles'?* Encourage them to use their dictionaries. (Many people go on a pilgrimage to save their *souls* /səʊlz/. But they often do a lot of walking so the *soles* /səʊlz/ of their feet get sore.)

Optional activity

What to bring on a walking holiday

- Tell students they are preparing for a walking holiday in the UK in August. They are going to spend their nights in bed and breakfasts.
- Students brainstorm things they would pack for their holiday. Encourage them to use their dictionaries.
- Write their ideas on the board. These might include: compass /'kʌmpəs/, map, waterproofs, walking boots, toothbrush and toothpaste, soap, sunglasses, jumper, t-shirts, shorts, long trousers, water bottle, penknife, plasters, mobile phone, binoculars /bɪ'nɒkjʊləz/. Draw quick sketches on the board to illustrate unknown vocabulary.
- Alternatively, bring in a backpack full of useful items. Show the items one by one to elicit the vocabulary.
- Tell students it's important that they travel light, because a heavy backpack will tire them out. They need to choose only ten things to bring with them.
- They work individually and select their ten items.
- Students compare their lists with a partner and decide on a joint list. Put some useful expressions on the board:

  We don't need a … because …;
  A … will be useful to …;
  If it rains / If it's hot / we'll need …

- This could be continued as a pyramid discussion (see Unit 1 page 26).

Vocabulary

1

- Students work individually and complete the tables with the prepositions.
- Check the answers with the class.

Answers

1 by 2 on 3 to 4 in 5 at (*in* is also possible)

2

- Students read the task. Check comprehension of vocabulary such as *tropical island, distance, covered.*
- Students complete the questions.
- Check the answers with the class.

Answers

1 at / in 2 to 3 on 4 by 5 in

3

- Students work with a partner. They ask and answer the questions in Ex 2.
- Ask some students to report back to the class. Find out who holds the class record for questions 3, 4 and 5.

Language study

say and *tell*

1

- Students complete the task.
- Check the answers with the class. Check comprehension of *order, report, direct / indirect speech.*

Answers

1 c 2 a 3 b

2

- Students complete the rules, referring to Ex 1 for help.
- Check the answers with the class.

Answers

1 tell 2 say

3

- Students complete the task.
- Check the answers with the class.

Answers

1 a 2 b 3 d 4 d 5 c 6 b 7 c

Take a break

Listening and vocabulary

Background information

British holidaymakers

The average adult in Britain goes on two holidays a year. About 55% of these holidays are within the UK, 30% to countries in the European Union, particularly France and Spain, and 15% to the rest of the world, eg Florida in the USA is a very popular destination.

1

- Read out the task.
- Students predict which person chooses each holiday.
- Listen to some suggestions, but don't confirm yet whether they are correct.

2

- 10 Students listen and check their ideas.
- Check the answers with the class. Ask: *Did any of the answers surprise you?*

Answers

1 Rebecca 2 Omar 3 Jun 4 Serena 5 Darren

Listening script 10

(I = Interviewer, O = Omar)

I: Where do you like going on holiday?

O: Everywhere. Anywhere. It must be exciting, though. I can't stand doing nothing. I need action to keep me interested. I love travelling. I've been to all five continents and visited more than sixty countries.

I: Where do you usually stay?

O: On a campsite if I can. I love camping – the feeling that you're sleeping under the stars with just a tent to cover you. It's not always possible to camp, so I rent an apartment – but always self-catering, so that I can cook my own food.

I: And what do you do during the day?

O: On my last holiday I went white-water rafting down the Zambezi River in Zambia. Extreme, but the Victoria Falls were absolutely incredible.

(I = Interviewer, S = Serena)

I: What is your ideal holiday destination?

S: Well, I spend the rest of the year working hard, so I prefer to go somewhere relaxing. I guess my ideal place would be some tropical paradise where I don't have to lift a finger. I can just chill out.

I: Where do you prefer to stay?

S: I only get the chance to take a break once a year from my busy life, so I usually stay in a resort. Everything is paid for: food, accommodation, drinks ... all I need to do is relax.

I: And what do you usually do with your time?

S: I usually spend my days sunbathing by the pool with a cool drink in one hand and a good book in the other.

(I = Interviewer, D = Darren)

I: Which type of place do you like going to?

D: Well, I haven't actually been anywhere as yet, but I'd want to go somewhere exotic. It would have to be somewhere with top quality service. Only the best. Everything deluxe. You know what I mean?

I: And what type of place would you like to stay in?

D: I could see myself in a private villa in the Maldives, with servants. You know, all the home comforts.

I: And what would you do during the day?

D: Nothing.

(I = Interviewer, R = Rebecca)

R: It's not really important where I go. And as far as accommodation is concerned, I usually stay in a two-star hotel – that's always good enough for me. I prefer to spend my money on other things.

I: And what do you usually do with your time?

R: I like shopping. I mean I really like shopping. I especially enjoy finding clothes that I can't get hold of at home. And I love picking up bargains – the cheaper the better. It feels great when you go home and people say, 'What a lovely top,' and I say, 'Yeah, and it only cost £5 – bargain!' I don't know which I love more, paying so little or seeing the faces of my friends when I tell them.

(I = Interviewer, J = Jun)

I: Where do you like going to on holiday?

J: I always try to travel to a country or city with plenty to see and do. I love historical cities like Moscow, Paris and my favourite, Kyoto, in Japan.

I: What type of accommodation do you choose?

J: I usually stay in a B & B, a bed and breakfast, as they are cheaper than hotels.

I: And what do you usually do?

J: I spend my days sightseeing – visiting all the famous places – oh, and I love visiting museums. It's so wonderful for me, you know, to walk around and find out about the customs of the local people.

3

- Students read the task. Check comprehension of *paradise, B & B, resort, self-catering, white-water rafting.*
- Students work in pairs and complete the table.

4

- Students listen again and check their answers.
- They compare their answers with their partner.
- Check the answers with the class.

Answers

	Words to describe location	Types of accommodation	Holiday activities
Omar	exciting	campsite, self-catering apartment	white-water rafting
Serena	tropical paradise, relaxing	resort	sunbathing
Darren	exotic, deluxe	private villa	
Rebecca		two-star hotel	shopping
Jun	historical	B & B	visiting museums, sightseeing

5

- Students work in pairs and answer the questions.
- They check their answers by referring to Listening script 10 on page 94.
- Check the answers with the class.

Answers

1 Omar 2 Darren 3 Serena 4 Kyoto 5 Rebecca

6

- Students work in pairs and discuss the question.
- Find out how many students think they are like each traveller.

Speaking

1

- Students follow the instructions on pages 93 and 96.
- Find out how many students fit each traveller type. Ask: *Do you agree with the results?*
- Ask students to explain some expressions from the text on page 96, eg *you work long hours* (you work a lot of hours every day), *you don't have to lift a finger* (you don't have to do anything), *picking up bargains* (buying things for a cheaper price than normal).

2

- Students read the task. Check comprehension of vocabulary such as *souvenirs* /suːvənɪəz/.

- Do the first sentence as an example. Make sure that students start their sentences with *I would* or *I'd*.
- Students discuss the questions and note down their partner's answers.

3

- Students complete the task. Encourage them to use the *say* and *tell* patterns they learnt on page 76.
- Ask some students to report back to the class. Ask: *Did your new partner guess the same traveller type for your first partner that the questionnaire came up with? Would you like to go with your first partner on his / her holiday? Why?/ Why not?*

Optional activity

Write a postcard

- Tell students they are going to write a postcard to the class from the destination they chose in Ex 1.
- Revise language for opening and closing a postcard and write it on the board:
  Hi X / Dear X; *See you soon*; *Love / Best wishes*
- Students write their card. Encourage them to give as much information as possible about their holiday, and to check their work carefully when they have finished.
- Display the cards around the classroom.

Revision activity

Consequences story

- Explain that students are going to play a traditional English game called *Consequences*. Say: *I'm going to give instructions to help you write a story.*
- Students take a sheet of A4 paper. Explain that after each step they must fold their paper so what they wrote cannot be seen, and pass the paper to the student to their left.
  1. At the top of the page, write the name of a man that everyone in the class knows or has heard of.
  2. This man met a woman. Write *met* and the name of a woman that everyone in the class knows or has heard of.
  3. Say where the couple met. Write a preposition and a place.
  4. The man said something to the woman. Write what he said. Use one of the *say* and *tell* patterns you have learnt in this unit.
  5. Write what the woman replied to the man. Use a different pattern with *say* or *tell*.
  6. Write what the man said next to the woman. Use a time sequencer such as *Then*, *After that*, *The next day* and a *say* or *tell* pattern.
  7. Write how the story ends. Start your sentence with *In the end …*
  8. Write what the world had to say on the subject: *The world said / told them to …*
- Students unfold the papers and read them out.
- Each group chooses the funniest to read out for the class. Note errors with *say* and *tell*.
- Write on the board and discuss any recurring errors.

Extra practice

Students complete the Extra practice material on page 88, either in class or for homework.

Extra practice answers

1 1 in 2 to 3 by 4 in / at 5 by 6 on 7 by 8 at 9 to

2 1 said 2 told 3 said to 4 told 5 said 6 told 7 said 8 said 9 said to 10 told her to

3 1 sightseeing 3 sunbathing, deluxe a Campsites c Self-catering apartments e paradise

4 1 d 2 b 3 e 4 c 5 a

References

Grammar reference Unit 3: Coursebook page 91
Wordlist Unit 3: Coursebook page 92
Communication activities: Coursebook pages 93 and 96
Photocopiable resources: Teacher's Book pages 108–109
Unit 3 test: Teacher's Book pages 147–148

CD-ROM

Unit 3 On the road again
Language exercise: Tell me what she said
Vocabulary activity: Travel prepositions
CEF-linked activity: I can summarise a story
Game: Witch's pot (words connected with travel)

UNIT 4

Out and about

Module 3

Topic	Language study	Vocabulary	Main skills
• Trouble in store (making complaints in shops) • What do I say? (shopping quiz)	• Talking about real and imaginary situations (first and second conditionals)	• Shopping vocabulary	• **Listening:** understanding mood and manner • **Reading:** understanding gist • **Writing:** a short dialogue • **Speaking:** buying and returning goods

Learning aims

- Can talk about real and imaginary situations (conditionals)
- Can buy and return goods
- Can use shopping vocabulary

Ideas for preparation

- a bag of recent purchases (see Warmer below)

Warmer

Last month's shopping

- Tell your class that you have a friend who has lots of money and loves shopping. Show them a shopping bag with some things that this person bought last month, eg clothes, books, magazines, CDs, DVDs, gadgets, rather than essentials like food. Show each item to the class and revise the vocabulary both for the item and where to buy it, eg *bookshop, newsagent's, chemist's, department store, supermarket, online.*
- Students work in pairs and discuss what they bought last month, and where they bought it.
- Students report back to the class.

Trouble in store

Lead-in

1

- Ask students to open their books on page 78. Students read the questions. Check comprehension of vocabulary such as *online, advantages, disadvantages.*
- Students work in groups and discuss the questions.
- Students report back to the class on their discussions. Ask: *Does anyone prefer to do all their shopping online?*

Listening and vocabulary

1

- **11** Students look at the picture, listen, and answer the questions.
- They compare their answers with a partner.
- Check the answers with the class.

Answers

1 A computer or office supplies shop, or an electrical retailer
2 Paula's printer isn't working properly, but the shop can't give her a refund or a replacement printer.

Listening script 11

(S = Shop assistant, P = Paula)

S: Can I help you?
P: Yes, I bought this printer a short time ago, and I'm having trouble with it already.
S: What seems to be the problem?
P: Sometimes it just stops printing half way through. Not every time, but frequently. It's very annoying. I'd like a refund, please.
S: Do you have a receipt?
P: Yes, here it is.
S: I'm sorry, you bought this five weeks ago. We can only give you your money back if the item is less than one month old.
P: But it's been breaking down since I bought it. I didn't do anything to it. I think there's a fault in the machine.
S: Once again, I can only say I'm sorry to hear about your printer. There is a one-year warranty on it. I'm sure the maker would agree to replace it. Why don't you call them and explain the situation?
P: Can't I just exchange it here?
S: I'm afraid that model is no longer in stock. It's not very reliable.
P: Now you tell me. I think I'll shop online next time. It's cheaper and more convenient. And now that I have to wait for the maker to send me a machine, it's exactly the same as buying online.
S: Yes, is there anything else I can help you with?
P: Like you helped me with this? I don't think so, thank you. Goodbye.
S: Thank you. Goodbye.

2
- Check comprehension of the adjectives in the box.
- Check the answers with the class.

Answers
a angry, disappointed b polite and helpful, until the end of the conversation where he becomes unhelpful

3
- Students predict the answers, then compare their answers with a partner.

4
- Students listen and check their answers from Ex 3.
- Check the answers with the class.

Answers
1 S 2 S 3 P 4 S 5 P 6 S 7 S 8 P 9 S 10 P

Optional activity

Disappearing dialogue
- Write a version of Paula's dialogue on the board:

S: Can I help you?
P: Yes, I bought this printer five weeks ago, but I think there's a fault in the machine.
S: What seems to be the problem?
P: It just stops printing sometimes, for no reason. I'd like a refund, please.
S: I'm sorry, that isn't possible. But there's a one-year warranty on it. I'm sure the maker would agree to replace it.
P: Can't I just exchange it here?
S: I'm afraid that model is no longer in stock.
P: That's very annoying. I'll shop online next time.

- Read out the dialogue line by line. With books closed, students listen and repeat.
- Rub off short phrases from the dialogue on the board. Students have to read out the whole dialogue, saying the missing words from memory. Make sure that they use the appropriate intonation.
- Repeat the process several times, each time rubbing off more of the dialogue. Eventually, students will be saying most of the dialogue from memory.
- Students role-play the dialogue in pairs.

5
- Students read and complete the summary.
- Check the answers with the class.

Answers
1 fault 2 refund 3 receipt 4 warranty 5 replace
6 exchange 7 model 8 in stock

6
- Check comprehension of *out of stock*.
- Students work in groups and discuss the questions. They decide who has experienced the worst problem with a purchase.
- Ask each group to report back to the class.

Reading

Background information

eBay
On the eBay website, sellers advertise items they no longer want. For a specified period, often a week, the advert appears on the relevant section of the website and buyers can bid for it. At the end of the period, the highest bidder buys the item and the seller arranges delivery. Some people even earn a living by selling second-hand goods on eBay.

1
- Students work in pairs. If you have students who aren't internet users, try to pair them with students who are.
- They discuss websites they visit.
- Students report back to the class. Ask: *Which websites do you visit most often?*

2
- Students complete the task. Check pronunciation of *browse* /braʊz/ and *auction* /ˈɔːkʃn/.
- Check the answers with the class.

Answers
1 browse 2 bid 3 tip 4 auction

3
- 12 Students read the text and match the headings. Encourage them to do this quickly without worrying about parts of the text that they don't understand.
- Check the answers with the class. You can also do this by playing the CD.

Answers
Buyers: 1 Read the description of the item carefully
2 Do your research 3 Check reviews
4 Be patient – don't act too quickly
Sellers: 1 Close at the right time 2 Use plenty of images
3 Keep it simple

4
- Students read the task. Check comprehension of *positive feedback, variety* /vəˈraɪəti/, *font size.*
- Students read the text again more carefully and complete the task.
- Check the answers with the class.

Answers
1 F (You can only get a refund if the item is different from the seller's description)
2 T
3 T
4 F (Prices are higher on Sunday evenings)
5 F (The buyer will be distracted and won't look at your item)

Optional activity

Vocabulary auction

- Write on the board ten vocabulary items and a brief definition for each. Some definitions should be wrong.
- Students work in pairs. Say: *Each pair has £10,000. Use the money to buy the correct definitions. The winners are the pair who buy the most correct definitions with the least money.*
- Sell the definitions. Read out each one and start the bidding.
- Write the names of the buyers and the amounts on the board.
- Check the definitions once they've all been bought, and work out the winner.

5

- Students work in pairs and discuss the questions.
- Ask some students to report back to the class. Ask: *What are the advantages and disadvantages of buying things at auction?*

Language study

Talking about real and imaginary situations

First and second conditional

1

- Tell students that they are going to practise conditional sentences. Ask: *Which word do conditional sentences often start with?* (if).
- Students read the sentences and complete the task.
- Check the answers with the class.

Answers

1 c, d 2 a, b

2

- Read out the task. Check comprehension of *contains, separated, comma.*
- Students complete the task. They can check their answers in the Grammar reference on page 91.
- Check the answers with the class.

Answers

1 both 2 1st conditional 3 1st conditional 4 2nd conditional 5 2nd conditional 6 both 7 both

3

- Write on the board: *If you use this face cream, you'll look ten years younger.* Ask: *Where do you see or hear sentences like this?* (in advertising). *What is this type of sentence called?* (a slogan).
- Students read the task. Check vocabulary such as *insurance* /ɪnˈʃʊərəns/ and *helmet.*
- Students complete the task, using the table in Ex 2.
- Check the answers with the class.

Answers

1 'll refund, find 2 eat, 'll be 3 'll pay, buy
4 'll be, wear 5 don't, won't

4

- Students read the text and choose the correct verb forms.

5

- 13 Students listen and check their answers to Ex 4.
- Check the answers with the class. Check comprehension of useful phrases such as *the car of my dreams, in the right mood, feel like staying in.*

Answers

1 'd do	7 'd spend
2 had	8 was
3 'd buy	9 had
4 could choose	10 'd go
5 had	11 felt like
6 'd drive	12 'd have

6

- Students read the instructions and question 1. Ask: *Is it possible that the weather will be good next weekend?* (Yes.) *So is this sentence talking about a real or an imaginary situation?* (real). *So should we use the first or second conditional?* (first). *How do we complete the sentence?*
- Students read questions 2–6. Check comprehension and pronunciation of *unlimited, fake.*
- Students complete questions 2–6.
- Check the answers with the class.

Answers

1 is, 'll 2 go, will 3 had, would 4 found, would
5 bought, would 6 go, will
Note: in 5 and 6 both forms are possible. In 5, the first conditional would be used if the person frequently bought fake designer items. In 6, the second conditional would be used if the person rarely went out.

7

- Students work in pairs. They ask and answer the questions.
- Ask some students to report back to the class. Say: *Let's find out how honest this class is. In question 4, who would keep the money? In question 5, who would say the designer bag was real?*

Optional activity

How honest are you?

- Explain that students are going to write three sentences describing situations in which they would be honest, and three in which they would be dishonest. Give them an example: *If I accidentally took something from a shop, I would / wouldn't take it back.*
- When students have written their sentences, they transform them into *yes / no* questions. Demonstrate with your example: *If you accidentally took something from a shop, would you take it back?*
- Students find a partner, ask them all their questions and note their answers. Encourage them to give alternative courses of action when they answer *no.*
- They move around the class, swapping partners until they have asked four people their questions.
- Students report back to the class.
- Write on the board and discuss any recurring errors.

What do I say?

Reading

1

- Students read the quiz and choose the correct answers.
- Students compare their answers with a partner.
- Check the answers with the class.

Answers

1 c 2 a 3 b 4 a 5 c 6 a 7 b

Writing and speaking

1

- Read out the instructions. Encourage students to look back through Unit 4 to help them structure their dialogues and to find useful phrases and vocabulary.
- Students write their dialogue with a partner. Go around the class giving help as necessary.
- They perform it for another pair, using lots of expression so it's easy to guess their adjectives.
- Find out how many adjectives were guessed correctly. Then choose one or two particularly good dialogues to be performed for the whole class.
- Write on the board and discuss any recurring errors.

Revision activity

Conditional chain game

- Students sit in circles of six to eight for a game.
- Explain that they are going to go round the circle saying conditional sentences. Each person must start their sentence with the second half of the previous person's sentence. Demonstrate by saying: *If there isn't any food in my fridge tonight, I'll go shopping. If I go shopping, I'll spend too much money. If I spend too much money, I won't be able to go out at the weekend.*
  Make sure students understand that the chain will be either of first conditional sentences or of second conditional sentences. They can't mix the two structures.
- Write some starter sentences on the board, for example:

  If I didn't work so hard, I'd have more free time.
  If I could live anywhere in the world, I'd live in the USA.
  If I miss the bus tonight, I'll get home late.
  If I go on holiday this year, I'll travel by plane.

- Students make a chain of conditional sentences until they can't think of a logical continuation. When this happens, the person who breaks the chain loses a life, and starts again with a new sentence from the board.
- Students report back to the class. Ask: *How long was your longest chain? Which starter sentence was the most difficult to make a chain from?*

Extra practice

Students complete the Extra practice material on page 89, either in class or for homework.

Extra practice answers

1 1 refund 2 receipt 3 fault 4 warranty 5 exchange 6 model 7 in stock

2 1 fault 2 receipt 3 warranty 4 exchange 5 in stock 6 model 7 refund

3 1 ~~you'd~~ you will 2 ~~went~~ go 3 ~~will~~ would 4 ~~had~~ have 5 ~~see~~ saw

4 (individual answers)

5 1 bid 2 angry 3 auction 4 disappointed 5 rude 6 confident 7 browse 8 tip extra word: internet

References

Grammar reference Unit 4: Coursebook page 91
Wordlist Unit 4: Coursebook page 92
Photocopiable resources: Teacher's Book pages 110–111
Unit 4 test: Teacher's Book pages 149–150

CD-ROM

Unit 4 Out and about
Language exercise: Shopping questionnaire
Vocabulary activity: Returning goods
CEF-linked activity: I can use shopping vocabulary
Game: Cats in hats (first and second conditionals)

Review

Ideas for preparation
- a counter per student and a dice for each group of four or five (see Vocabulary game on Coursebook page 83)

Warmer
- Tell students they are going to review the module, *Motion*. Write *Travel* on the board.
- Students work in groups of three and brainstorm words connected with travel.
- They categorise the words that they have written down into groups, eg transport, words connected with holidays or reasons to travel.

Lead-in

1
- Students read the questions. Elicit examples of driving jobs, eg *taxi driver, train driver, lorry driver, racing driver.*
- Students work in pairs and discuss the questions.
- Find out which is the most popular way to travel to English class. Then ask students for advantages and disadvantages of a driving job.

Language study

1
- Students read the text and correct the mistakes.
- Check the answers with the class.
- Quickly revise any areas of grammar that are causing problems and refer students to the Grammar reference on pages 90–91.

Answers
1 told me / said to me / said 2 for 3 'll 4 get 5 said / told me 6 since 7 best 8 'd 9 told / said to 10 've been 11 than 12 began 13 friendly 14 won

2
- Read out the task. Check comprehension and pronunciation of problematic vocabulary such as *previous* /'priːviəs/, *ambition* /æm'bɪʃn/.
- Students write a text about Sarah Harris, using the text in Ex 1 as a model. Go around the class giving help as necessary.
- Students check their work carefully for errors in grammar, spelling and punctuation, then swap texts with a partner. They check their partner's work.
- Ask some students to read out their texts to the class.

Possible answer
Sarah Harris, 32, is an underground train driver in Liverpool in the UK. She told me, 'I've lived in Liverpool since 1999 and I've been a train driver for five years – it's a really interesting job. I used to work as a shop assistant, which was very tiring. Before that I was a secretary, which was very boring. One day I'd like to have flying lessons. If I could choose any job in the world, I'd be a pilot.'

Optional activity

Write a personal profile
- Students write notes about themselves, using Sarah Harris's information as a model.
- Each student gives his / her notes to a partner. The partner uses the notes to write a short biography.
- Partners exchange biographies and correct factual errors or mistakes in grammar, punctuation or spelling.

Vocabulary

1
- Explain that students are going to play a game. Give each person a counter, or ask them to find a small coin to use instead. Organise them into groups of four or five, and give each group a dice.
- Read out the instructions for the game.
- A pair of students demonstrates the game, until one lands on a transport square and has to answer a question. The rest of the class judges whether the question has been answered correctly. If it has, the player moves forwards two squares.
- Students play the game. Go around the class giving help and adjudicating.
- Check the answers with the class.

Possible answers
2 on 4 deluxe, luxury, exotic, relaxing 7 skateboarding, swimming 10 begin / start 12 by 14 self-catering apartment, B & B, private villa 15 for 17 piano, guitar, flute 18 from 21 white-water rafting, sightseeing, sunbathing 23 confident, shy, polite 29 friendly, happy, interesting 32 ice hockey, squash 35 got 38 refund 40 receipt

Song

1

- Students look at the picture. Ask: *Does anyone know who this person is? Do you know any of her songs, or anything about her life?*
- Students read the task. Check comprehension of vocabulary such as *influenced* /ˈɪnfluənst/, *sign a contract*.
- Students read the factfile and answer the questions.
- Check the answers with the class.

Answers
1 Piano and guitar 2 Billie Holiday 3 When she went to a school for the Performing and Visual Arts 4 Blue Note Records 5 *Feels like home*

2

- Students read the words in the box.
- Students work in pairs and discuss their predictions.
- Ask some students to report back to the class.

3

- 14 Students listen to the song with books closed and check if their predictions from Ex 2 were correct.
- Ask: *Do you like the song?*
- Students open their books. Play the song again. This time students can read along.
- Students work in pairs and discuss what the song is about.
- Check the answer with the class.

Answers
She wants the person she is singing to to come with her and live a simple life in the countryside. It isn't clear if she is thinking of a holiday or a more permanent arrangement.

4

- Students look at the lyrics and answer the questions.
- Check the answers with the class.

Answers
1 In the night 2 A song 3 By bus 4 Clouds and rain 5 Fields, mountains

5

- Students work in pairs and discuss the question.
- Ask some students to report back to the class.

Speaking: a survey

1

- 15 Students work in pairs. Explain that they are going to conduct a shopping survey.
- **Step 1:** students look at the words in the box and tick the information they hear.
- Check the answers with the class.
- Students read the questionnaire and the examples. Elicit the question for item 1 (*What's your name?*).
- Students work in pairs. They prepare questions for items 2–3 and 6–9 in the survey. Encourage them to use the Listening script 15 on page 95 to help them. Go around the class giving help as necessary.
- Check the questions with the class.
- **Step 2:** students write three extra questions.
- **Step 3:** students carry out the survey.
- They return to their original partner and compare survey results.
- **Step 4:** students suggest contenders in the three categories.
- Have a class vote for the winners of each category. Ask: *Did the winners give real or imaginary answers.*

Answers
Age, Occupation, Credit card, Places the person would like to go shopping

Possible answers
1 What's your name?
2 What's your occupation? / What do you do?
3 How old are you?
4 How often do you go shopping?
5 How much do you spend on clothes / entertainment / electronic goods every month?
6 How do you usually pay?
7 How many times have you done internet shopping?
8 Where would you go shopping if you could?
9 How often do you complain? Why do you complain?

Listening script 15

A: Excuse me. Can I ask you a few questions for a shopping survey?
B: Yes, of course.
A: How old are you?
B: I'm 26.
A: What do you do?
B: I'm a computer programmer.
A: Hm-mm. Do you have a credit card?
B: Yes, I do.
A: How long have you had it?
B: I've had it for about three years.
A: How often do you go shopping?
B: Mm. I usually go every weekend. I love shopping.
A: Where would you go shopping if you could afford it?
B: I'd go to Paris if I had the opportunity. There are some wonderful designer shops in Paris.

Reference

Module 3 test: Teacher's Book pages 151–153

Additional material

Photocopiable resources

Photocopiable tests

UNIT 1

What makes good parents?

1 Look at the sentences. Do you agree or disagree with them?

(1 = I strongly agree; 4 = I disagree strongly)

	1	2	3	4
1 It's not important if your parents are rich or poor.				
2 People over 40 are too old to be good parents.				
3 Children should look after their parents when they are older.				
4 Parents should teach children their religion.				
5 Parents should be married.				
6 It's better for children to live with relatives than adopted parents.				

2 Work in pairs and compare your ideas. Give reasons for your choices.

Example:
I don't think that people over 40 will be good parents because they don't have enough energy.

3 Look at the information about three couples who want children.
Which couple do you think will make the best parents?

Khulu is 29 and from South Africa. He lives with his partner, Susannah, in West London. They met five years ago and bought a flat three years ago. They both have good jobs and they enjoy travelling.

Justin and Veronica are in their early thirties. They got married three years ago. Veronica is a school teacher and Justin is an office manager. They live in a small house in Liverpool with a garden, and go to the local church.

Amina and Rehan Shah are from Pakistan and are in their forties. They got married in 1984. They have two sons who are both at university. Amina and Rehan own a busy pharmacy in Bradford, and live in a house with a small garden.

4 Work in groups and compare your ideas. Give reasons for your choices.

Useful language
I think x and y will be the best parents because ...
x and y are the best choice because ...
I think x and y are the best couple because ...
I don't think x and y are a good choice because...

5 Work in groups and discuss these questions.

1 What do you think makes a good parent?

2 What are the easiest / most difficult / most fun parts of being a parent?

6 Work in pairs and discuss the question.

Do you think you are / will make a good parent? Why? / Why not?

Think about:

1 your character

2 your energy levels

3 your age

4 other responsibilities

5 how much time you have

6 your lifestyle:
- Do you work long hours?
- Do you practise a hobby regularly?
- Do you like going out in the evenings?

Perfect partner

My answers	love	like	don't mind	don't like	can't stand
spicy food					
rap music					
sleeping					
dogs					
horror films					
skiing					
chocolate					
museums					

1 Name ________	love	like	don't mind	don't like	can't stand
spicy food					
rap music					
sleeping					
dogs					
horror films					
skiing					
chocolate					
museums					

2 Name ________	love	like	don't mind	don't like	can't stand
spicy food					
rap music					
sleeping					
dogs					
horror films					
skiing					
chocolate					
museums					

3 Name ________	love	like	don't mind	don't like	can't stand
spicy food					
rap music					
sleeping					
dogs					
horror films					
skiing					
chocolate					
museums					

4 Name ________	love	like	don't mind	don't like	can't stand
spicy food					
rap music					
sleeping					
dogs					
horror films					
skiing					
chocolate					
museums					

5 Name ________	love	like	don't mind	don't like	can't stand
spicy food					
rap music					
sleeping					
dogs					
horror films					
skiing					
chocolate					
museums					

Useful language
My perfect partner is ...
We both like ...
He / She likes xx more than me ...
I like xx more than him / her ...
We're very similar because ...

UNIT 2

The right thing?

1 Work in pairs. What do you think is most important for the future of the world? Rank these ideas. Add ideas of your own if you want to. (1 = most important)

protecting the environment	☐	helping poor countries	☐	educating young people	☐
developing drugs to treat illness	☐	developing new technology	☐	making goods cheaper for everyone	☐
____________	☐	____________	☐	____________	☐

2 Read the article and answer these questions.

1 What does the charity want to do?

2 Why isn't the computer company helping?

3 Who do you think is right?

> We often hear that developing countries need food, clean water and medicine, but we don't often think about technology. One international charity is hoping to change this. It wants to provide enough laptop computers for every child in the developing world. These special computers are cheap to make and they are clockwork so they don't need electricity.
>
> The charity asked to buy cheap software from a large computer company. However, the company is worried. It says that it wants to help, but selling software cheaply in one area of the world reduces prices worldwide. At the moment, the company is refusing to provide the cheap software.

3 Work in pairs and discuss these issues.

1 Do children in the developing world need laptop computers? Why? / Why not?

2 If worldwide software prices fall, what will happen to …

a the company?

b the development of new software?

3 Could the government pay for the software?

4 Work in pairs and discuss possible solutions to the problem. Use the phrases in the box to help you.

Useful language

The main problem is that ...
The most important thing is ...
The charity / company / government should ...
One solution is to ...
I agree / don't agree with you ...
That's a good / bad / terrible idea.
Without computers, people can't ...

5 Work in pairs. Roleplay this situation. At the end of your conversation, agree on a solution.

Student A

You are the manager of the computer company. Explain why you are worried about providing cheap software.

Student B

You work for the charity. Explain why you need to have cheap software.

Happy endings

UNIT 3

Dilemmas

1 Work in pairs and discuss these questions.

1 When you have a problem do you try to solve it on your own?
2 Who do you go to when you need advice?
3 Have you ever accepted advice from a total stranger?
4 Are there advice columns in newspapers and magazines in your country?
5 What kind of problems do people write about?

2 These three letters appeared on a discussion website. What advice would you give each person?

Useful language
You should / shouldn't ... because
You ought to ...
You could ...

My son loves motorbikes and wants one for his 18th birthday. He works hard at school and is very sensible. However, I think that motorbikes are very dangerous. My sister lives in the USA and we haven't visited her for ten years. Should I buy my son a motorbike or take the family to the USA for a holiday?

Rose

I work in a shop. A colleague wants me to write a job reference for her. She wants to be a bus driver. She passed the test and it's a good opportunity for her. However, she has problems sleeping at night and is often tired at work. Once I found her asleep in the staff room.

Should I write the reference? What if she falls asleep when she's driving?

Mike

I'm doing my final exams at university. I have a wonderful girlfriend. She's really intelligent, very pretty, and I love being with her.

She's going to work in London after university, and already has a job there. She wants me to go to London too. But I want to go on a trip round the world with my friends. What should I do?

Tom

3 Work in pairs and compare your advice.

4 Work in pairs and discuss these questions.

1 Whose dilemma do you think is the most difficult? Why?
2 How do you think Rose's son will feel if Rose doesn't buy him a motorbike?
3 If Tom goes travelling, do you think his relationship with his girlfriend will continue? Why? / Why not?

5 Think of a dilemma you've been in and tell your partner about it.

- What was the problem?
- When did it happen?
- Where were you?
- Who were you with?
- How did you feel?
- What did you do?

Dear Jane

1 Read the problems and match them to the correct titles.

1 Jealous of my friend ☐
2 Money can't buy me love ☐
3 Is she cheating? ☐
4 I lied online ☐
5 I hate my job ☐

a

Dear Jane,

I've been seeing my boyfriend, Ben, for a year. He's kind, caring and very generous. For my last birthday, he bought me a new car. The problem is, I don't love him. I feel so guilty when he buys me expensive presents.

Monica

b

Dear Jane,

I started a new job recently, but I don't like it. The work is boring and my boss is horrible to me. I really want to leave, but I'm worried about how I'll pay my rent.

Sophie

c

Dear Jane,

A few weeks ago, I found a text message on my girlfriend's phone. It was from another man, asking her to go for a drink. I want to ask my girlfriend who he is, but she'll be angry that I looked at her messages.

Toby

d

Dear Jane,

My best friend, Amy, has everything – good looks, a great job and a wonderful boyfriend. I feel so dull and boring in comparison. When we go out together, people ignore me and just talk to Amy. I'm so jealous. I don't know what to do.

Ellen

e

Dear Jane,

A month ago I met a girl through an internet dating site. We chat every day and we get on really well. Now she wants to meet me. The problem is that I haven't been honest about my appearance. She thinks I'm tall, dark and handsome, but I'm not.

Peter

2 Write a reply to one of the problems. Use the phrases in the box to help you.

Dear ______________________

____

____

____

____

____

____

Useful language
My advice is to ...
You should / shouldn't ...
You (really) must ...
You mustn't ...

3 Read other students' replies. Decide which you think gives the best advice for each problem.

4 Work with a partner and roleplay the situation between one of these pairs.

Student A	**Student B**
Monica	Monica's boyfriend, Ben
Sophie	Sophie's boss
Toby	Toby's girlfriend
Ellen	Ellen's friend, Amy
Peter	Peter's internet date

UNIT 4 Taking time out

1 Work in pairs and discuss these questions.

1 Why do people take time out from work or education?

2 What do people do with their time out?

3 Would you like to take some time out? Why? / Why not?

4 In some countries, all government workers are given three months' paid holiday after ten years in their jobs. Is this a good idea? Why? / Why not?

2 Look at the advertisements and answer these questions.

Which jobs / experiences involve …

1 working with children?

2 travelling?

3 working as a volunteer?

4 studying?

a
Want to see the world? Take the bus!
We have routes across Europe, America, Asia, Africa and Australia.
Ticket prices from £800.
Air travel not included.

b
Cruise the Caribbean
Singers, dancers, waiting staff and cleaners required for luxury cruise ship.
Meals and accommodation provided.

c
Au pairs wanted for work in central London.
Contracts: three months to two years.
Accommodation, basic wage and English course provided.

d
An unforgettable experience!
Work abroad as a volunteer builder, teacher or engineer.
We have vacancies in **Africa and Asia.**
Airfare and accommodation provided.

e
Need a change?
Train for a new career in just three months.
Courses in journalism, retail, catering and leisure.
Prices start at just £120.

f
Time to spare?
Local charity for children with disabilities needs help with summer sports club.
All meals provided.

3 Work in pairs and interview your partner. Complete the questionnaire with his / her responses.

1 Which word best describes you?
- a hard-working ☐
- b adventurous ☐
- c relaxed ☐

2 Where do you like to spend your time?
- a Outdoors, in the open air. ☐
- b Indoors, where it's comfortable. ☐
- c Moving around, on trains, planes or buses. ☐

3 What is the best reason to take time out from work or education?
- a To help people. ☐
- b To find out more about my future career. ☐
- c To travel. ☐

4 Who do you most like to spend your time with?
- a adults ☐
- b children ☐
- c I like spending time alone. ☐

4 Choose an advertisement for your partner. Explain your decision. Use the language in the box to help you.

Useful language

I think you should go to / do ... because ...	You're (+ adjective)
You like / don't like ...	You want to / don't want to ...
You're good at ...	You like being with ...

Best person for the job

Vet

I'll be ____________

I'll always ____________

I'll never ____________

I won't ____________

Lion tamer

I'll be ____________

I'll always ____________

I'll never ____________

I won't ____________

Secretary

I'll be ____________

I'll always ____________

I'll never ____________

I won't ____________

Astronaut

I'll be ____________

I'll always ____________

I'll never ____________

I won't ____________

Teacher

I'll be ____________

I'll always ____________

I'll never ____________

I won't ____________

President

I'll be ____________

I'll always ____________

I'll never ____________

I won't ____________

Shop assistant

I'll be ____________

I'll always ____________

I'll never ____________

I won't ____________

Stuntperson

I'll be ____________

I'll always ____________

I'll never ____________

I won't ____________

Postal worker

I'll be ____________

I'll always ____________

I'll never ____________

I won't ____________

Pop star

I'll be ____________

I'll always ____________

I'll never ____________

I won't ____________

UNIT 1

Public and private

1 Work in pairs and discuss these questions.

1 Why do you think celebrity gossip magazines and websites are popular?

2 Do you ever read them? Why? / Why not?

2 Work in pairs and look at these events.
Which stories would interest you in a celebrity magazine?
Why? / Why not?

a singer has a new boyfriend / girlfriend	a princess is getting divorced
a footballer got drunk at a party	a model has put on weight
an actor is getting married	an actress has had plastic surgery
an actress is pregnant	a singer has bought a new house

Useful language

I would / wouldn't be interested in ...
It would be interesting because ...
xxx would be boring because ...
I'd like to / wouldn't like to read about ...
I love reading about xxx because ...
It has nothing to do with me.

3 Read the article from a magazine. Describe the relationships between Gina, Anton and Storm.

Gina's new love?

Gina Richards, 24, star of *Hope Valley Close*, has split up with her boyfriend of two years, Anton Benson, 27, singer with pop sensation Brixton.

One friend, who did not wish to be named, said 'We're really surprised. I saw them last week and they seemed really in love.'

There are rumours that Anton was unhappy with Gina's close friendship with fellow actor, Storm Davis, 25.

A waiter from a London restaurant told us 'Gina and Storm came here for dinner the other night. They didn't kiss each other, but they looked very happy together.'

We contacted Gina's publicity agent, who said, 'Ms Richards has a right to a private life. She will make a statement later this week.'

4 Work in groups and discuss these questions. Give reasons for your answers.

1 Imagine you are a friend of Gina's. Would you answer questions from newspapers / magazines about her? Why? / Why not?

2 Can you read stories like this in your country's newspapers and magazines?

3 Do you think that famous people should have more privacy? Why? / Why not?

4 Would you ever answer questions about a celebrity for money? Think about:
- the behaviour of the celebrity towards you or other people
- the type of celebrity (eg pop star, footballer, politician)
- the amount of money.

Finished or unfinished?

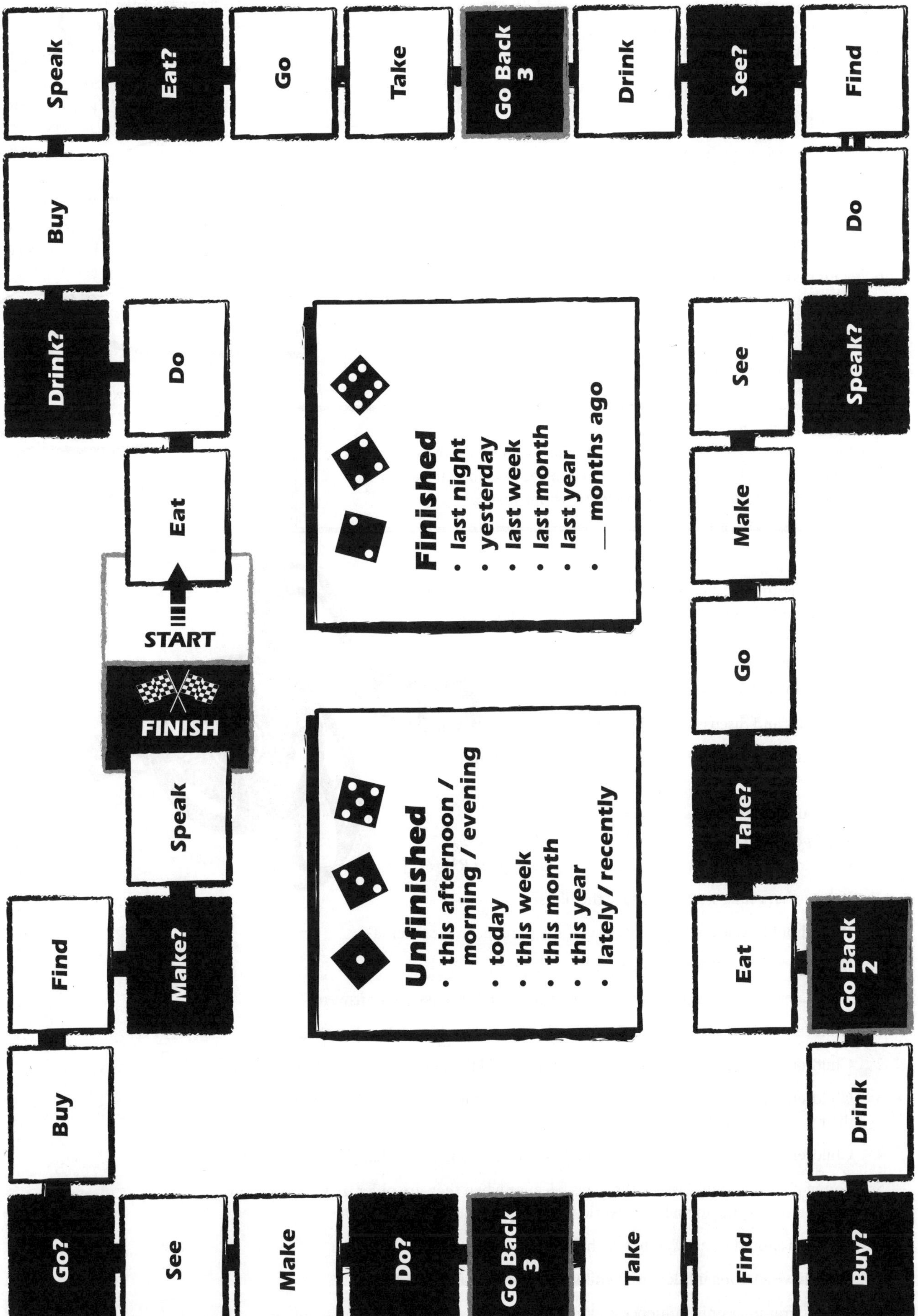

UNIT 2

See no evil?

1 Read the speech bubbles and the scenarios and decide which viewpoint is closest to yours for each scenario. Work in pairs and compare your opinions.

1 a love story with a 65-year-old woman and a 25-year-old man ☐
2 a burglar shooting a dog ☐
3 a charity worker who has been taken hostage asking his / her government to give the terrorists what they want ☐
4 a married politician coming out of a hotel with his girlfriend ☐
5 your country's dead soldiers – they have been killed in a war ☐
6 your country's football team captain drunk in a nightclub after winning the World Cup ☐
7 people dying of hunger ☐
8 a woman being attacked in the street ☐

a Nobody has the right to censor the news – we need to be sure it is true.

b Some things are too horrible to put on TV – people could see them by accident.

c I don't want my children to see something like that.

d It's different when it's real – in a film you know that everyone's OK in the end.

e Even famous people should have a private life.

f We need to know what is happening in the world. We can't ignore things just because they're horrible.

Useful language

I don't like seeing ...
I think it's wrong to show ...
I believe TV should show xxx with a warning because ...
I don't think TV should show xxx because ...
We need to see xxx, so that we can ...

2 Films are classified in the UK to try and stop people the wrong age from seeing things that they shouldn't. The ratings are:

- U for everyone
- PG for children accompanied by an adult
- 12, 15 and 18 for people over these ages.

Work in pairs and discuss these questions.

1 Do you think it is necessary to give each film a rating? Why? / Why not?
2 Do you agree with these ratings:
   - *Spiderman* (12)
   - *Mr and Mrs Smith* (15)
   - *Shrek 2* (PG)
   - *Lord of the Rings* (PG)
3 If not, what rating would you give the films?
4 Who should decide what children see – the parents or the cinema?

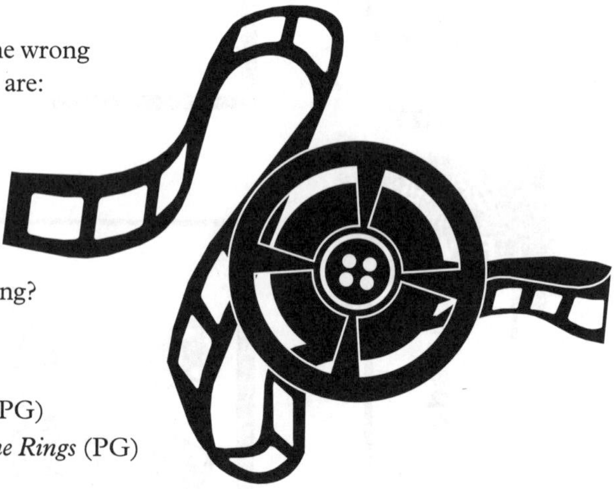

3 Tick the statements you agree with. Work in groups and discuss your answers.

1 Children who watch films with lots of violence will become violent later on. ☐
2 Children who see programmes that scare them will then become frightened in real life. ☐
3 Children who see programmes about divorced parents will be better prepared if their parents get divorced. ☐
4 Children who only watch family comedies and cartoons will be happy. ☐
5 Young children should watch the news because when they are older they will be more interested in trying to make the world a better place. ☐
6 Children should be allowed to watch TV when they want. ☐
7 Films have a strong influence on children's opinions and beliefs. ☐
8 TV programmes only influence children, not adults. ☐

Desert island iPod

1 You are going to spend a year alone on a desert island. Before you leave, you can load your iPod with the following:

- five pieces of music
- two film / TV clips
- the full text of one book

You can also take your favourite possession with you.

What would you choose and why? Use the Useful language box to help you.

Useful language

Because _____ reminds me of my ...	I've chosen this because ...	My parents gave this to me when ...
It reminds me of ...	I saw this when ...	I bought this when ...
When I went on holiday to ...	I've always loved ...	My ____ gave me this as a present ...
I first heard this ...	I thought this was fantastic because ...	I got this on my _____ birthday ...
This track makes me think about ...		

Choice	Reason
Music 1:	
Music 2:	
Music 3:	
Music 4:	
Music 5:	
Film 1:	
Film 2:	
Book:	
Favourite possesion:	

2 Work in pairs and compare your lists.

3 Your teacher will give you another list. Could you live for a year with the new list? Why? / Why not? Discuss in your pairs.

4 Find the person whose list you have.

Module 2

UNIT 3

How tasty is that?

1 Work in groups and discuss these questions.

1 What is the typical dish of your country or region? What are the ingredients?

2 What food from other countries have you tried? Do you eat it often?

3 What is the most unusual thing you have ever eaten?

2 Jacob Mullens is a travel writer with experience of food in many countries. Here are two texts about typical dishes that he's eaten. Read the texts and complete the table.

1 **Haggis**

This is a traditional Scottish dish and it's basically lamb, onion, wheat and salt put in a sheep's stomach and boiled. There are vegetarian alternatives that taste very similar. I ate it with mashed potato and vegetables – very tasty.

2 **Kimchee**

I ate this in Korea and it is usually made from cabbage but you can use other vegetables too. You leave the uncooked cabbage in a mixture of garlic, red pepper, ginger and salt. It is very spicy and Koreans eat it with everything. It's delicious.

	Haggis	Kimchee
Where is it from?		
How is it prepared?		
What are the ingredients?		
Does Jacob Mullens like it?		

3 Work in pairs and discuss these questions.

1 Which of the dishes would you try?

2 Is there a dish you would or wouldn't try? Why?

3 In which countries do people eat these things for breakfast?

rice beans biscuits pancakes sausage

4 Which of these foods is unusual in your country and which have you tried?

horse dog snake monkey frog ready-made meals rice with jam strong-flavoured cheese peanut butter and jelly chilli sweets

5 Describe the strangest thing that people in your country eat.

4 Work in groups of four and ask your partners the questions on your card about food and eating in their country.

Student A

What's a typical breakfast / lunch / evening meal in your country?

What do people usually drink with their meals?

Student B

How often do you go to restaurants in your country?

What's your favourite restaurant?

What foreign restaurants do you have in your country?

Is it expensive to eat out?

Student C

Who is the best cook you know and what dishes do they make?

What food do you hate the most?

What food do you love the most?

What dishes can you cook?

Student D

Do you eat lots of fruit and vegetables?

How often do you eat fast food?

What is typical fast food in your country?

Do people in your country have an unhealthy diet?

5 Report the most interesting thing you learned about one of your partners to the class.

Are you a healthy eater?

1 Complete the questions with *much* or *many*.

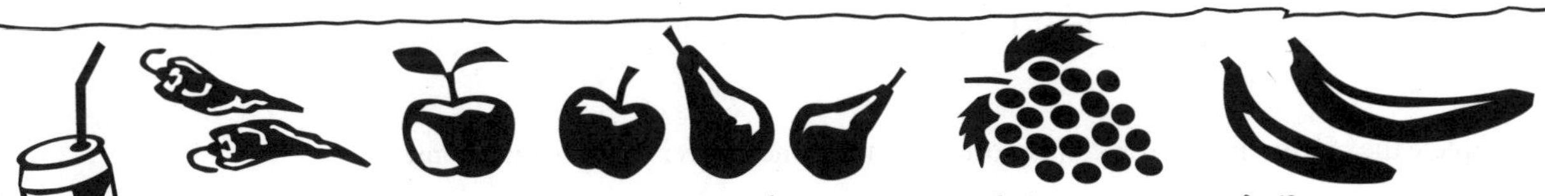

1 How ______ food do you eat in one meal?
- a I eat until I'm full.
- b I eat as much as I can.
- c I don't eat meals. I just have snacks when I feel hungry.

2 How ______ time do you spend preparing food?
- a As little as possible – I just put something in the microwave.
- b About an hour. I need enough time to make a proper meal.
- c Hours! I like to cook a lot of food.

3 How ______ times a week do you eat fast food?
- a Once or twice, if I need something quick.
- b None. I never eat fast food.
- c I go as often as I can. I love burgers and chips.

4 How ______ salt do you put on your food?
- a A little, if the food needs it.
- b Lots! Food doesn't taste good without it.
- c None. I like to taste the flavour of the food I'm eating.

5 How ______ portions of fruit and vegetables do you eat in a day?
- a At least five. I love fruit!
- b About two or three.
- c As few as possible.

6 How ______ water do you drink a day?
- a None. I prefer fizzy drinks.
- b Two or three glasses, but I drink other things, too.
- c Lots! I always drink plenty of water.

7 How ______ packets of crisps and sweets do you eat?
- a I never eat sweets or crisps. I don't want spots!
- b I sometimes eat them, if I want a treat.
- c I eat sweets and crisps every day.

2 Work in pairs and interview your partner. Complete the quiz with his / her responses. Then add up the scores.

My partner has

Mostly As ☐ = Very healthy

Mostly Bs ☐ = Neither good nor bad

Mostly Cs ☐ = Very unhealthy

Patient's name ______________________

Comments on diet ______________________

____

____

Recommendations ______________________

____

____

3 Complete the doctor's report card for your partner. Use the words in the box to help you.

Useful language
- Your diet is (+ adjective)
- You eat too much ...
- You don't eat enough ...
- You need to eat more / less / fewer ...
- You eat a lot of ...
- You eat too many ...
- You need to drink more / less ...

4 Exchange cards with your partner and read your report. Do you agree with your partner's advice?

Body beautiful

1 Match the words with the pictures in the questionnaire.

tattoo ☐ wrinkles ☐ facelift ☐ bald ☐ piercing ☐

2 Complete the questionnaire. You can choose more than one answer to some questions.

1 Do you have any piercings?
- a None.
- b One.
- c Two or more.

2 Would / Do you have a piercing in
- a a nostril?
- b your tongue?
- c your belly button?

3 How often do you change your hair style?
- a Every six months.
- b When I go to party.
- c Hardly ever.

4 When would you shave your head?
- a To look fashionable.
- b When I start losing my hair.
- c Never.

5 Have you ever had a henna tattoo?
- a No.
- b Yes, when I was on holiday.
- c Yes, at a music festival.

6 Would / Do you have a tattoo on
- a your shoulder?
- b your arm?
- c your ankle?

7 Why would you have a tattoo?
- a I wouldn't. It's too painful.
- b To show how much I loved someone.
- c To be trendy.

8 When would you have a facelift?
- a When I get a few wrinkles.
- b When I have enough money.
- c Never.

a

b

c
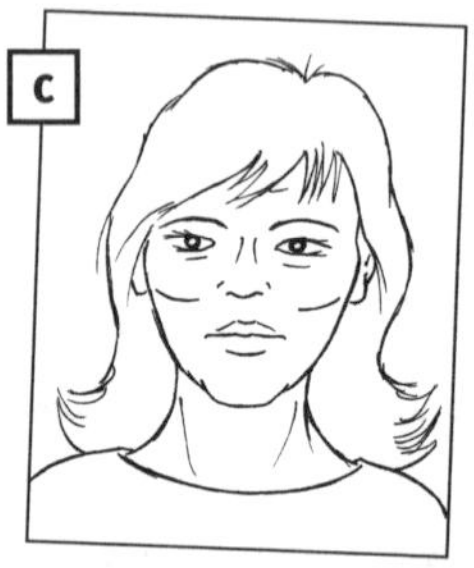

d
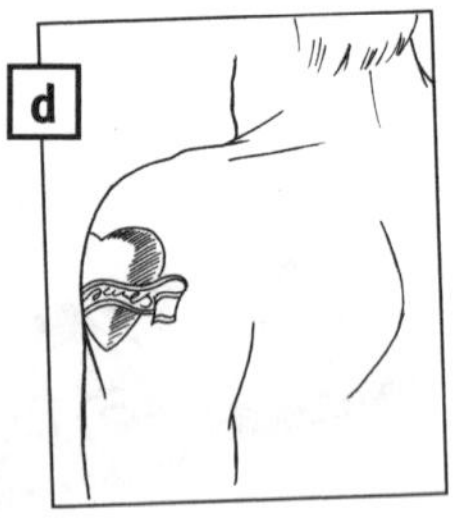

e
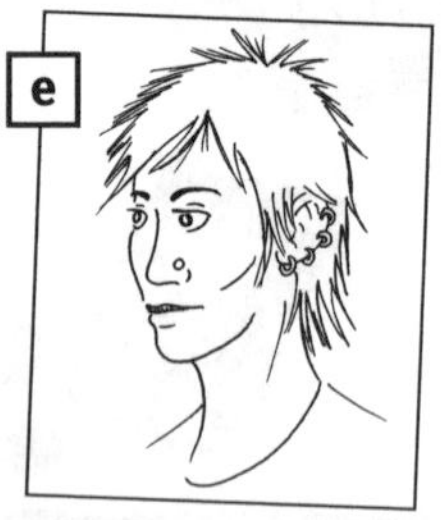

3 Work in pairs and compare your answers.

Useful language
I'd have a ...
I think that would look ...
Really? I wouldn't. I think it would be ...
I'd feel ...

4 Work in groups and discuss the statements in the speech bubbles. Use the questions below to help you.

1 Do you agree that it is better to grow old naturally? Why? / Why not?

2 Do you think liposuction is a good solution to putting on weight? Why? / Why not? How would you solve a weight problem?

3 What are the advantages of having a tattoo? Can you think of any disadvantages of having a tattoo?

4 Should people only have cosmetic surgery for medical reasons, eg to mend a broken nose? Why?

5 Do some people think about their appearance more than others? If so, who and why? How important is it to care about your appearance? Why?

1 A lot of people have cosmetic surgery nowadays, but I don't think it's necessary. I think it's better to grow old naturally.

2 Liposuction is the quickest and easiest solution to putting on weight.

3 I love my girlfriend so much that I have her name in a tattoo on my arm. I think it looks great!

4 I'm so glad I had laser eye surgery. My quality of life has improved so much since the operation.

5 I don't think I can go to that party tonight. My face looks terrible, my hair is a mess and I'm so fat.

Three in a row

Preposition cards

on	**after**	**up**
up	**off**	**after**
away	**off**	**up**

UNIT 1

The big event

1 Work in groups of three and discuss these questions.

1 What type of music do you like listening to, eg pop, rock, jazz?

2 Do you ever go to concerts? How often?

3 Do you think that live music is better than listening to a CD? Why? / Why not?

4 Have you ever been to a music festival or watched one on TV?

2 Read the article. Work in pairs and answer these questions.

1 Would you like to go to Glastonbury festival?

2 Why? / Why not?

Last year, I went to Glastonbury festival. My ticket cost £125. It was expensive, but some of my favourite bands were playing, so I thought it was worth it. When I saw the first band, it was amazing. We were near the stage, so we had good views and the atmosphere was incredible.

Staying in a tent was fun, but it was noisy at night and hard to sleep. On the second day, it rained a lot and the fields got very muddy. I couldn't wash properly because the facilities weren't very good.

Overall, I had a great time. I saw 12 bands in three days. I'll go again, but next time I'll take my own food. The meals we bought from stalls were disgusting.

Jenny, London

3 What is most important at a music festival? Work in pairs and rank these ideas in order of importance.

(1 = most important, 7 = least important)

- comfortable accommodation ☐
- good view of the stage and performers ☐
- moderately priced tickets ☐
- great music ☐
- clean toilets and washing facilities ☐
- a good atmosphere ☐
- good choice of food ☐

4 Work in groups and compare your answers.

5 Work in groups and plan your own music festival. Make notes on these categories.

the style of music

____

which bands you would like to book

____

____

____

the duration (one to three days)

____

the type of venue (indoor or outdoor)

____

the type of accommodation for festival goers

____

the type of accommodation for bands and singers

____

the facilities for festival goers

____

the price of the tickets

____

6 Tell the class about your group's music festival.

For or since?

A

five years

... I was young

2000

about a year

B

... I left

a few days

this morning

last night

a long time

three years

... I was eleven

C

1 January

a fortnight

a few weeks

yesterday

D

two months

... I met

last summer

a couple of days

last week

ages

... I started learning English

- use the internet
- go to a carnival
- go to the cinema
- see my friends
- visit my grandparents
- go abroad
- buy clothes
- live in the same house
- play the piano
- make a phone call
- read a book
- eat hamburgers
- drink champagne
- go to a wedding
- drive a car
- watch a horror film
- go to a museum
- buy a CD

UNIT 2

Which sport?

1 Work in groups of three and discuss these questions.

1 What are your favourite outdoor sports or leisure activities?

2 Why do you like them?

3 What equipment do you need?

4 Are there any dangers involved?

2 Your teacher will give you an article about an outdoor sport. Read it and then tell your group about the sport.

3 Work in groups and compare the sports. Use the words and phrases in the box to help you.

Which would you most / least like to do? Why?

4 Tell your group about a sport or a memorable sporting / outdoor experience you've had. Think about these questions.

1 What were the best parts?

2 What were the difficulties?

3 Would you do it again? Why? / Why not?

Useful language

I would / wouldn't like to do sport climbing because ...
Wakeboarding is easier / more difficult / faster than ...
Running is the best / worst / easiest sport because ...

Adjectives

dangerous	easy	good
safe	difficult	bad
scary		

Student A

Marathon running

The great thing about running is that anyone can do it – all you need is a good pair of trainers.

Six years ago, I did my first marathon in London. I had a good start, but after eighteen miles I was dehydrated and exhausted. These are the most common problems that runners experience, especially when they aren't used to long distances.

I didn't give up and since then, I've done marathons in New York, Sydney and Singapore. Next year, I'm planning to do the Great Wall marathon in China. Running has taken me all over the world.

Student B

Wakeboarding

If you haven't heard of wakeboarding, think of water-skiing with a surfboard. It's a really wild sport and I love it!

The advantage of using a surfboard is that you can do some amazing tricks. As the boat speeds up, the water rises on either side of you. You can use this to help push yourself into the air. You never fall off because the board is attached to your feet.

It looks fast and dangerous, but in reality it's a slower sport than water-skiing. It's also surprisingly easy to pick up. The only problem is that the equipment is expensive to hire.

Student C

Sport climbing

I started climbing about four years ago at an indoor wall near my home. After about a year, I thought I ought to try a real rock face, so I joined a sport climbing group.

Sport climbing is safer than traditional climbing because we use special climb routes with bolts placed closely together in the rock. This means that if we fall, the rope only slips one or two metres.

But these extra safety measures don't make the sport any easier. Many of the sport climbing routes are in places that would be impossible to climb in any other way. In this sport, you can be as adventurous as you like.

UNIT 2

Sport dominoes

	play		go		do
	play		go		do
	play		go		go
	play		go		go
	play		do		go
	go		go		play
	go				

UNIT 3
Holiday friends

1 Work in pairs and discuss these questions.

1 Do you try to meet people when you are on holiday?

2 Do you exchange addresses or emails?

3 Do you think you will see these people again?

Hi Neil,

Do you remember me? We met during your holiday in Mexico. It was quite a few months ago, wasn't it? We had such a good time.

I've got some great photos of the scuba-diving trip and a really good one of you at the top of that pyramid at Chichen Itza.

Anyway, the reason I'm writing is because I'm coming to England in June and I was hoping we could meet up. I'm planning to be in London for at least a week because there's so much to see.

Can you give me some advice on the best places to stay and what to see and do?

Hope to hear from you soon.

Jim

2 Read the email and decide if the statements are true or false.

1 Jim and Neil went on holiday to Mexico together.

2 They had a good time in Mexico.

3 They haven't seen each other for a while.

4 Jim is looking forward to seeing Neil.

3 How do you think Neil will feel when he receives this email?

4 Work in groups and discuss these questions.

1 Would you remember someone you met on holiday a year ago?

2 How would you feel if they contacted you?

3 What would you do if they asked for advice about where to stay? Would you invite them to stay with you? Why? / Why not?

4 Would you ever contact someone you had met on holiday? Why? / Why not?

5 When you go away on holiday do you like to stay in hotels or do you prefer to stay at someone's house? Why?

5 What are the main reasons you go away on holiday? Rank these ideas. (1 = main reason)

1 To meet new people. ☐

2 To make new friends. ☐

3 To have fun. ☐

4 To learn more about the customs and culture of the country. ☐

5 To learn a new language. ☐

6 To have new experiences. ☐

7 To try out different food and drink. ☐

8 To relax and do nothing. ☐

9 To practise your favourite sport. ☐

10 To visit famous landmarks. ☐

Useful language

I go on holiday to ...
I want to ...
For me, the most important reason for going on holiday is to ...
I don't want to ...
I think you can do xxx in your own country.
You don't need to go away to do xxx.

6 Work in groups and compare your answers.

1 What was the most popular reason for going on holiday?

2 How important was meeting people or making friends?

Say, tell maze

1 Work in pairs and do the maze.

START
She told to me 'I love you.'
✓ Go to 6.
✗ Go to 1.

1
She told me forget about the idea.
✓ Go to 13.
✗ Go to 6.

2
'Give me another chance,' Jean told me.
✓ Go to 11.
✗ Go to 14.

3
She told that he won't be late.
✓ Go to 8.
✗ Go to 7.

4
Mark told me to sell the flat.
✓ Go to 9.
✗ Go to 15.

5
'Take the money and leave,' they said.
✓ Go to 14.
✗ Go to Finish.

6
'I'll see you in Rome,' Natasha said.
✓ Go to 10.
✗ Go to 13.

7
'I don't feel well,' he told me.
✓ Go to 12.
✗ Go to 15.

8
'You're the best brother,' he said me.
✓ Go to 10.
✗ Go to Finish.

9
They told to find a new one.
✓ Go to 3.
✗ Go to 2.

10
She said, 'I really don't care any more.'
✓ Go to 13.
✗ Go to 9.

11
'Maria said, 'I'm getting married.'
✓ Go to 5.
✗ Go to 7.

12
She told, 'It won't work.'
✓ Go to 8.
✗ Go to 15.

13
She said me, 'Tuesday is perfect.'
✓ Go to 2.
✗ Go to 4.

14
Ali told to me that he wasn't coming.
✓ Go to 12
✗ Go to 3.

15
You told me that you wanted one.
✓ Go to 8.
✗ Go to 10.

FINISH

2 Work in small groups. Choose three of the sentences. If they are wrong, correct them.
Write a story which includes the three sentences you have chosen. Read your story to another group.

UNIT 4

Who are you?

1 There are lots of ways of keeping in touch and your personal details can be everywhere: on envelopes, on the internet, in marketing questionnaires. Do this quick quiz to find out how safe your personal information is.

1 How do you throw away letters and envelopes with your name and address on?
a Tear up all letters and envelopes
b Put them in the bin
c Tear up confidential letters only

2 When you use the internet, are your passwords a mixture of letters and numbers?
a Yes b No c Sometimes

3 Do you use 'easy' passwords?
a No
b Yes
c Sometimes

4 Do you give personal details, eg credit card numbers, on public computers?
a No b Yes c Sometimes

5 How often do you check your computer for viruses and 'spyware'?
a Every day b Once a month
c Every week

6 Do you give personal information, eg what town you live in, when you are in internet chat-rooms?
a Yes b No c Sometimes

7 How often do you check your credit card / bank statements?
a Monthly b Never
c Every few months

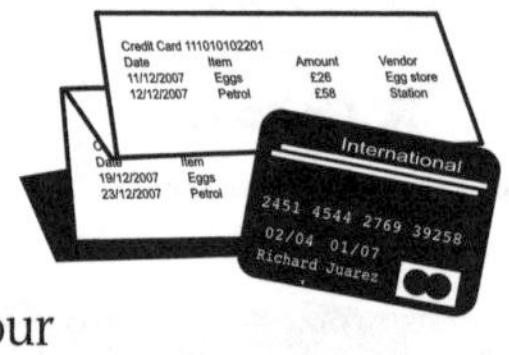

8 Do you ever complete questionnaires with your personal information for people in the street?
a No b Yes
c Sometimes

Key

Mostly A answers – Congratulations! You take care of your personal details, keep it up!

Mostly B answers – Be careful! You need to take more care with your personal information.

Mostly C answers – OK, you are trying to be careful, but you could do more!

2 Work in pairs and compare your answers.

3 Identity theft is a modern crime. What do you think it is? Read the text to find out.

Who are you?

... and can you prove it?

Imagine waking up to find a credit card bill for thousands of pounds in your name or the news that 'you' have taken out a loan with a bank and cannot pay it back. You wake up and find the police at your door, investigating a crime 'you' have committed – except ... it wasn't you at all. You are one more victim of identity theft. This is when criminals 'steal' your identity, and use it to borrow money, buy goods and commit crimes.

4 Work in groups and discuss these questions.

1 What information do criminals need to steal someone's identity?

2 How do you think they get this information?

3 What can you do to stop them stealing your identity?

Shopping

- START
- If my credit card wasn't accepted, …
- I'd be very disappointed if …
- I'll pay more if …
- Would / you buy / something / auction?
- If I bought a TV with a fault, …
- GO BACK 3
- If it's out of stock, …
- What / you buy / if / you go / supermarket after lesson?
- If I got a discount …
- GO FORWARD 3
- What would you do / if / something you buy online / not arrive?
- I'd sell my car if …
- If the shop is too crowded, …
- What / you buy first / if you / win / lottery?
- I'll exchange it if …
- GO BACK 2
- What / you do / if / you / can't find / right size?
- I'd buy something online if …
- If a shop assistant was rude to me, …
- If I lose the receipt, …
- If there is a sale, …
- GO BACK 3
- If the jeans don't fit me, …
- What / car you buy / if / have / a lot of money?
- GO FORWARD 2
- I'd buy you some flowers if …
- If it was your birthday today, …
- GO BACK 1
- I'll get a refund if …
- FINISH

Teacher's resource notes

Module 1

Unit 1 What makes good parents?

Lead-in

Brainstorm adjectives to describe good parents, eg *patient, caring*.

Procedure

1 Students work individually to read the statements and complete the grid. Make sure students understand the meaning of *should* before they complete the grid.
2 Students work in pairs and compare their answers. Encourage them to justify and expand on their opinions wherever possible.
3 Students work individually to read the texts and decide who they think will make the best parents and why.
4 Students work in groups and compare their opinions. Then open the discussion up to the class.
5 Students work in groups and discuss the questions.
6 Students work in pairs and discuss whether they think they will make / are good parents and why / why not.

Vocabulary

adopted, partner, pharmacy, character, lifestyle

Unit 1 Perfect partner

Lead-in

Ask: *What do you love? What do you like? What can't you stand?*

Procedure

1 Students work individually to complete the table headed *My answers*, by ticking the correct column for each item.
2 Students go round asking and answering the question *Do you like xx?* to complete the other five tables on their worksheet.
3 Students work in pairs and discuss who their perfect partner is and why. Point out the phrases in the Useful language box which can help them.
4 Students then tell the class who their perfect partner is and why.

Vocabulary

spicy food, both, similar

Unit 2 The right thing?

Lead-in

Ask students to identify some of the problems in the world today. Ask: *What can we do about these problems?*

Procedure

1 Students work in pairs and rank the ideas in order of importance and add their own ideas. Ask different students to share their opinions with the class.
2 Students read the text and then discuss the answers in pairs.
3 Go through the answers as a class.
4 Students work in pairs and discuss the issues and possible solutions to the problem, using the words in the Useful language box for help.
5 Students swap pairs and roleplay a conversation between the charity representative and the company manager. In the end, they agree on the solution they reached in Ex 4.
6 Some of the pairs act out their roleplays for the class.

Answers

2 1 The charity wants to provide enough laptop computers for every child in the third world.
2 they say that producing software cheaply in one area of the world reduces prices worldwide.

Vocabulary

environment, aid, technology, clockwork, software, to refuse, solution, to develop, to provide

Unit 2 Happy endings

Lead-in

Revise the pronunciation of the past simple of regular verbs. See p7 of the Coursebook.

Procedure

1 Students can work individually or in pairs.
2 Students find their way from *start* to *finish* by looking for words with the same *-ed* sound. They must change to the other verb on the hexagon every time they land on a new hexagon and they cannot use that verb again. They can only choose from the two hexagons directly in front of them (one hexagon if they are in the top or bottom row) and the other verb *must* end in a different sound to the first one.
3 Go through the example with students. Ask: *How do you say 'want' in the past simple?* Then ask: *How do you say 'start', 'enjoy', 'like' and 'return' in the past simple? Which one has a similar ending to 'wanted'?* They should answer '*started*'. Say: *So, you move to 'start' and then choose the verb 'enjoy' and find a verb in the next column with a similar ending.*
4 The first student or pair to reach *finish* is / are the winners.
5 Check the path the students chose.

Answers

start, paint, talk, brush, change, discover, attract, invent, push, work, believe, travel, treat, decide, promise, like, love, live, develop, finish

Vocabulary

Past simple of regular verbs

Unit 3 Dilemmas

Lead-in
Review language for advice on p12 of the Coursebook.

Procedure
1 Students work in pairs to discuss the questions.
2 Students read the three letters and think about what advice they would give each person. Encourage them to look at the language box for some useful phrases.
3 Students work in pairs and compare their advice.
4 Students remain in their pairs and discuss the questions.
5 Students remain in their pairs and discuss a dilemma they have had to deal with.

Vocabulary
sensible, opportunity, reference

Unit 3 Dear Jane

Lead-in
Ask: *Do you ever read problem pages in magazines or newspapers. Do you think agony aunts give good advice?*

Procedure
1 Students work in groups of five. If the class doesn't divide exactly, some groups can have fewer students.
2 Students read the problems and match them to the correct titles. Go through the answers.
3 Students stay in their groups. Each student chooses a different problem to reply to. Set a time limit of ten minutes for students to write their answers. Encourage them to use the phrases in the Useful language box to help them.
4 Display the letters on the wall, grouping all the answers to one problem together.
5 Students stand up and read the letters. After they have finished, discuss which is the best answer to each problem.
6 Students work in pairs. They choose one of the pairs listed and prepare a roleplay in which Student A explains his / her problem to Student B and Student B responds.
7 Some of the pairs act out their roleplays for the class.

Answers
1d, 2a, 3c, 4e, 5b

Vocabulary
jealous, cheating, generous, guilty, dull, to ignore

Unit 4 Taking time out

Lead-in
Tell students that taking time out from work or education is becoming increasingly popular in Britain. For example, people might take a break from university to travel or do voluntary work. Discuss with the class the advantages and disadvantages of taking time out.

Procedure
1 Students work in pairs and discuss the questions. Then they share their ideas with the class.
2 Students look at the advertisements. Explain any unfamiliar words or phrases. Students work in pairs and answer the questions.
3 Students work in pairs and complete the questionnaire for their partner.
4 Students use their partner's answers to choose a time out experience for them. They explain their choice, using the words and phrases from the Useful language box.
5 Discuss the activity with the class. Ask: *Do you agree with the choice your partner made? Why? / Why not?*
6 Follow-up: students write a letter in response to the advertisement that their partners chose for them.

Answers
1 c, f; 2 a, b, c (You have to travel to London for this job) d;
3 d, f; 4 c, e

Vocabulary
time out, route, basic wage, vacancy, journalism, retail, catering, adventurous

Unit 4 Best person for the job

Lead-in
Ask the class to name as many different types of jobs as they can. Teach or elicit the jobs on the worksheet.

Procedure
1 Copy enough job cards for everyone in the class. In order for the game to work, there must be at least two students for each job.
2 Give out the cards. Make sure that students are not sitting next to anyone with the same card as their own.
3 Say: *Imagine you are competing with each other for job vacancies. You have to show that you are the best person for the job on your card.*
4 Students complete the sentences on their card to make a series of promises. For example, *Lion tamer: I'll be very brave. I'll always feed the lions. I'll never make them angry. I won't be late for work.*
5 Call all of the lion tamers to the front of the class. They take turns to tell the class why they are the best person for the job. Other students can ask questions, if they like. When the lion tamers have finished talking, the class takes a vote on who is the best one for the job.
6 Call another group of students to the front of the class and repeat the process.
7 The game finishes when everyone has spoken and all of the vacancies have been filled.

Vocabulary
vet, secretary, shop assistant, postal worker, lion tamer, astronaut, president, stuntperson, pop star

Module 2

Unit 1 Public and private

Lead-in

Ask: *What stories about famous people are in the news at the moment?*

Procedure

1 Students work in pairs and discuss the questions.
2 Students decide which stories they would / wouldn't be interested in. Then they compare their ideas with a partner. Encourage them to give reasons for their answers and to use the Useful language box to help them. Teach the useful language as fixed phrases; don't try to explain the grammar.
3 Students read the article and describe the relationship between the three people.
4 Students work in small groups. They discuss their answers to the questions. After students have discussed in their groups, elicit whole class feedback to generate cross-class discussion.

Vocabulary

celebrity, pregnant, to have a relationship, split up, privacy, behaviour

Unit 1 Finished or unfinished?

Lead-in

Review the present perfect and past simple on page 36 of the Coursebook.

Procedure

1 Students work in small groups. Give each group a copy of the board game and a dice. Make sure each student has a counter.
2 Players throw the dice and move the number of squares indicated.
3 If students roll an odd number (1, 3 or 5), they make a sentence using the word in the square in the present perfect with one of the unfinished time phrases. For example, if a student throws a one, he / she could say *I have eaten a lot of chocolate today.* If students roll an even number (2, 4 or 6), they make a sentence using the word in the square in the past simple with a finished time phrase. For example, if a student throws a four, he /she could say *I didn't buy any clothes last week.* If students land on a black square, the same rules apply, but he / she must ask a question to someone in the group and that person should give an answer. For example, if a student throws a three, he / she could ask *Have you drunk any coffee today?*
4 Other students can challenge the sentence or question, if they think there is something wrong.
5 The winner is the first player to arrive at the finish.

Unit 2 See no evil?

Lead-in

Ask: *What kind of films / TV programs do you like to watch? Are there any that you hate watching? Why?*

Procedure

1 Students read the speech bubbles and programme scenarios and decide which opinion they most closely agree with for each one.
2 Students work in pairs and discuss their opinions. Encourage them to look at the Useful language box for some helpful phrases.
3 Students work in pairs and discuss the questions.
4 Students read the statements and tick the ones they agree with. Then they work in groups to discuss their ideas.

Vocabulary

censor, burglar, charity worker, hostage, classified, ratings, influence

Unit 2 Desert island iPod

Lead-in

Ask: *What kind of music do you like to listen to? What are your favourite films?*

Procedure

1 Build the scenario that students are about to spend a year alone on a desert island. Say: *You are going to spend a year alone on a desert island. You can take two things with you: an iPod and your favourite possession.*
2 Give students the worksheet. Students work individually to complete the table for themselves.
3 Students discuss their choices with a partner. Make sure they discuss reasons for their choices. Encourage them to use the Useful language box examples.
4 Collect in the worksheets and then redistribute them. Students look at their new choices and discuss them with a partner. Encourage students to give reasons why they could or couldn't live with the new selection.
5 Ask students to stand up and go around the room asking questions until they find the person whose worksheet they have.

Vocabulary

It reminds me of …, I first heard this …, It makes me think about …,

Unit 3 How tasty is that?

Lead-in

Ask: *What is your favourite food? Is there anything that you can't stand? Do you like to try new food?*

Procedure

1 Students work in groups and discuss the questions.
2 Students work individually to read the texts and complete the table.
3 Go through the table with the class.
4 Students work in pairs and discuss the questions.
5 Students work in groups of four. Each student chooses a card and asks the others in the group the questions on the card. They discuss the answers.
6 Students report to the class on the most interesting thing they learned about one of the people in the group.

Answers

2

	Haggis	Kimchee
Where is it from?	Scotland	Korea
How is it prepared?	It is boiled in a sheep's stomach.	The uncooked cabbage is mixed with the other ingredients.
What are the ingredients?	lamb, onion, wheat, salt	cabbage, garlic, red pepper, ginger and salt
Does Jacob Mullens like it?	Yes	Yes

Vocabulary

Scottish, wheat, ginger, savoury, food items

Unit 3 Are you a healthy eater?

Lead-in

Ask different students around the class if they believe they are healthy eaters. Encourage them to give reasons for their answers.

Procedure

1 Students work in pairs and complete the questions with *much* or *many*.
2 Go through the answers with the class.
3 Students work in pairs and ask each other the questions. When they have finished they add up their partner's score and tick the appropriate box.
4 Students use the information from the questionnaire to fill out a doctor's report card for their partner.
5 Students exchange cards and read their partner's advice. They discuss whether or not they agree with it. Ask different students to share their opinions with the class.

Answers

1 1 much, 2 much, 3 many, 4 much, 5 many, 6 much, 7 many

Unit 4 Body beautiful

Lead-in

Ask students to think about how much care they take over their appearance. Ask questions like: *How long do you take to get ready in the morning? Do you have to put on make-up? Do you think it is important to follow the latest fashions?*

Procedure

1 Students match the words with the pictures in the questionnaire.
2 Check the answers with the class.
3 Students complete the questionnaire for themselves.
4 Students work in pairs and compare their answers.
5 Students work in groups and discuss the statements. Encourage them to use the discussion questions and the phrases in the Useful language box.

Answers

a bald b wrinkles c facelift d tattoo e piercing

Vocabulary

facelift, liposuction, laser eye surgery, cosmetic surgery

Unit 4 Three in a row

Lead-in

Review the use of phrasal verbs on pages 46–48 of the Coursebook.

Procedure

1 Students work in pairs. Give each pair a verb grid and a set of preposition cards.
2 Students shuffle the preposition cards and place them face down.
3 Student A begins the game. He / She picks up the first preposition card and tries to find a verb on the grid to match it. He / She makes a sentence containing the phrasal verb, using the pictures for help.
4 If Student A is successful, he / she writes his / her initials on the appropriate square of the verb grid and copies down the sentence in his / her notebook. If Student A cannot make a sentence, he / she returns the preposition card to the bottom of the pile.
5 Student B picks up a preposition card and continues the game in the same way.
6 Students continue to take turns until someone makes a line of three with their initials on the verb grid.
7 If no one has made a line of three before all of the verbs have been used, the student with the most correct sentences is the winner.

Answers

Sentences should contain the following phrasal verbs: try on, take after, dress up, get up, go off, look after, give away, call off, make up

Module 3

Unit 1 The big event

Lead-in
Ask: *What is a music festival? Can you give any examples?*

Procedure
1 Students work in pairs and discuss the questions. Ask some of the students to share their answers with the rest of the class.
2 Students read the article and then form pairs and discuss Jenny's experience at Glastonbury. They say whether or not they would like to go to this festival, giving reasons.
3 Students swap partners and think about what would be most important to them if they were going to a music festival. They rank the ideas.
4 Pairs of students join up to form groups of four. Students compare and explain their answers.
5 Students use their ideas from Ex 3 to decide what kind of festival they would like to organise. In the same groups, they complete the notes.
6 Each group tells the class about their festival.

Vocabulary
it was worth it, atmosphere, muddy, facilities, stalls, disgusting, moderately, duration

Unit 1 *For* or *since*?

Lead-in
Review the use of *for* and *since* on page 68 of the Coursebook.

Procedure
1 Students work in groups of four. Make sure that each group has a copy of the game and a dice, and each student has a counter.
2 Each student places his / her counter on a square: A, B, C or D. They take it in turns to throw the dice. All students should move their counters around the board in a clockwise direction.
3 There are two types of square. The black squares require students to use the word *for* to make a sentence and the white squares require students to use the word *since* to make a sentence.
4 When students land on a square, they choose a cue from the centre and make a sentence in the present perfect using the time phrase on their square and the correct word *for* or *since*. For example, if a student starting on 'B' throws a two, he / she moves to the square 'a few days' and could say, eg *I haven't used the internet for a few days*.
5 Emphasise that students should make sentences that are true about themselves where possible and that they don't have to use the cues if they have their own idea. Other students should then ask follow-up questions to find out more information.
6 Other players can challenge the sentence if they think something is incorrect. If the whole group agrees that the sentence is incorrect, then the student must remain on that square on his / her next turn and try again.
7 The game finishes when the first student returns to their home square.

Unit 2 Which sport?

Lead-in
Ask: *How many different types of outdoor sports or leisure activities can you name?* Write the answers on the board. If you like, take a vote to find out which one is most popular.

Procedure
1 Students work in groups of three.
2 Give each group a copy of Exercises 1–4. Students discuss the questions in Ex 1 together and then share their opinions with the class.
3 Give each person in the group a different sports text. Students read about the person's experiences and then take turns to tell the rest of the group about what they have read. They should do this in their own words, without reading directly from the texts.
4 Students discuss the sports together. They say which sports they would / wouldn't like to try, giving reasons. Encourage them to use comparative structures like those in the Useful language box.
5 Students tell their group about a memorable sporting or other outdoor experience they have had. Ask a few students to share their experiences with the class.
6 Follow-up: Students write about their experiences for homework.

Vocabulary
dehydrated, exhausted, wakeboarding, tricks, bolts, to slip

Unit 2 Sport dominoes

Lead-in
Ask: *What kind of sports do you like playing / doing? How often do you play / do them?*

Procedure
1 Cut the dominoes where indicated.
2 Students work in groups of three. Give each group a set of dominoes and tell them to place one domino on the table and to divide the other dominoes evenly amongst them.
3 A student begins by placing one of his / her dominoes next to the domino on the table, so that the verb or activity on their domino matches the verb or activity on the table domino. He / She should say the collocation as he / she does so, eg *do karate*.
4 Students take it in turns to place their dominoes. If a student cannot place a domino, he / she misses a turn.
5 The first player to place all his / her dominoes wins.

Unit 3 Holiday friends

Lead-in

Ask: *What kind of holiday do you like to go on? What kinds of things do you like to do? Do you like to meet other people?*

Procedure

1 Students work in pairs and discuss the questions.
2 Students work individually to read the email and decide if the statements are true or false.
3 Discuss the statements with the class.
4 Discuss with the class how they think Neil will feel when he reads the email.
5 Students work in groups and discuss the questions.
6 Students work individually to rank the reasons for going on holiday.
7 Students work in groups and discuss their answers. Encourage them to look at the Useful language box for some helpful phrases.

Answers

2
1 false 2 true 3 true 4 true

Vocabulary

pyramid, customs, culture, landmark

Unit 3 *Say*, *tell* maze

Lead-in

Review the use of *say* and *tell* on p76 of the Coursebook.

Procedure

1 Students work in pairs. They go through the maze identifying correct and incorrect sentences with *say* and *tell*.
2 Explain the game. Students begin at the *Start* square. They decide if the sentences are correct or not. If they are correct then they follow the directions next to the tick, if they are incorrect they follow the directions next to the cross. Say: *You will probably visit every square before you arrive at the finish.*
3 The first pair to reach the finish are the winners.
4 Check the path they took with the class.
5 Students work in small groups and choose three sentences from the maze. They decide if the sentences are right and correct them if they are not. Then they write a story which includes the three sentences.
6 When each group has finished writing their story, they tell it to another group.

Answer

Start, 1, 6, 10, 13, 4, 9, 2, 11, 5, 14, 3, 7, 12, 15, 8, Finish

Vocabulary

give me another chance

Unit 4 Who are you?

Lead-in

Write the question *Who are you?* on the board and ask a few students for an answer. Ask: *What information do you usually give to prove who you are?* Elicit name, date of birth etc. Make sure students know that this information is called personal information or personal details.

Procedure

1 Students do the quiz to find out how safe their personal information is and then compare answers in pairs.
2 Brainstorm the meaning of the phrase *identity theft* and then ask students to read the text to check their ideas.
3 Students work in groups to discuss the questions. Discuss their opinions with the class.

Vocabulary

to throw away, to tear up, password, personal information, identity, to prove

Unit 4 Shopping

Lead-in

Review first and second conditionals on page 80 of the Coursebook.

Procedure

1 Students work in groups of three or four. Give each group a copy of the game and a dice. Make sure everyone has a counter.
2 Students take it in turns to throw the dice and move around the board.
3 There are three types of square. Students have to either complete a 'main clause' or an 'if-clause', ask the group a question from the word cues on the square or follow directions to move forwards or backwards. For example, if a student throws a three, he / she has to complete the main clause, eg *I'll pay more if it's good quality.*
4 When a student lands on a square where he / she forms a question, he / she asks the question to the group and everyone should give their answer.
5 Other players can challenge if they think a sentence / question is incorrect. If a player makes a mistake then they remain on the same square and try again on their next turn.
6 The winner is the person who gets to the finish first.

Vocabulary

out of stock, discount, sale

Move placement test

Name: ______________________________

Section 1 Language: Total ____/50
Section 2 Vocabulary: Total ____/25
Section 3 Writing: Total ____/25
Section 4 Speaking: Total ____/25

Total score ____/____

Section 1 Language

Circle the correct alternative – *a*, *b* or *c*.

1 ______ a bank near here?
a Is b Is it c Is there

2 Sam speaks English very ______.
a good b well c bad

3 My mother is ______ teacher.
a – b a c one

4 What ______?
a Sam does want b does Sam wants
c does Sam want

5 We had ______ rain last night.
a a lot b a little c a few

6 Sam is ______ than Dave.
a more old b more older c older

7 ______ out last night?
a Did you go b Have you been
c Have you gone

8 She's in the same class ______ me.
a to b like c as

9 Who ______ this book?
a gave you b did give you c did you give

10 ______ the newspaper.
a I always read b I read always c Always I read

11 Where ______?
a is Harry going b Harry is going c is going Harry

12 This picture ______ by my friend.
a painted b was painting c was painted

13 A: I love Indian food. B: ______.
a I do so b So do I c So I do

14 There's a no-smoking sign. You ______ smoke here.
a don't have to b don't must c mustn't

15 If you're hot, I ______ the window.
a 'll open b am going to open c open

16 I'm going out ______ some milk.
a for get b for to get c to get

17 Try ______ late.
a to not be b to be not c not to be

18 ______ here before.
a I think I haven't been b I don't think I've been
c I don't think I haven't been

19 Someone ______ the meeting was cancelled.
a said me b told me c told to me

20 If you ______ me your email address, I'll write to you.
a will give b give c gave

21 Life would be easier if I ______ a bit more money.
a would have b have c had

22 I'm late for school ______.
a sometimes b never c always

23 I look forward ______ you next week.
a seeing b to see c to seeing

24 He speaks with ______ strong accent.
a – b the c a

25 I'm going to the hairdresser's ______.
a to get my hair cut b to get cut my hair
c to cut my hair

26 I ______ in Rome since 2003.
a 'm living b 've lived c live

27 Is it alright ______ I open the window?
a – b that c if

28 We complained to the waiter ______ the food.
a for b of c about

29 ______ it was raining we went for a walk.
a However b But c Although

30 Sam was only pretending ______ upset.
a be b to be c being

31 My parents never let me ______ computer games.
a play b to play c playing

32 I ______ call you yesterday, but I didn't have time.
a would b would be going to c was going to

33 Peter came out with us last night ______ feeling ill.
a yet b although c despite

34 I was surprised ______ Tom at the party last night.
a to see b seeing c for seeing

35 If you're tired, ______ to bed.
a go b you go c you will go

36 Have you any idea where ______?
a does she live b she does live c she lives

37 I wish I ______ to David yesterday.
a had spoken b would have spoken c spoke

38 A: What does this word mean?
B: Look ______ in the dictionary.
a up b it up c up it

39 This time next week, I ______ on a beach in Greece.
a 'm lying b 'll lie c 'll be lying

40 I could see a small road ______ into the distance.
a disappearing b was disappearing
c disappeared

41 It ______ Pete who broke the window – he wasn't here at the time.
a mustn't have been b couldn't be
c can't have been

42 This is the first time ______ Vietnamese food.
a I've eaten b I'm eating c I eat

43 I can't give you a lift because my car is ______.
a still repairing b still being repaired
c still repaired

44 ______, that everyone stayed indoors.
a The weather such was b Such was the weather c Such the weather was

45 Phone me when you ______.
a have arrived b will arrive c will have arrived

46 I'd rather you ______ in the house.
a didn't smoke b not smoke c don't smoke

47 Nobody rang me, ______?
a did anybody b did he or she c did they

48 ______ realised, I would've told you.
a Had I b Would I have c If I would have

49 Sam doesn't work, ______ he always seems to have a lot of money.
a whereas b yet c however

50 ______ all the questions, James felt quite pleased with himself.
a Has finally answered b Finally answering
c Having finally answered

Total mark ______ / 50

Section 2 Vocabulary

Add the missing word.

1 I ______ born in Paris.

2 I ______ 21 years old.

3 My birthday is ______ July.

4 Last month, I went ______ the USA.

5 I stayed in New York ______ two weeks.

6 Did you ______ many photos on holiday?

7 What does Katy's new boyfriend look ______?

8 Did you ______ your homework last night?

9 It's a good idea to try ______ clothes before you buy them.

10 As ______ as I'm concerned, internet shopping is a great idea.

11 Oxford is famous ______ its university.

12 Have you any ______ what time it is?

13 I get on really ______ with my brothers and sisters.

14 We went to lots of places last night, but we ended ______ in *Bar Soleil.*

15 Sue's new dress is very eye- ______.

16 We used to be friends, but we lost ______ a few years ago.

17 I don't know how old he is, but he looks to be in ______ late twenties.

18 The sea was very cold – in fact it was absolutely ______.

19 Can you ______ a secret?

20 Lizzy has got a great ______ of humour.

21 After being off school for a week, he found it difficult to ______ up with the work he'd missed.

22 You're the only person I've told. No-one knows about it ______ from you and me.

23 The advantages far ______ the disadvantages.

24 Central Park in New York is a great place to while ______ a few hours.

25 She'll be very successful – she's a real go- ______.

Total mark ______ /25

This page contains guidance for teachers for Section 3 Writing and Section 4 Speaking.

Section 3 Writing

Ask students to write about one of the following topics. Write a maximum of 150 words.

a My family
b My home town or city
c My job / studies
d My hobbies and interests

Give a score out of 25
out of 5 points for accuracy
out of 5 points for vocabulary use
out of 5 points for cohesion
out of 5 points for complexity of language used
out of 5 points for general impression

Section 4 Speaking

Choose from the following questions / instructions. Within each section the questions become progressively more challenging.

Home town / city

Where are you from?
How long have you lived there?
Can you tell me something about (student's home town / city)?
How do you feel about living in (student's home town / city)?

Family and friends

Do you have a large or small family?
Can you tell me something about your family?
What kinds of things do you do together as a family?
Can you tell me something about your friends?
What kinds of things do you do with your friends?
What do you think are the important qualities of a good friend?

Work / study

Do you work or are you a student?
What do you do / study?
How long have you had this job / been a student?
Can you tell me something about your work / studies?
What do you enjoy most about you work / studies?
Is there anything you don't like?

Leisure

Have you got any hobbies or interests?
How did you become interested in (student's hobby or interest)?
Are you interested in sports / music / cinema / reading etc?
What's your favourite sport / kind of music / film / book etc?
What else do you like to do in your free time?
What do you generally do in the evenings and at weekends in (student's home town / city)?

Future plans

What do you hope to do in the next few years?
Do you have any long-term plans?
Where do you see yourself in ten years' time?

Learning English

How long have you been studying English?
Why are you learning English?
How do you feel about learning English?
How important is English for you?

What do you want to gain from this English course?

Which areas of English are the most important for you to work on during this course?
– speaking
– writing
– reading
– listening
– grammar
– vocabulary
– pronunciation

Give a score out of 25
out of 5 points for accuracy
out of 5 points for vocabulary use
out of 5 points for cohesion
out of 5 points for complexity and language used
out of 5 points for general impression

See page 154 for answers to Section 1 Language and Section 2 Vocabulary

Most students should be able to complete sections 1 and 2 in approximately 30 minutes.

Test

Name: ______________________________

1 Complete these sentences with the correct form of the verbs.

a I really hate __________ (get up) early and equally don't like __________ (go to) bed very late.

b I don't mind __________ (play) football but I enjoy __________ (watch) it more.

c I love classical music but I can't stand __________ (listen to) hip-hop.

d I don't like __________ (learn) grammar. I much prefer __________ (read) English magazines.

e I enjoy __________ (hang out) with my friends but I can't stand crowded places.

2 Underline the correct alternative to agree or disagree with the first statement.

a A: I don't enjoy science fiction at all. (disagree)
B: *Really? I do. / Me neither.*

b A: I can't stand speed-dating. I never have enough time to get to know the other person. (agree)
B: *Me too. / Me neither.*

c A: I love playing basketball – in fact, I like all team games. (agree)
B: *Me too. / Me neither.*

d A: My favourite music is reggae, but I can't stand listening to rap. (disagree)
B: *Really? I like it. / Me too.*

e A: I prefer reading to watching TV. (disagree)
B: *Really? I do. / Do you? I don't.*

f A: I really enjoy watching horror films. (agree)
B: *Really? I do. / Me too.*

3 Rearrange these words to make full sentences.

a hanging out / I / like / really / at weekends

______________________________.

b prefer watching / I / like / really / don't / I / reading much, / films

______________________________.

c after dark / hates / horror stories / She / reading

______________________________.

d hate doing / but / enjoy cooking / I / the washing up / I

______________________________.

e mind listening / can't stand / music or / I don't / to classical / reggae / pop but I

______________________________.

4 Put these sentences in the correct order starting with the most positive (1) to the most negative (7).

a I really don't mind looking after young children. ☐

b I hate watching fantasy films. ☐

c I like going out for a walk when it's raining. ☐

d I don't like listening to rap. ☐

e I really enjoy eating out with my friends. ☐

f I can't stand doing boring housework. ☐

g I love playing tennis – especially when I win! [1]

5 Choose the correct alternative.

a When I was young, my grandparents looked *at / after / on* me.

b Most children want to grow *into / on / up* quickly nowadays.

c I'm looking forward to the holidays because then I have time to hang *up / on / out* with my friends.

d She loves music so much that she wants to go *into / on / at* the music industry.

e My friend says I take *up / on / after* my father – we both have the same eyes and hair.

6 Replace the underlined words with an expression in the box.

becomes an adult	looks and behaves like	
spends time	start work in	take care of

a When John finishes school, he wants to go into TV.

b What does Mark want to do when he grows up?

c When my parents go out, I look after my little sister.

d Lucy takes after her mother.

e My brother hangs out with his friends in the sports centre every Saturday.

7 Underline the odd word out in each group.

a comedy / science fiction / basketball / horror

b listening to music / karate / hanging out with friends / going out

c go into / take after / hang out / watch films

d football / swimming / reading / karate

e hip-hop / reggae / watching TV / pop

8 Read the article. Is each sentence true or false, according to the article? Write T (true) or F (false) in the boxes.

1 a It's important for your child to have a healthy diet. ☐

b Your child will be clever if they study a lot. ☐

2 a Exercise such as walking and swimming doesn't help children's brains. ☐

b They should do exercise every day. ☐

3 a It isn't important when children go to bed. ☐

b Children need plenty of sleep so they don't get tired. ☐

4 a It's important for a child's development to have lots of friends. ☐

b Hanging out with friends is a waste of time. ☐

5 a Watching TV with friends helps children to become clever. ☐

b Staying in isn't as good as doing things with friends. ☐

Make you and your children happy

All children need the right conditions to help them develop. Here are some things that are important for your child to grow up healthy, happy and balanced.

People usually think that the most important thing for your child to be clever is that she studies a lot. But studying hard doesn't always help. In fact, one of the most important things is that your child has a healthy diet. Children often miss breakfast or eat lots of fast food and neither of these is good.

Regular exercise is also very good for children. Walking, riding a bike or swimming every day will help their brains! It's also important that they don't get tired. So, on school nights they should go to bed early and get plenty of sleep.

Finally, it's very good for your child to mix with other children. Children who have lots of friends are usually happier and develop well. Encourage your child to hang out with their friends and do things together. It's much better for them than staying in and watching lots of TV.

Exercise	Score
1 Language	________ / 8
2 Language	________ / 6
3 Language	________ / 5
4 Language	________ / 6
5 Vocabulary	________ / 5
6 Vocabulary	________ / 5
7 Vocabulary	________ / 5
8 Reading	________ / 10
Total:	________ / 50
	________ %

Test

Name: ______________________________

1 Complete these sentences with the past simple or past continuous. Use the verbs in brackets.

a I ____________ (make) lots of friends when I ____________ (study) at the college.

b The police ____________ (stop) Kate while she ____________ (drive) to the party.

c Sara ____________ (have) lunch with her boss when her mobile ____________ (ring).

d The computer ____________ (crash) when I ____________ (write) an email.

e Julia ____________ (dream) about a holiday on the beach when the alarm clock ____________ (ring).

2 Correct the grammar mistake in each sentence.

a I was watched the TV when the phone rang.

______________________________.

b I was working for a computer company when we meet.

______________________________.

c She was talking to her friends when I was arrived.

______________________________.

d They were meeting when they were 18.

______________________________.

e What was he doing when you were seeing him?

______________________________?

3 Put the words in the correct column according to the pronunciation of the *-ed* ending.

asked	discovered	introduced	invented
produced	pushed	returned	started
wanted	worked		

/d/	/t/	/ɪd/

4 Choose the correct alternative.

a *Do / Make* me a favour and get some milk from the shop.

b How many phone calls have you *done / made* recently?

c Don't *make / do* me laugh; this is not funny at all.

d Look at your grades! You haven't *made / done* badly at all.

e When you have a cold, a warm lemon drink *does / makes* you good.

f How much money did you *do / make* when you sold your house?

g You have to *make / do* a decision now, because the shop is closing in a few minutes.

h Be careful or you'll *make / do* a mistake!

5 Match these words to the definitions.

gizmo	innovative	policy	produce
retirement	scent		

a a set of plans or actions the government, a political party or a business agree on

b the time when people stop working, usually at the age of 60

c a pleasant smell

d new and advanced

e a gadget or piece of high-tech equipment

f to make something

6 Complete the short biography with the words from Ex 5.

When most people are thinking about (a) ____________ Josh Steiner was starting a new company. At the age of 63 Josh invented his first (b) ____________, a key chain that glowed in the dark. Two years later and his company – Nopoint – now (c) ____________ about 5000 key chains each month. Josh's (d) ____________ ideas have become popular in many countries. His company have a (e) ____________ of introducing a new product every month. His latest idea is a small button that you fix to your clothes. The button gives off a (f) ____________, making everything smell nice and fresh.

7 Read the webpage and answer the questions.

Invention or accident?

One night in the early 1930s, Percy Shaw was driving home along a country road late at night. The road was really dark and Percy began to think about how useful it would be to have lights along the road. Of course, the problem was that it was very expensive. Then, as he was driving round a corner, he saw two lights at the side of the road. He slowed down to have a look and he saw a big black cat. He noticed that the cat's eyes reflected from the lights of his car. When he got home he sat down and invented Catseyes. Now, around the world, there are millions of these small metal and glass balls in the middle of roads showing us the way.

a Who was driving home late at night?

b Where was the road?

c Why were there no lights?

d What reflected the lights of the car?

e How do Catseyes help drivers?

Exercise	Score
1 Language	________ / 10
2 Language	________ / 5
3 Pronunciation	________ / 10
4 Vocabulary	________ / 8
5 Vocabulary	________ / 6
6 Vocabulary	________ / 6
7 Reading	________ / 5
Total:	________ / 50
	________ %

Test

Name: ______________________________

1 Read these two letters and underline the correct words to complete the letters giving advice.

> Dear John,
> I am worried! Next week I have an important exam and I'm very nervous about it. What shall I do? Please, give me some advice.
> Jack

> Dear John,
> It's my girlfriend's birthday next Saturday. I want to surprise her, but I haven't got much money. What shall I do?
> Mike

> Dear Jack,
>
> Try not to worry but you (a) *should / shouldn't / don't have to* leave the revision until the last minute. You (b) *should / shouldn't / don't have to* plan how much time you spend studying each day and you (c) *must / mustn't / should* stay up late the night before the exam or you will be too tired the next day.

> Dear Mike
>
> Try not to worry! You (d) *must / mustn't / don't have to* buy expensive presents. It's more important to know what your girlfriend likes and I'm sure she'll be happy that you remember her birthday. You (e) *should / must / don't have to* organise a birthday party for her but you (f) *mustn't / don't have to* ruin the surprise – keep the party secret!

2 Choose the sentence a or b that means the same as the first sentence.

1 It isn't necessary to be an expert.
- a You don't have to be an expert.
- b You mustn't be an expert.

2 It's a good idea to listen to his advice.
- a You must listen to his advice.
- b You should listen to his advice.

3 It's necessary to be quiet.
- a You must be quiet.
- b You should be quiet.

4 It isn't a good idea to leave it until Friday.
- a You shouldn't leave it until Friday.
- b You mustn't leave it until Friday.

5 It's necessary not to worry.
- a You don't have to worry.
- b You mustn't worry.

3 Three of these sentences have a grammar mistake. Put a ✔ or a ✘ in the boxes.

- a You should try to relax. ☐
- b You mustn't to think about anything else. ☐
- c She doesn't have listen to your advice. ☐
- d I must be careful and pay attention. ☐
- e You ought to try to remember your dreams. ☐
- f I shouldn't not worry. ☐

4 Correct the three sentences from Ex 3 that are wrong.

a ______________________________.

b ______________________________.

c ______________________________.

5 Match these adjectives to the people in the picture.

a	confident	☐	e	sensible	☐
b	friendly	6	f	sensitive	☐
c	helpful	☐	g	suspicious	☐
d	selfish	☐	h	boring	☐

6 Complete these sentences with the words from Ex 5.

a She's such a ____________ person. She's always thinking about other people's feelings.

b He's very ____________. He always does things in the house and he also does the shopping for me.

c Stop being so ____________. You always think about yourself.

d She's a very ____________ person. I've never seen her get nervous.

e He's so ____________. When he needs some help he always asks.

f It's nice when people are ____________ and talk to you.

g You must learn to trust people. Try not to be so ____________ all the time.

h I don't want to sit next to him at the party. I'm sorry, but he's so ____________. When he talks, I want to fall asleep.

7 Complete these sentences with the words in the box.

believe	interpret	psychic	sense	symbols

a Tarot cards have pictures and ____________ with different meanings.

b People try to ____________ or understand the meanings of the pictures.

c Many people ____________ their dreams have special meanings.

d Some people believe in a sixth ____________.

e A person with ____________ powers knows what people are thinking or what will happen in the future.

8 Match these headings to the paragraphs in the article.

Do you remember your dreams?
What does your dream mean?
Do dreams come true?
What do people dream about?
Do you dream every night?

9 Read the text again and choose the correct alternative, according to the text.

a *It is true* / *It isn't true* that some people never dream.

b We remember our dreams better when we wake up *suddenly* / *slowly*.

c People *often* / *never* dream about flying.

d Experts *can* / *can't* explain what every dream means.

e *It is possible* / *It isn't possible* to predict the future in our dreams.

Dreams!

(a) ____________

Some people say they never dream, but that isn't true. We all dream for about an hour a night but many of us just don't remember our dreams. We dream when we are sleeping lightly and not when we are fast asleep.

(b) ____________

Most people find it easy to remember bad dreams or nightmares. This is because you often wake up suddenly and when this happens you are more likely to remember the dream than when you wake up slowly.

(c) ____________

The most common dreams are about falling, flying and running. We also dream about people and places we know well. But the situations we meet them in can be strange and we may not have thought about these people for a long time or visited the places for years.

(d) ____________

Most of us have asked the question 'What does it mean?'. Interpreting dreams – saying what they mean – is big business and there are lots of books about dreams, but the truth is that nobody really knows.

(e) ____________

When a dream comes true it's either an amazing coincidence or you have made it come true. Whatever people might say or think, you can't really predict the future in your dreams.

Exercise	Score
1 Language	____ / 6
2 Language	____ / 5
3 Language	____ / 6
4 Language	____ / 3
5 Vocabulary	____ / 7
6 Vocabulary	____ / 8
7 Vocabulary	____ / 5
8 Reading	____ / 5
9 Reading	____ / 5
Total:	____ / 50
	____ %

Test

Name: ______________________________

1 Read these sentences and choose the alternative that best describes each one.

1 I'll have the roast beef with the salad.

a request / order b prediction c promise / offer

2 I won't forget to make an appointment for you.

a request / order b prediction c promise / offer

3 It'll be sunny and warm later this week.

a request / order b prediction c promise / offer

4 I'll do the shopping on the way home.

a request / order b prediction c promise / offer

5 Will you turn the music down, please?

a request / order b prediction c promise / offer

6 It'll take another half an hour to finish this exercise.

a request / order b prediction c promise / offer

2 Complete these sentences with *will*, *'ll* or *won't*.

a Yes, please. I ______ have two.

b I ______ phone you later. Is that OK?

c Don't worry. We ______ be late.

d ______ you help me, please?

e You ______ be able to lift that. It's too heavy.

f I'm sorry, but I ______ see you later.

g It's OK. I ______ be fine, really.

3 Complete these dialogues with the sentences 1–7 from Ex 2.

a A: ______________________________.

B: Yes, I will. I'm very strong.

b A: ______________________________.

B: That's fine. I should be home by 8pm, so anytime after that.

c A: ______________________________.

B: I'm sorry, but I can't.

d A: I'm really worried. Can I help you at all?

B: ______________________________.

e A: Hurry up! Look at the time!

B: ______________________________.

f A: You can give me the money after dinner this evening.

B: ______________________________.

g A: Do you want any of these cakes?

B: ______________________________.

4 Write full sentences to complete the dialogues. You need to use *will* or *won't*.

a A: Please try to be on time. I don't want to wait too long.

B: I / not / late

______________________________.

b A: I'm really worried about the test next Monday.

B: Everything / fine

______________________________.

c A: I don't understand this question. It's so difficult.

B: I / help

______________________________.

5 Rearrange the words in brackets to complete the definitions.

a An ______________ (ctrichtea) designs all sorts of buildings, from houses to sport centres.

b An ______________ (reneeing) designs roads, railways and different machines.

c A ______________ (mepublr) fits and repairs pipes that supply and store water in the buildings.

d A ______________ (suner) helps the doctors to look after the patients in hospitals or surgeries.

e A ______________ (cutmorep amgromperr) writes instructions that tell computers how to work.

f A ______________ (hercate) works in a school and helps others to learn.

g An ______________ (rutallurigca krower) works in an industry that produces fruit and vegetables.

6 Replace the underlined words with words in the box that mean the same.

aim	abroad	a charming	crazy
developed	skills	superficial	

a You have the ability to do well in this job.

b What an attractive and pleasant person your girlfriend is!

c How many times have you been to a different country this year?

d I think his interest in business studies is not too deep.

e You need to work a lot harder if you want to achieve your target.

f It's amazing what he's achieved! His business has grown into a multinational company.

g That's a very silly idea!

7 Read the text and answer these questions.

1 What kind of text is it?

a An information leaflet b A job advert

2 Is it from

a a newspaper? b a book?

Volunteers needed

Do you want to work abroad? Do you want to help people? Do you have any of the skills we need?

We are a leading charity organisation looking for volunteers for the following jobs:

- teachers in China and Vietnam
- nurses in Indonesia, Thailand and Sri Lanka
- plumbers in Mozambique, Angola and Namibia

All flights and accommodation are provided as part of the contract. You will also receive a local salary. Contracts are for 3 months to 1 year.

All enquiries to Melanie Cox at:
112b Porchester Road
London W1
Or email: mel@vols.co.org

8 Read the text again. Write T (true) or F (false) in the boxes.

a The organisation is looking for skilled people to do voluntary work abroad. ☐

b They are looking for nurses in China and Vietnam and plumbers in Thailand. ☐

c Three countries need volunteers who can work as plumbers. ☐

d The volunteers are paid the same as other people working in the country. ☐

e The volunteers have to pay for their flight and accommodation. ☐

f The length of the contracts is between three months and one year. ☐

g You can find out more by sending an email. ☐

h If you're interested, you should phone the charity organisation. ☐

Exercise	Score
1 Language	____ / 6
2 Language	____ / 7
3 Language	____ / 7
4 Language	____ / 6
5 Vocabulary	____ / 7
6 Vocabulary	____ / 7
7 Reading	____ / 2
8 Reading	____ / 8
Total:	____ / 50
	____ %

Module test

Name: ________________________

1 Complete the dialogue with the words and phrases in the box.

can't stand	love	Me neither	prefer	Me too

A: I really (a) ____________ going to the cinema. I go about five times a month.

B: (b) ____________. What kind of films do you like?

A: Well, I like action films, but I (c) ____________ horror films. They're awful!

B: (d) ____________. I don't mind action films, but I (e) ____________ comedies.

2 Choose the correct alternative.

a My first great idea *came / was coming* to me when I *drank / was drinking* a cup of coffee one morning.

b She *talked / was talking* to me on the phone when you *arrived / were arriving*.

c John Anderson *worked / was working* as a teacher when he *wrote / was writing* his first novel.

d I *had / was having* a bath when I *thought of / was thinking of* my latest gizmo.

e Sorry I couldn't answer your call. I *dried / was drying* my hair when you *phoned / were phoning*.

3 Complete the second sentence using *must, mustn't, should, shouldn't* or *don't have to* so the meaning is similar to the first sentence.

a It's not necessary to pack a lot of clothes.

You ______________________________.

b It's a good idea to take plenty of money.

You ______________________________.

c Don't worry too much. It's important to relax.

You ________ worry. ____________________.

d Don't be late!

You ______________________________.

e It's necessary to bring your passport.

You ______________________________.

4 Match each sentence to a category in the box.

prediction	promise	request

a I'll show you where you can buy souvenirs after the lesson. ________

b Will you call me later? ________

c Don't jump! It's too high and you'll hurt yourself. ________

d Come on! You can tell me. I won't tell anyone else. ________

e It'll be really hot in Spain. ________

5 Choose the correct phrasal verb.

a What kind of music did you listen to when you were *growing up / looking after*?

b I often *looked after / grew up* my brother when we were kids.

c I can't decide what to *take after / go into* after I finish university.

d Would you like to *hang out / go into* with me later?

e A: Here's a photo of my son.

B: Wow! He really *looks after / takes after* you.

6 Four of these sentences have a mistake with *make* or *do*. Put a ✔ or a ✘ in the boxes. Correct the four that are wrong.

a You really need to be careful or you'll do a mistake. ☐

b Wow! You've done really well in your exam. Well done! ☐

c He made badly in his driving test. ☐

d Excuse me! Could you make me a favour? ☐

e I hate doing difficult decisions. ☐

f Steve's a fantastic friend – he makes me laugh. ☐

1 ______________________________

2 ______________________________

3 ______________________________

4 ______________________________

7 Choose the correct alternative.

1 You only think of yourself! You are so ______.

a sensitive
b sensible
c selfish

2 Be careful what you say to her. She's over-______ and she might start crying.

a sensitive
b sensible
c demanding

3 Don't be so ______. You have to trust people.

a sensitive
b suspicious
c demanding

4 You're so ______. All you talk about is football, football, football!

a friendly
b boring
c demanding

5 My boss is really ______. He wants me to work until 8pm every night!

a friendly
b boring
c demanding

6 Don't worry if Max doesn't say much – he's usually a very ______ person.

a quiet
b boring
c helpful

7 Jack is such a ______ person. He's always ready to do things for you.

a quiet
b demanding
c helpful

8 I'm sure I can do it. I'm a very ______ person.

a confident
b selfish
c shy

9 Don't do anything silly. I know you aren't always ______.

a helpful
b friendly
c sensible

10 I really like John – he's such a ______ person.

a friendly
b boring
c demanding

8 **02** Listen to three people meeting at a speed-dating evening. Do these statements refer to Ben, Layla or Ian? Write B, L or I in the boxes.

a He / She studies business at university. ☐
b He / She finds the subject boring. ☐
c He / She plays music in a band. ☐
d He / She loves listening to reggae. ☐
e He / She agrees that hanging out with friends is good. ☐
f He / She doesn't study at the moment. ☐
g He / She likes science fiction films. ☐
h He / She prefers comedies. ☐
i He / She doesn't like horror films. ☐
j He / She enjoys reading. ☐

9 Listen again. Are these statements true or false? Write T (true) or F (false) in the boxes.

a Ben and Layla both study business at university. ☐
b Ben would like to go and watch Layla's band. ☐
c Ben and Layla like the same kind of music. ☐
d Ian studies scientific research at university. ☐
e Layla prefers watching TV to reading. ☐

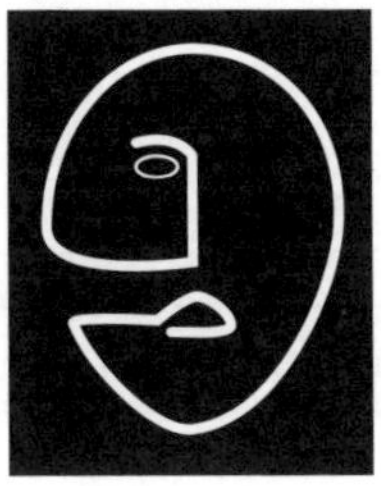

Hi, my name's Hannah and I come from Sweden. I grew up in Stockholm and I still live there. I study music at university and I work as a waitress. I enjoy listening to good music, watching films and hanging out with my friends. My favourite kind of film is comedy but I can't stand science fiction or horror films. My friends say that I'm very friendly but a little bit quiet. I don't agree because I think I'm confident but I just don't like gossiping, so that's why I don't talk so much. I like working with people and when I finish university I want to work as a volunteer for a year abroad. I also like playing sports. I'm quite fit because I go running every day. I enjoy in-line skating and I love skiing. I don't mind other sports like football or basketball, but I don't really like watching them on TV. I'm looking for pen pals from different countries to write to and hang out with online.

10 Read the chat room message and answer these questions

- a Where did Hannah grow up?
- b What does she study?
- c What does she enjoy doing in her free time?
- d What kind of films **doesn't** she like?
- e What do her friends think about her?
- f Why does Hannah prefer being quiet?
- g What does she want to do when she finishes university?
- h How often does she go running?
- i What other sports does she enjoy doing?
- j Why is she looking for pen pals?

11 Write a reply to Hannah. Tell her about your likes and dislikes and what you do in your leisure time. Write about 100 words.

Exercise	**Score**
1 Language	________/ 5
2 Language	________/ 5
3 Language	________/ 5
4 Language	________/ 5
5 Vocabulary	________/ 5
6 Vocabulary	________/ 10
7 Vocabulary	________/ 10
8 Listening	________/ 10
9 Listening	________/ 5
10 Reading	________/ 20
11 Writing	________/ 20
Total:	________/ 100
	________%

UNIT 1 Test

Name: ______________________________

1 Tick ✔ the correct sentences.

1 a I haven't kept in touch with my friends lately.
  b I didn't keep in touch with my friends lately.

2 a She bought a new computer last month.
  b She has bought a new computer last month.

3 a It wasn't me! I didn't spread any rumours recently!
  b It wasn't me! I haven't spread any rumours recently!

4 a He has spent a summer with his parents in Australia two years ago.
  b He spent a summer with his parents in Australia two years ago.

5 a We had a big party to celebrate my father's retirement last Saturday.
  b We have had a big party to celebrate my father's retirement last Saturday.

2 Choose the correct alternative.

a She *put on* / *has put on* some weight recently.

b I *saw* / *have seen* this film four times this month.

c *Did you read* / *Have you read* any good books lately?

d He *split up* / *has split up* with his girlfriend last night.

e I *heard* / *have heard* a lot of gossip about my neighbour recently.

3 Complete these sentences using past simple or present perfect.

a I ______________ (not / see) Paul this week.

b She ______________ (publish) her third book last autumn.

c This is the third time Jennifer ______________ (call) this evening.

d ______________ you ______________ (buy) any new clothes recently?

e How many points ______________ you ______________ (get) in your last test?

4 Complete the table with the missing verb forms.

Infinitive	Past simple	Past participle
become		
	bought	
		broken
eat		
fall		
	had	
		heard
see		
	spoke	
		taken

5 Complete these sentences with an appropriate form of the phrases in the box.

have a chat	keep a secret	spread rumours
form a bond	keep in touch	

a I don't like magazines which ______________ about celebrities.

b When was the last time you ______________ with your friend?

c A: Can you ______________ ?
  B: Yes, of course I can. What is it?

d After you leave home, make sure you ______________ with your parents; they want to know how you are doing.

e When I moved here I found it hard to ______________ with my next-door neighbour.

6 Rewrite the sentences using the expressions in Ex 5 to replace the underlined words in italics. Be careful! Sometimes you have to change the form.

a If you tell me where Sarah is going, I promise I won't tell anyone.

____

____

b She is upset because her friend has told stories about her private life.

____

____

c The students in my group are very friendly, so it's been easy to get close to them.

____

____

d Why don't you talk to Judy? She seems to be very lonely.

____

____

e Promise me you'll write or phone regularly as I want to know how you are doing in your new school.

____

____

7 Complete these two emails with the expressions in the boxes.

Email A

According to   Apparently   have you heard
they split up   you won't believe it

Hi Jenny,

Thanks for your last email. It's great to hear that you've got a new boyfriend – you look really happy in the photo!

So, (a) ___________ the latest gossip? Do you remember Mary from school? Well, I saw her recently and (b) ___________ – she's had a baby! Yeah! I know, it's amazing.

(c) ___________ she was dating Jack! I never knew that – did you? (d) ___________ Suzy, they were together for about three months but then (e) ___________. I've heard they're back together now and really happy about the baby.

So, that means John's an uncle! That's amazing too!!

Anyway, must go – the football's on TV.

Love,

Phil

Email B

last week   Keep in touch   having a chat
guess what   Can you keep a secret?

Hi Phil,

It was great to get your email, and really very funny.

It's amazing about Jack and Mary, really, but (f) ___________? I saw Jack just (g) ___________ and we were (h) ___________ in the new café on King Street. He told me all about Mary and the baby. (i) ___________ According to him, they split up after only one month and then she was dating Mark! Still, they're back together now and really love being parents.

(j) ___________ and write back soon,

Jenny

Exercise	Score
1 Language	________ / 5
2 Language	________ / 5
3 Language	________ / 5
4 Language	________ / 10
5 Vocabulary	________ / 5
6 Vocabulary	________ / 10
7 Reading	________ / 10
Total:	________ / 50
	________ %

Module 2

UNIT 2
Test

Name: ____________________

1 Choose the correct alternative.

A: *What did you think of / If you ask me* the film?

B: I didn't enjoy it at all. I really *didn't think / thought* Johnny Depp was very good.

A: Didn't you? *In my opinion / Same here* he was much better in this film than in that comedy everyone thought was so brilliant.

B: Really? *What do you think / If you ask me,* he is a fantastic director but a really average actor.

A: *Oh, come on / Me too.* You can't be serious!

B: But I really thought that Gwyneth Paltrow was good.

A: *Oh, come on / Me too.* At last we agree on something!

2 Rearrange these words to make correct sentences.

a all / are / Hollywood / In / movies / my / opinion, / terrible

____________________.

b great / are / on. / come / of / Oh, / Some / them

____________________.

c you / the / really / me, / is / If / bad / ask / acting

____________________.

d OK/ I / Really? / it's / think

____________________.

e Johnny Depp / do / think / you / of / What

____________________?

f I'm / as / Leonardo DiCaprio / As / better / is / far / concerned,

____________________.

3 ~~Cross out~~ the alternative which is not possible.

1 ______ Tom Cruise is a fantastic actor.

a In my opinion, c If you ask me,

b What did you think

2 ______ He's not that good.

a Really? b Oh, come on! c Same here.

3 A: I think action films are really boring.

B: ______.

a In my opinion b Me too c Same here

4 A: If you ask me, there are too many special effects in films now.

B: ______ I think they're great.

a Really? b Me too. c Oh, come on.

5 ______ comedies are the best.

a In my opinion, c Really?

b As far as I'm concerned,

4 Match the words in the box to these definitions.

biography	convincingly	hesitation
role	to devote	

a a book written about somebody's life

____________________.

b the character that is played by an actor or actress in a film or play

____________________.

c do something in a way that we believe it is true or good

____________________.

d a pause before doing something

____________________.

e spend a lot of time and effort to do something

____________________.

5 Complete these sentences with the words from Ex 4.

a I agreed with his suggestion without ____________. It was such a good idea.

b Have you read David Beckham's ____________?

c As an actor he became famous in the ____________ of Martin Luther King.

d He played the role so ____________, nobody realised it was his first major role.

e You need ____________ more time to this project.

6 Complete these sentences with the words in the box.

character	close-up	in the background
played by	scene	set

a Look! The ________________ shows that she is wearing a watch and she is supposed to be a Roman goddess!

b I thought that the actions of the main ________________ were not convincing.

c In this ________________, the focus is on the love story.

d Who is Mr Bennet's character ________________?

e Can you see those old ruins ________________?

f The story of Romeo and Juliet was ________________ in Verona.

7 Underline the stressed syllable in these adjectives.

Example: *boring*

a gorgeous
b fantastic
c impressive
d spectacular
e brilliant
f funny
g childish

8 Read the reviews and match the type of film in the box to the title of each film. Be careful! There are seven film types and only four films.

comedy	historical drama	horror	martial arts
romance	science fiction	western	

a Kick out ________________
b Time's up! ________________
c The long road ________________
d 2120 ________________

9 Read the texts again. Write T (true) or F (false) in the boxes.

a The film with lots of fighting in it did not get a good star rating. ☐
b There is lots of dialogue in the martial arts film. ☐
c The story in the comedy is excellent. ☐
d The horses and guns in *The long road* made this a really good film. ☐
e The writer doesn't usually like westerns. ☐
f *2120* is a film about the future. ☐

Star Rating

★★★★★ = Excellent – go and see it immediately
★★★ = Good
★★ = OK, but there are better films
★ = Terrible

Kick out ★

This film is set in Hong Kong. As you would expect there is a lot of fighting and not much dialogue. In fact, there's often so much action that it's difficult to understand the story. It's very boring.

Time's up! ★★★★★

I couldn't stop laughing from the start to finish. Although the story isn't very good, the jokes are so funny it doesn't matter. This is one of those films you can go and see again and again and even though you know the jokes you'll still laugh!

The long road ★★

I don't usually like this kind of film with lots of guns and horses. The story isn't very complicated, but the scenery was spectacular and the acting was fairly good. Go and see it if you like this kind of film.

2120 ★★★

From the title you would think it's a film about the future, but you'd be wrong. This is a really good film set in a hotel and, in particular, room 2120. I don't want to spoil the story, but if you like love and crying then this film is for you.

Exercise	Score
1 Language	______ / 6
2 Language	______ / 6
3 Language	______ / 5
4 Vocabulary	______ / 5
5 Vocabulary	______ / 5
6 Vocabulary	______ / 6
7 Pronunciation	______ / 7
8 Reading	______ / 4
9 Reading	______ / 6
Total:	______ / 50
	______ %

UNIT 3 Test

Name: ______________________________

1 Choose the correct alternative.

a How *many* / *much* eggs do you need for the cake?

b How *many* / *much* time do we have before the restaurant closes?

c How *many* / *much* wine do you want?

d How *many* / *much* people are coming to the meal tonight?

e How *many* / *much* does it cost?

2 Choose the correct alternative.

1 They've moved around frequently; that's why they have only got ______ friends.

a a few b a lot of

2 ______ research has been done to find out the link between the food colour and our appetite.

a A few b A lot of

3 I try to spend ______ time every day revising for my exams.

a any b some

4 Have you bought ______ fruit today?

a any b some

5 I see you've prepared almost everything. There isn't ______ work for me to do.

a many b much

6 How ______ times do I have to tell you the answer?

a many b much

7 Your mailbox is almost full! ______ people have replied to your ad so far.

a A few b A lot of

8 I don't know how to solve this problem. Can you give me ______ advice?

a any b some

9 Can you spend ______ minutes helping me?

a a few b a little

10 I only have ______ time left, so we need to hurry.

a a few b a little

3 Complete the dialogue with the words in the box.

some	few	any	a lot of	little

A: Do you have ________ close friends? You know, people you can tell all your secrets.
B: Yes, I've got a ________ really close friends. I've known them since university.
A: Do you stay in touch with ________ friends from your student days?
B: Not really. I have very ________ time to spend writing letters and emails to them.
A: That's a shame!
B: Yes, I'd love to see ________ of them more often, but they live in a different city.

4 Choose the correct alternative.

1 I'd like to ______ a table for two for tonight.

a buy b order c book

2 Do you have a ______ in English?

a menu b receipt c order

3 Are you ready to ______?

a buy b order c book

4 Can you ______ a wine to go with the fish?

a offer b recommend c pour

5 I'll ______ the soup of the day, please!

a get b take c have

6 I'd like to pay now. Can I have the ______, please?

a bill b buy c receipt

7 Would you like anything for ______?

a eat b main c dessert

8 The waiter will ______ the wine into your glass.

a offer b recommend c pour

5 Are these sentences polite (P) or impolite (I)? Choose the correct alternative.

a I want the soup. P / I

b Excuse me, I'd like to book a table for lunch. P / I

c No. The bill. P / I

d Could I have a bottle of white wine, please? P / I

e Certainly, sir. Anything else? P / I

f No, thank you. P / I

6 Put the dialogue in the correct order, 1–6.

a Certainly sir, and would you like anything to drink? ☐

b Could I see the menu, please? ☐

c Yes, the Australian white is really nice. ☐

d Yes, I'd like the fish, please. ☐

e Yes, can you recommend a wine to go with the fish? ☐

f Here you are. Are you ready to order? ☐

7 Read the letter and restaurant review and answer the questions.

a What is the name of the restaurant? ______________

b Who cooked the food mentioned in the letter? ______________

c Why is the food at Giuseppe's so nice? ______________

d Who was rude? ______________

e When should you eat in the restaurant? ______________

f What does Joel always do? ______________

g How did Judy describe Marge's food? ______________

h What should you eat at Giuseppe's? ______________

i What does Judy want? ______________

j What makes the perfect meal? ______________

Dear Marge,

I'm just writing to say thank you for the wonderful meal last Friday. The food was absolutely delicious and also looked fantastic. You'll have to give me the recipes sometime so that I can try and cook the same dishes. I'm sorry about Joel, he really has no manners. Of course he ate too much, but he always does.

Thanks again,

Judy

Giuseppe's is one of the best restaurants in town. Go in the middle of the week when it is quieter and you'll get fantastic service as well as really tasty food. One reason the food is so good is that it is freshly prepared and they use no artificial colours or flavours. Try the risotto as it's delicious – some mushrooms, a little bit of fish and a bit of onion and parsley – amazing! Have a glass of white wine and a lovely dessert and you've got a perfect meal.

Exercise	Score
1 Language	______ / 5
2 Language	______ / 10
3 Language	______ / 5
4 Vocabulary	______ / 8
5 Vocabulary	______ / 6
6 Vocabulary	______ / 6
7 Reading	______ / 10
Total:	______ / 50
	______ %

UNIT 4 Test

Name: ______________________________

1 Complete these sentences using an appropriate form of the phrasal verbs in the box.

call off	come across	dress up	go off
look after	take after	turn off	turn up

a I feel so embarrassed! The alarm clock on my mobile phone ______________ during the speech.

b As this is a special party you should make the effort and ______________.

c Have you ever ______________ anyone with a tattoo?

d I can't go out tonight! There's no-one to ______________ my little sister.

e Poor Alex! His girlfriend's changed her mind and has ______________ the wedding.

f If you aren't watching the TV, why don't you ______________ it ______________?

g Pete ______________ his mum – he has her eyes and nose.

h Everyone was shocked when Steve ______________ unexpectedly.

2 Choose the correct phrasal verbs to complete the short story.

A few weeks ago I (1) ______ for a party at a friend's house. I knew that a boy I liked would be there, so I decided to (2) ______. I also wore a necklace that (3) ______ my green eyes. When I arrived I saw that everyone else was wearing casual clothes, like jeans and a T-shirt – I was so embarrassed. Luckily, my friend realised and told me to go upstairs. We went to her room and she gave me some of her clothes to (4) ______. I found a pair of jeans and a T-shirt that were the right size so I (5) ______. Now I think I'm going to (6) ______ the dress because it reminds me of that evening.

	a	b	c
1	a gave away	b turned up	c showed off
2	a dress up	b put on	c try on
3	a tried on	b turned up	c showed off
4	a try on	b give away	c turn up
5	a tried them on	b showed them off	c put them on
6	a try on	b give away	c dress up

3 Tick ✔ the correct sentence in each pair.

1 a Where did you come across this beautiful necklace? ☐
  b Where did you come this beautiful necklace across? ☐

2 a Could you dress it up for the theatre? ☐
  b Could you dress up for the theatre? ☐

3 a Both of Mark's children take after him. ☐
  b Both of Mark's children take him after. ☐

4 a I'm late because my alarm clock hasn't gone it off. ☐
  b I'm late because my alarm clock hasn't gone off. ☐

5 a Due to lack of interest, the organisers called off it. ☐
  b Due to lack of interest, the organisers called it off. ☐

6 a I don't like the way they always show off. ☐
  b I don't like the way they show always off. ☐

4 Complete these words with the vowels *a, e, i, o, u*.

5 Complete these sentences with the words from Ex 4.

a He's always dressed in the latest __________ clothes.

b I want a __________ wedding with a white dress.

c He's got a __________ with a heart and her name on his arm.

d I buy all my __________ at a shop in the centre of the city.

e You need to wear __________ clothes when you go to meet her parents.

f Those jeans are so __________! Look! They're really dirty.

g She's really __________. She doesn't need to wear any make-up.

h I'm not wearing that! It's so __________. It looks like something my grandfather wears.

i That's a really nice __________. Where did you buy it?

j You can come in __________ clothes – just some jeans and a T-shirt.

6 Read the magazine article and match the types of body art in the box to the paragraphs 1–4.

Henna	Mohican	Piercing	Tattoo

Body Art

In this section we will take a quick look at body art. Here are four of the most popular.

(a) __________

This hairstyle became very popular in the 1970s and was connected to punk music. The hairstyle was very different and quite unique. Sometimes the hair was dyed in different colours.

(b) __________

This kind of decoration is very popular in countries like Morocco and India. Women have patterns painted on their hands and feet. Only two colours are used: red or black, but the patterns are very beautiful.

(c) __________

This kind of body art is not new and is popular in many countries. Now many famous people have one or more. Sometimes they have a meaning, but often they are just for decoration.

(d) __________

This kind of body art is becoming very popular. Thirty years ago you just saw people with rings and studs in their ears. Nowadays, it's just as common to see people with their nose, tongue or eyebrows done as well.

7 Read the text again and then write P (piercing), H (henna), M (mohican), or T (tattoo) next to each sentence.

a This kind of body art is often connected to a type of music. ☐

b You might see a well-known person with one of these. ☐

c This kind of body art is very common for women in some countries. ☐

d Lots of different colours can be used to make the decoration even more unusual. ☐

e This kind of body art is often connected to people's faces. ☐

f This kind of body art can sometimes be more than just a decoration. ☐

Exercise	Score
1 Language	__________ / 8
2 Language	__________ / 6
3 Language	__________ / 6
4 Vocabulary	__________ / 10
5 Vocabulary	__________ / 10
6 Reading	__________ / 4
7 Reading	__________ / 6
Total:	__________ / 50
	__________ %

Module test

Name: ______________________

1 Choose the correct alternative.

Anna: Have you (a) *see / saw / seen* Jane recently?

Bill: Yes, I (b) *see / saw / seen* her last week.

Anna: Really? (c) *Did she tell / Has she told* you any gossip?

Bill: Not really. We (d) *didn't have / haven't had* much time.

Anna: Oh! That's a pity because I've (e) *hear / heard* a rumour that she's getting married soon.

2 Complete the dialogue using the expressions in the box.

If you ask me, Me too What did you think of it? Oh, come on Really?

Dave: Hi! Have you seen the new Spielberg film?

Mike: Yes, I saw it last week.

Dave: (a) ______________

Mike: I didn't think it was very good.

Dave: Why not?

Mike: (b) ______________ the acting was bad.

Dave: (c) ___Really?___ I thought it was OK.

Mike: You're joking! It really wasn't very good.

Dave: Well, I still think he's great director.

Mike: (d) ______________.

Dave: So you like his films.

Mike: Yes, but recently his films haven't been very good.

Dave: (e) ______________. What about *War of the Worlds*?

Mike: Was that him? Oh, well, that was excellent.

3 Three of these sentences have a grammar mistake. Put a ✔ or a ✘ in the boxes.

a How many fruit do you eat everyday? ☐

b I don't eat some fruit. ☐

c Do you want any wine? ☐

d How much wine do you want? ☐

e I usually have a few milk in my coffee. ☐

4 Choose the correct sentence in each pair.

1 a I really think you take after your sister.
  b I really think you take your sister after.

2 a Have you heard? Brad and Jenny have split up.
  b Have you heard? Brad and Jenny have split it up.

3 a You really should try on.
  b You really should try it on.

4 a I'm sorry but we'll have to call off.
  b I'm sorry but we'll have to call it off.

5 a She's got a new car and wants to show off.
  b She's got a new car and wants to show off it.

5 Complete these sentences with the verbs in the box. You need to use one verb twice.

form have keep spread

a I hate it when people __________ rumours.

b Can you __________ a secret?

c I find it difficult to __________ a bond with people who have different tastes from me.

d You will promise to __________ in touch, won't you?

e Wow! Kate, I haven't seen you for ages. Let's go to the café and __________ a chat then we can catch up on all the gossip.

6 Match the words in column A to the definitions in column B.

1	animation	a	the place where a film is made
2	character	b	a person in a film or book
3	scene	c	images or sounds in a film that are created using technology like computers
4	set	d	a part of a film where things happen in the same place
5	special effects	e	a kind of film using cartoons or drawings

7 Complete the dialogue with the words and phrases in the box.

the menu	the bill	recommend a good wine
ready to order	booked a table for one	

Customer: Excuse me! I've (a) ________________.

Waiter: What's your name?

Customer: Smith. Phil Smith.

Waiter: Ah yes! This way please.

Customer: Can I have (b) ________________, please?

Waiter: Certainly sir.

Waiter: Are you (c) ________________?

Customer: Yes. I'll have the soup as a starter and then the fish.

Waiter: Anything to drink, sir?

Customer: Can you (d) ________________ that will go with the fish?

Waiter: The Chardonnay's good.

Customer: That's fine.

Waiter: Would you like any dessert or coffee?

Customer: No, thanks. Just (e) ________________, please.

Waiter: Of course, that's £19.

8 Replace the underlined words with a word from the box with a similar meaning. Be careful! There are two extra words.

accessories	attractive	casual	
old-fashioned	scruffy	smart	trendy

a Do you think she's <u>beautiful</u>?

b His clothes are always so <u>up-to-date</u>.

c I think your taste in clothes is quite <u>traditional</u>.

d Can't you wear something else? That's just so <u>untidy</u>.

e Where do you buy all your <u>jewellery</u>?

9 **27** Listen to the person talking about good manners and choose the correct alternative.

1 Why was the woman worried in Canada?
   a It was a formal dinner.
   b She didn't know which knife to use first.

2 Why is it easy to remember which knife to start with?
   a It's the same everywhere.
   b It doesn't matter.

3 Where did the man finally put his chopsticks?
   a On the table
   b Across the plate

4 Which hand should you use to pick up your food in Tunisia?
   a Your right hand
   b Your left hand

5 Which hand do you use to shake hands in Tunisia?
   a The same one that you eat with
   b The one you don't use to eat with

6 What do people in Britain argue about?
   a How to make tea properly
   b Making a noise when you drink your tea

7 Is it OK to make a noise or slurp when you are eating or drinking in Britain?
   a Yes
   b No

8 Should you make a noise or slurp when you are eating noodles in Japan?
   a Yes
   b No

9 Where is the person from?
   a Australia
   b Europe

10 If you are invited to a barbecue in Australia, what should you do?
   a Take a bottle of wine
   b Relax and enjoy yourself

Tasty!

For many people taste is very important. It's not just taste in food, but taste in clothes and how they look, taste in music or films they like to watch and taste in who they are friends with. Here is what five young people had to say about taste.

For me it's important to look good. Although clothes are important I think that my hair is what makes me different. I've got a Mohican and people often look at me when I'm walking down the street.

Brendan, 19

I spend a lot of money on food. I love eating out and trying food from different countries. Sometimes I have dinner parties at my house. I like to spend time on making the food look good as well as taste good.

Jenny, 24

How I look and what I wear is really important to me. I like to be up-to-date and wear quite trendy clothes. I've also got two tattoos – a flower and a bird, and a heart with my name.

Petra, 35

I think it's important that my friends have the same tastes as me. Not in clothes and food but in music and films. I like to go to the cinema and watch science fiction films. We're friends because we like the same kind of films.

Joe, 29

It's something to gossip about. When people have different tastes in boyfriends or clothes or even music, you can talk about these things. It would be very boring if we all had the same tastes.

Sam, 15

10 Read the magazine article. Write T (true) or F (false) in the boxes.

- a For Brendan, the clothes he wears are as important as his hairstyle. ☐
- b People look at Brendan because of his hairstyle. ☐
- c Jenny enjoys trying food from different countries. ☐
- d She cares more about how the food tastes than how it looks. ☐
- e Petra has a taste for fashionable clothes. ☐
- f One of her tattoos is a flower and her name, the other one is a bird in a heart. ☐
- g For Joe, it is important that his friends share the same tastes in everything. ☐
- h His friends watch science fiction films as well. ☐
- i Sam likes to gossip about differences in taste. ☐
- j She isn't interested when her friends talk about music she doesn't like. ☐

11 A friend from another country is coming to stay with you. Write a letter (about 80 words) telling them about manners in your country.

Exercise	Score
1 Language	______ / 5
2 Language	______ / 5
3 Language	______ / 5
4 Language	______ / 5
5 Vocabulary	______ / 5
6 Vocabulary	______ / 5
7 Vocabulary	______ / 5
8 Vocabulary	______ / 5
9 Listening	______ / 20
10 Reading	______ / 20
11 Writing	______ / 20
Total:	______ / 100
	______ %

Test

Name: ____________________

1 Underline *since* or *for* to complete each sentence.

a I've lived in this house *since* / *for* I was born.

b I've had this violin *since* / *for* three years now.

c I've been thinking about you *since* / *for* you phoned me last night.

d I haven't played any instruments *since* / *for* two months.

e She's been practising every day *since* / *for* she got the part in the play.

f I haven't seen you *since* / *for* ages.

2 Rewrite the sentences in the present perfect using *since* or *for* and the words in brackets.

a I moved to Spain in 2003. (lived)

____

b I bought my car in 2000. (had)

____

c I started collecting stamps when my father gave me his old ones. (been)

____

d Mary started dancing five years ago. (been)

____

e I had my first English lesson when I was 12 years old. (learning)

____

3 Use the prompts to make questions.

a Who / best friend? How long / you / know him?

____

____

b What / most expensive / possession? How long / you / have / it?

____

____

c Who / next-door neighbour? How long / you / know each other?

____

____

d Where / your language school? How long / going there?

____

____

4 Choose the correct preposition from the box to complete the sentences.

for	from	in	of	with

a A big crowd gathered in the main square when the rock band arrived ______ town.

b The origin of the festival comes ______ the time when the harvest was done by hand.

c Urban music is mixed ______ African tribal music to create a new style of music.

d Rio de Janeiro is famous ______ the carnival.

e When you think ______ New Orleans, the Mardi Gras festival comes to mind.

5 Put the words in the box into the correct column.

classical	carnival	festival	guitar	jazz
parade	steel drums	calypso	trumpet	

Types of music	Instruments	Celebrations

6 Complete these sentences using the appropriate words from Ex 5.

a The Mardi Gras is possibly the most famous __________ in the world.

b At the end of the week there is a big __________ through the streets with people dressed in colourful costumes.

c Although New Orleans is famous for lots of different kinds of music, __________ is probably the most popular.

d __________ were originally just the lids of dustbins that people hit.

e It is unusual to hear __________ music at a carnival. Usually an orchestra plays this type of music at a concert.

f __________ originally came from Trinidad.

La Tomatina

La Tomatina is one of the most unusual festivals in Europe. It takes place on the last Wednesday of every August in the town of Buñol near Valencia, Spain. In the morning local people and tourists go to the square and lorries carrying 125,000 kilograms of tomatoes drive into the town. At eleven o'clock everybody starts throwing tomatoes at each other. This lasts for about two hours and then everybody stops. The first tomato 'fight' took place in 1944 and in 1959 the Town Hall made the fight an official part of the celebrations. Nowadays, La Tomatina attracts many tourists to the small town of Buñol.

7 Read the article and match the numbers in a–e to what they represent 1–5.

a	1944	1 The time that the tomato fight starts.
b	11	2 The amount of tomatoes.
c	2	3 The year the tomato fight became an official part of the carnival.
d	1959	4 The year the carnival started.
e	125,000	5 The number of hours the fight takes.

8 Read the text again. Write T (true) or F (false) in the boxes.

a La Tomatina takes place on the first Wednesday of August every year. ☐

b The festival takes place in a small town. ☐

c Only local people go to the festival. ☐

d People have to bring their own tomatoes. ☐

e Lots of tourists go to the town because of the festival. ☐

Exercise	Score
1 Language	______ / 6
2 Language	______ / 10
3 Language	______ / 4
4 Language	______ / 5
5 Vocabulary	______ / 9
6 Vocabulary	______ / 6
7 Reading	______ / 5
8 Reading	______ / 5
Total:	______ / 50
	______ %

UNIT 2

Test

Name: ____________________________

1 Complete the sentences with the correct form of the adjective in brackets.

a If you want to be the ____________ (fast) swimmer in your club, you should practise at least two hours a day.

b In the last match he played ____________ (good) than any time before.

c A special ceremony was held last night to award the ____________ (successful) young sportsperson of the year.

d Skateboarding is ____________ (not dangerous) as in-line skating.

e Cycling to work is ____________ (healthy) than driving.

f The ____________ (scary) moment was when I almost crashed.

g I love scuba diving. I think it's ____________ (beautiful) sport in the world.

h John is ____________ (good) basketball player in the school because he is tall and very fit.

2 Three of these sentences are incorrect. Put a ✔ (correct) or a ✘ (incorrect) in the boxes.

a Snowboarding is easyer than in-line skating. ☐

b John is the youngest player on the team. ☐

c Tim Henman is the most successful tennis player from Britain. ☐

d She's the badest gymnast I've ever seen. ☐

e In-line skating isn't most dangerous as free running. ☐

f You aren't as fast as Matt. ☐

3 Rewrite the three incorrect sentences from Ex 2 making them correct.

a ____________________________.

b ____________________________.

c ____________________________.

4 Choose the correct alternative.

a How long have you been *playing / doing* tennis?

b Can you *play / do* karate in this sports centre?

c As he lives near the sea he *does / goes* scuba diving regularly.

d Every Christmas I spend a few days in the mountains and *go / do* skiing.

e My favourite lesson at school was when we were *doing / playing* exercises.

f He joined the local team at the age of 12 and ever since he has been *playing / doing* football.

5 Replace the underlined words with a phrase from the box. Sometimes you need to change the form.

get angry	get better	get fit	get in shape
get into	get lost		

a It was so dark and foggy that I <u>wasn't sure of my location</u>.

b Maggie has <u>become slimmer</u> now that she goes swimming every week.

c I hope you'll <u>improve</u> soon.

d First I didn't enjoy playing tennis at all but soon I <u>started to enjoy</u> it.

e He always <u>becomes annoyed</u> when his team loses the match.

f It's important to <u>become healthy</u>. You'll feel better and you'll be happier as well.

6 Choose the correct alternative.

1 ______ I have started exercising every day, I'm still not very fit.

a Although b However c But

2 Swimming isn't very difficult ______ it's a good way of staying healthy.

a finally b but c then

3 ______ I found skateboarding fun, but after a while it became a bit boring.

a To begin with b Finally c Although

4 I really don't want to exercise a lot because I'm rather lazy. ______, I don't want to become unhealthy.

a To begin with b Then c On the other hand

7 Put the words from the box in the correct column.

athletics	cycling	gymnastics
judo	karate	swimming	tennis

■ ▪	▪ ■ ▪

8 Read the article about *Street sports* and answer these questions.

a Why is in-line skating popular?

b What equipment do you need for in-line skating?

c Where can you see lots of people doing in-line skating?

d Where did free running become very popular?

e Which is more dangerous, free running or in-line skating?

f What makes free running dangerous?

g How does the writer describe free running?

h How is street basketball different from the normal basketball?

i Where is it popular?

j Who is street basketball for?

Street sports

One of the most popular sports and certainly one that gets you fit, in-line skating is the 'in thing'. One of the reasons for its popularity is that it isn't too expensive – all you need are the skates and some knee pads, although a helmet is a good idea too. In some places, like Los Angeles, you can see hundreds of people skating down the streets, often with earphones and an iPod.

Another sport that has really taken off in more ways than one is free running. It became extremely popular in France in the late 1990s. It's not the most dangerous sport, but is certainly more dangerous than other street sports like skateboarding or in-line skating. There are no rules to free running; all you do is run through a town or city, jumping from building to building. At its best it can be described as an 'extreme sport' with people trying harder and harder routines, jumping across bigger gaps and from taller buildings. It's exciting to watch and even more exciting to do!

Street basketball is fast and energetic. Unlike normal basketball the street version has very few rules. It's faster and much better. Street basketball started in the USA but in the last twenty years it has become popular in many countries. It's also very easy to learn – if you can bounce a ball, run and don't mind getting physical, then street basketball is for you.

Exercise	Score
1 Language	________ / 8
2 Language	________ / 6
3 Language	________ / 3
4 Vocabulary	________ / 6
5 Vocabulary	________ / 6
6 Vocabulary	________ / 4
7 Pronunciation	________ / 7
8 Reading	________ / 10
Total:	________ / 50
	________ %

Test

Name: ____________________________________

1 Choose the correct alternative.

1 Peter ______, 'Let's meet for a drink after work!'

a told b tells c said d said me

2 Lara ______ that she was too tired to come to my party.

a said me b tells me c told me d say

3 'Take my advice and pack casual clothes!' my friend ______.

a told b said me c say d said

4 Daniel ______ that he wanted to rent an apartment in the city centre.

a say to Karl b said c told d tells to Karl

5 'When I am on holiday I want to enjoy the luxury of a five-star hotel,' Carol ______.

a says me b told me c tell d tells

6 Sarah ______ she wanted to go sightseeing.

a told John b told c said John d says

7 'I prefer staying at a campsite,' ______.

a told Tom b told c said d said Tom

2 Rearrange the words into full sentences.

a Jenny / that her / went / parents / abroad / told Tom

______________________________________.

b my friend that / her / I couldn't / I told / after class / meet

______________________________________.

c said that / holiday / the best / to choose / She / this was

______________________________________.

d he prefers / Tim told / a relaxing / me / holiday

______________________________________.

e 'I go / when I / said John / have a break,' / to the mountains

______________________________________.

f she / hotels / Carol said / like / didn't

______________________________________.

3 Complete these sentences with the correct preposition.

a In the first part of our journey we travelled ______ bus, but we got to the hotel ______ foot.

b Travelling ______ plane is a lot faster than travelling ______ train.

c On our holiday we flew ______ Marrakech where we stayed ______ a beautiful hotel for a few days.

d Flying ______ New York has become a lot quicker in the last few years.

e After a delay of several hours we finally arrived ______ London.

f If you want an exotic holiday, why don't you go ______ Fiji?

g I don't really like travelling ______ train.

4 Match the words in the box to the definitions.

campsite	exciting	historical
paradise	resort	self-catering
sightseeing	sunbathing	

a When something is interesting and fun __________

b When you cook your own food on holiday __________

c Sitting or lying in the sun so that your skin gets darker __________

d Connected with history __________

e A place where people go on holiday __________

f A perfect place __________

g Travelling around a place in order to see buildings that are interesting __________

h A place where you can stay in tents __________

5 Put the words in the box into the correct column.

apartment	exciting	exotic
paradise	sightseeing	sunbathing

■ ▪ ▪	▪ ■ ▪

6 Complete the email with six of the words from Ex 4.

Last year I went on holiday with my boyfriend and two of my best friends. We went to a beach (a) ______________ in Thailand. It was almost like (b) ______________. We stayed at a local (c) ______________ because it was much cheaper than the hotels. We didn't do any (d) ______________, we just relaxed on the beach and spent most of the day (e) ______________. I also went windsurfing and scuba diving! It was one of the most (f) ______________ holidays I've ever had and I want to go back again next year.

7 Read the extract from a holiday brochure. Write M for Marrakech and E for Essaouira next to each statement.

a is not far from the sea. ☐
b is a good place to go if you like sunbathing. ☐
c is an old city. ☐
d is near the mountains. ☐
e feels like you could be somewhere like Spain or Italy. ☐
f has wonderful views. ☐
g is a good place to go if you like playing golf. ☐
h isn't too noisy. ☐
i is a popular resort with people who don't need to be active. ☐
j has luxury accommodation. ☐

Holiday experiences

Do you enjoy active holidays? We have the perfect experience for you. Choose from one of the following options:

Golf at the bottom of the Atlas mountains

Enjoy a week of luxury at one of the best hotels and holiday resorts in Morocco. The D'Or Golf Club has a great golf course in fantastic surroundings. Five-star accommodation and a golf course designed by a leading expert just thirty minutes from the centre of Marrakech and with a view of the stunning Atlas mountains.

Sand, sea and surf

Enjoy a fantastic holiday in the beautiful surroundings of the ancient city of Essaouira. Situated on the Atlantic coast, the town has a real Mediterranean feel. Its quiet beaches are very popular with windsurfers, sunbathers and people who simply want to relax and have fun.

For more information contact **Moroccan Experiences** at:
231 St Marks Lane
London
W1 4SR
Tel: 021 887 5...

Exercise	Score
1 Language	______ / 7
2 Language	______ / 6
3 Vocabulary	______ / 7
4 Vocabulary	______ / 8
5 Pronunciation	______ / 6
6 Vocabulary	______ / 6
7 Reading	______ / 10
Total:	______ / 50
	______ %

Test

Name: ________________________________

1 Choose the correct alternative.

a If you *want* / *'ll want* to look for a new coat, I *'ll go* / *go* shopping with you.

b We *'ll be* / *are* late if we *don't leave* / *won't leave* now.

c We *don't go*/ *won't go* anywhere if it *is raining* / *will be raining.*

d If you *shop* / *'ll shop* online you *will find* / *find* a bargain.

e If I *don't have* / *won't have* much time, I *'ll buy* / *buy* the cheapest swimming costume that fits me.

2 Complete the sentences using a first or second conditional.

a I __________ (buy) four Mercedes if I __________ (have) enough money.

b __________ you __________ (give) me a refund if this programme __________ (not run) on my computer?

c __________ you __________ (buy) designer clothes if they __________ (go) out of fashion?

d If you __________ (lose) your passport on holiday, what __________ you __________ (do)?

e Where __________ you __________ (live) if you __________ (can) choose?

3 Correct the most likely mistake in three of these conditional sentences.

a If I have more money, I'd buy lots of things.

b I usually relax if I feel tired.

c If you will find one cheaper, we'll refund your money.

d I'd go shopping with you if you asked.

e If I were you, I'll choose that one.

f If these shoes fit, I'll buy them.

a ________________________________

b ________________________________

c ________________________________

4 Choose the correct alternative.

a A *receipt* / *refund* is a piece of paper you get in a shop, showing that you have paid for the goods.

b A *fault* / *model* is a particular type of goods a company makes.

c When something is *exchanged* / *in stock* it's available to buy in the shop.

d *An exchange* / *A refund* is when you return an item to the shop and get a new one instead.

e A *model* / *warranty* is the company's promise to repair or replace a faulty item free of charge.

f A *fault* / *warranty* is a problem that stops the item from working properly.

g A *receipt* / *refund* is when you get money back when you return something to a shop.

5 Complete these sentences with the words from Ex 4.

a My computer is only a few months old and there's already a __________ in it.

b When you buy an expensive item, it usually comes with a one-year __________.

c Always keep your __________ in case you want to return the goods.

d If there is a fault with a new TV, the maker usually gives you a __________.

e I wanted the same __________ as you have but unfortunately it wasn't __________.

f This shirt is too small for me. Can you __________ it for a bigger size?

6 Rearrange the letters to make adjectives that complete the sentences.

a The shop assistants in that store are really ___________ (plufleh).

b When I got the new TV home I was really quite ___________ (depinatodips). I thought it would be much better than it is.

c I got quite ___________ (grayn) when they didn't give me a refund.

d He told me there was no warranty, so I was rather ___________ (sipusicsou).

e Shop assistants have to be really ___________ (itlope) even when the customers are rude.

7 Complete the article using these phrases.

1 get a refund if you prefer
2 if you enjoy window shopping
3 If the item you buy has a fault
4 if you like shopping and you haven't tried it yet
5 If you're worried about security
6 you don't need to wait

Winners all round

Online shopping is now the most popular way to buy things. It's easy, cheap and safe.

(a) ______, don't be. You are less likely to lose money than if you walk down the street! (b) ______, it is easy to send it back and replace it with a new item or (c) ______.

One of the main advantages of online shopping is that you can do it at anytime of the day or night – (d) ______ until the shops are open. And, (e) ______, then you're sure to like surfing the internet looking at all the different things you can buy if you want – on the internet the choice is endless.

Another advantage is that you can often find great bargains because the companies don't have to pay for a shop and lots of shop assistants.

So, (f) ______, go online and open up a whole new world.

8 Read the text again and answer these questions.

1 Which of these sentences is **not** true?
a Online shopping is dangerous.
b Online shopping is very popular.
c You can return items and get a refund if you want.

2 According to the article, when you shop online
a you can shop when you want.
b you'll spend more money than usual.

3 According to the article, online shopping is like window shopping because
a you can do it when the shops are closed.
b you don't have to buy anything.

4 According to the article, online shopping
a is cheaper than normal shopping.
b isn't good for the companies.

Exercise	Score
1 Language	________/ 5
2 Language	________/ 10
3 Language	________/ 6
4 Vocabulary	________/ 7
5 Vocabulary	________/ 7
6 Vocabulary	________/ 5
7 Reading	________/ 6
8 Reading	________/ 4
Total:	________/ 50
	________%

Module test

Name: ______________________________

1 Complete the sentences with *for* or *since*.

a Pete and Sally have known each other __________ they were young.

b They've only been married __________ last week.

c They've lived in the same house __________ a few months.

d Sally has played the piano __________ a long time.

e They've been on holiday __________ yesterday.

2 Choose the correct alternative.

a What's *scarier / the scariest* thing you've ever done?

b I think parkour is *more / most* dangerous than skiing.

c I think I'm as *good / better* as you at skiing.

d That's *faster / the fastest* I've ever run.

e Do you think it can get any *worse / the worst*?

3 Three of these sentences are incorrect. Put a ✔ (correct) or a ✘ (incorrect) in the boxes.

a 'What did she told you?' ☐

b 'I'll meet you at ten,' said Joanne. ☐

c She said me, 'I'll see you later.' ☐

d Everybody told me she was a good student. ☐

e 'Let's go,' she told. ☐

4 Match the beginnings to the endings of the sentences.

a If you find it cheaper in another shop,

b If I get paid tomorrow,

c I wouldn't be upset

d What will you do

e I won't buy it

1 I'll take you out for a meal.

2 if it's too expensive.

3 if I am late?

4 we will refund the difference.

5 if you said 'No'.

5 Complete each sentence with *go, do* or *play*.

a I really don't __________ enough exercise.

b How often do you __________ basketball?

c Scuba diving is one of the most dangerous sports to __________.

d I __________ swimming every morning.

e I've heard that you __________ ice hockey. Is that true?

6 Choose the correct alternative.

Interviewer: Why do you come to the gym?

Denise: I know that it's really important for me to (a) *get fit / get angry*, but it's difficult to find enough time. I (b) *get angry / get into* when I think about how fit I used to be and how unfit I am now. I guess the only way to (c) *get into / get in shape* is to exercise regularly. I'm sure I'll (d) *get into / get fit* it and enjoy it a lot and I'll (e) *get lost / get better* faster.

7 Choose the correct alternative.

Sandra: Where did you go last year then?

Lizzie: Last year I went (a) *at / in / to* Florida with my boyfriend. We travelled there (b) *by / in / on* plane and it took seven hours. We arrived (c) *at / in / to* Miami late in the evening and we stayed (d) *to / on / at* a really nice five-star hotel. In the mornings we went (e) *by / in / on* foot to the beach. It was a wonderful holiday.

8 Complete the sentences by rearranging the letters in brackets to make words.

a I'm sorry but I can't give you a (a) __________ (underf) unless you have a (b) __________ (icepetr).

b Would you like to (c) __________ (eachgnex) it for something else?

c I'll just check to see if we have that model in (d) __________ (costk).

d The best way to shop is to (e) __________ (sowerb) on the internet.

9 **05** Listen to an interviewer asking three people about *parkour*. Are these sentences true (T) or false (F)?

a *Parkour* is like basketball. ☐

b *Parkour* is becoming more popular around the world. ☐

c Free running is another name for *parkour*. ☐

d You can stop in *parkour*. ☐

e Sam describes *parkour* as a game. ☐

f It started in Paris. ☐

g Spider has been doing *parkour* since he was ten. ☐

h People who do *parkour* are called *traceurs*. ☐

i Monkey has never hurt himself doing *parkour*. ☐

j *Parkour* isn't good for your health. ☐

10 Read the advertisements and choose the best heading for each paragraph.

Party time!
Activity is the new relaxation
Spectacular views with a difference

Amazing breaks!

Are you bored with holidays where all you do is lie on the beach or go sightseeing? Would you like a holiday with a difference? Here are three to choose from.

(a) __________

Spend two weeks on our 'Action break' holidays. We have a lot of different activities for you to choose from including skydiving, white water rafting, climbing and scuba diving as well as more traditional sports like basketball, tennis and cycling. You don't need to be fit although it does help if you are in shape. If you choose one of the more dangerous sports you will spend the first week training and learning about the sport with one of our professional coaches. Come along and enjoy a holiday you'll remember.

(b) __________

Travel to Peru and visit one of the most amazing places you will ever see – Machu Picchu. You'll need to be in good shape as we walk from the nearest town and camp each night in the hills. Although the accommodation isn't five-star, the scenery is probably the most beautiful in the world – it'll take your breath away. This holiday is more like a pilgrimage than a traditional sightseeing break.

(c) __________

Do you like music, dancing and great food? Then come to the biggest and the most famous carnival in the world – Rio. Carnival starts seven weeks before Easter Sunday and lasts for four days. Probably the best part of Carnival is the Samba Parade with the amazing costumes, fantastic music and tasty food. So, if you want to be part of the best party in the world – come and join us in Rio.

11 Read the texts again. Which text are these sentences about? Write A for the action break, P for the holiday in Peru or C for the carnival in Rio.

a On this holiday you can learn a new sport. ☐

b The accommodation won't be top quality. ☐

c You can only go on this holiday at a particular time of the year. ☐

d This holiday is perfect for people who love music. ☐

e This holiday can be dangerous. ☐

f You have to be fit for this holiday. ☐

g You can choose what you want to do on this holiday. ☐

12 Think of a festival or celebration in your city or country. Write an email to a friend and tell them about it. Include what it's called, when it takes place, how long it lasts, when it first took place, what happens, about any special food or music, etc. Write about 80 words.

Exercise	Score
1 Language	______ / 5
2 Language	______ / 5
3 Language	______ / 5
4 Language	______ / 5
5 Vocabulary	______ / 5
6 Vocabulary	______ / 5
7 Vocabulary	______ / 5
8 Vocabulary	______ / 5
9 Listening	______ / 20
10 Reading	______ / 6
11 Reading	______ / 14
12 Writing	______ / 20
Total:	______ / 100
	______ %

Placement test answers

Section 1 Language

(One point for each correct answer)

1	c
2	b
3	b
4	c
5	b
6	c
7	a
8	c
9	a
10	a
11	a
12	c
13	b
14	c
15	a
16	c
17	c
18	b
19	b
20	b
21	c
22	a
23	c
24	c
25	a
26	b
27	c
28	c
29	c
30	b
31	a
32	c
33	c
34	a
35	a
36	c
37	a
38	b
39	c
40	a
41	c
42	a
43	b
44	b
45	a
46	a
47	c
48	a
49	b
50	c

Section 2 Vocabulary

(One point for each correct answer)

1	was
2	am
3	in
4	to
5	for
6	take
7	like
8	do
9	on
10	far
11	for
12	idea
13	well / badly
14	up
15	catching
16	touch / contact
17	his
18	freezing
19	keep
20	sense
21	keep / catch
22	apart
23	outweigh
24	away
25	getter

Score banding

0–30 Elementary
31–40 Pre-intermediate
41–50 Intermediate
51–60 Upper-intermediate
61–75 Advanced

Unit tests answers

(One point for each answer unless stated otherwise)

Module 1 Unit 1

1 a getting up, going to b playing, watching c listening to d learning, reading e hanging out

2 a Really? I do. b Me neither. c Me too. d Really? I like it. e Do you? I don't. f Me too.

3 a I really like hanging out at weekends.
  b I really don't like reading much, I prefer watching films.
  c She hates reading horror stories after dark.
  d I hate doing the washing up but I enjoy cooking. OR I enjoy cooking but I hate doing the washing up.
  e I don't mind listening to classical music or pop but I can't stand reggae.

4 a 4 b 7 c 3 d 5 e 2 f 6 g 1

5 a after b up c out d into e after

6 a start work in b becomes an adult c take care of d looks and behaves like e spends time

7 a basketball b karate c watch films d reading e watching TV

8 1a T b F 2 a F b T 3 a F b T 4 a T b F 5 a F b T

Module 1 Unit 2

1 a made, was studying b stopped, was driving c was having, rang d crashed, was writing e was dreaming, rang

2 a I was ~~watched~~ watching the TV when the phone rang.
  b I was working for a computer company when we ~~meet~~ met.
  c She was talking to her friends when I ~~was~~ arrived.
  d They ~~were meeting~~ met when they were 18.
  e What was he doing when you ~~were seeing~~ saw him?

3 /d/ discovered, returned
  /t/ asked, introduced, produced, pushed, worked
  /ɪd/ invented, started, wanted

4 a Do b made c make d done e does f make g make h make

5 a policy b retirement c scent d innovative e gizmo f produce

6 a retirement b gizmo c produce(s) d innovative e policy f scent

7 a Percy Shaw b In the country c They were too expensive. d (The) cat's eyes e Drivers can see the middle of the road.

Module 1 Unit 3

1 a shouldn't b should c mustn't d don't have to e should f mustn't

2 1 a 2 b 3 a 4 a 5 b

3 a ✔ b ✘ c ✘ d ✔ e ✔ f ✘

4 a You mustn't ~~to~~ think about anything else.
  b She doesn't have to listen to your advice.
  c I shouldn't ~~not~~ worry.

5 a 2 b 6 c 4 d 1 e 8 f 3 g 7 h 5

6 a sensitive b helpful c selfish d confident e sensible f friendly g suspicious h boring

7 a symbols b interpret c believe d sense e psychic

8 a Do you dream every night?
  b Do you remember your dreams?
  c What do people dream about?
  d What does your dream mean?
  e Do dreams come true?

9 a It isn't true b suddenly c often d can't e It isn't possible

Module 1 Unit 4

1 1 a 2 c 3 b 4 c 5 a 6 b

2 a 'll b 'll c won't d Will e won't f won't g 'll

3 a e b b c d d g e c f f g a

4 **(Two points each)**
  a (Don't worry) I won't be late.
  b (Don't worry) Everything will be fine.
  c I'll help (you).

5 a architect b engineer c plumber d nurse e computer programmer f teacher g agricultural worker

6 a skills b a charming c abroad d superficial e aim f developed g crazy

7 1 b 2 a

8 a T b F c T d T e F f T g T h F

Module 2 Unit 1

1 1a ✔ 2a ✔ 3b ✔ 4b ✔ 5a ✔

2 a has put on b have seen c Have you read d split up e have heard

3 a haven't seen b published c has called d Have / bought e did / get

4 **(Half point for each word)**

Infinitive	Past simple	Past participle
become	became	become
buy	bought	bought
break	broke	broken
eat	ate	eaten
fall	fell	fallen
have	had	had
hear	heard	heard
see	saw	seen
speak	spoke	spoken
take	took	taken

5 a spread rumours b had a chat c keep a secret d keep in touch e form a bond

6
a If you tell me where Sarah is going, I promise I'll keep it a secret. OR I promise to keep it a secret.
b She is upset because her friend has spread rumours about her private life.
c The students in my group are very friendly, so it's been easy to form a bond (with them).
d Why don't you have a chat with / to Judy? She seems to be very lonely.
e Promise me you'll keep in touch as I want to know how you are doing in your new school.

7 a have you heard b you won't believe it c Apparently d According to e they split up f guess what g last week h having a chat i Can you keep a secret? j Keep in touch

Module 2 Unit 2

1
A: *What did you think of* the film?
B: I didn't enjoy it at all. I really *didn't think* Johnny Depp was very good.
A: Didn't you? *In my opinion* he was much better in this film than in that comedy everyone thought was so brilliant.
B: Really? *If you ask me,* he is a fantastic director but a really average actor.
A: *Oh, come on.* You can't be serious!
B: But I really thought that Gwyneth Paltrow was good.
A: *Me too.* At last we agree on something!

2
a In my opinion, all Hollywood movies are terrible.
b Oh, come on. Some of them are great.
c If you ask me, the acting is really bad.
d Really? I think it's OK.
e What do you think of Johnny Depp?
f As far as I'm concerned, Leonardo DiCaprio is better.

3 1 b 2 c 3 a 4 b 5 c

4 a biography b role c convincingly d hesitation e to devote

5 a hesitation b biography c role d convincingly e to devote

6 a close-up b character c scene d played by e in the background f set

7 a <u>gor</u>geous b fan<u>tas</u>tic c im<u>press</u>ive d spec<u>tac</u>ular e <u>bril</u>liant f <u>fun</u>ny g <u>chil</u>dish

8 a martial arts b comedy c western d romance

9 a T b F c F d F e T f F

Module 2 Unit 3

1 a many b much c much d many e much

2 1 a 2 b 3 b 4 a 5 b 6 a 7 b 8 a / b 9 a 10 b

3
A: Do you have <u>any</u> / <u>a lot of</u> close friends? You know, people you can tell all your secrets to?
B: Yes, I've got a <u>few</u> really close friends. I've known them since university.
A: Do you stay in touch with <u>a lot of</u> friends from your student days?
B: Not really. I have very <u>little</u> time to spend writing letters and emails to them.
A: That's a shame!
B: Yes, I'd love to see <u>some</u> of them more often, but they live in a different city.

4 1 c 2 a 3 b 4 b 5 c 6 a 7 c 8 c

5 a I b P c I d P e P f P

6 a 4 b 1 c 6 d 3 e 5 f 2

7 a Giuseppe's b Marge c It's freshly prepared and they use no artificial colours or flavours. d Joel e The middle of the week f He eats too much. g (Absolutely) delicious h The risotto is amazing. i The recipes j A glass of white wine and a (lovely) dessert

Module 2 Unit 4

1 a went off b dress up c come across d look after e called off f turn (it) off g takes after h turned up

2 1 b 2 a 3 c 4 a 5 c 6 b

3 1a ✔ 2b ✔ 3a ✔ 4b ✔ 5b ✔ 6a ✔

4 a trendy b accessories c tattoo d traditional e necklace f scruffy g attractive h old-fashioned i smart j casual

5 a trendy b traditional c tattoo d accessories e smart f scruffy g attractive h old-fashioned i necklace j casual

6 a Mohican b Henna c Tattoo d Piercing

7 a M b T c H d M e P f T

Module 3 Unit 1

1 a since b for c since d for e since f for

2 **(Two points each)**
(Assuming it is 2006)
- a I've lived in Spain since 2003 / for three years.
- b I've had my car since 2000 / for six years.
- c I've been collecting stamps since my father gave me his old ones.
- d Mary has been dancing for five years / since 2001.
- e I've been learning English since I was 12 years old.

3
- a Who is your best friend? How long have you known him?
- b What's your most expensive possession? How long have you had it?
- c Who's your next-door neighbour? How long have you known each other?
- d Where is your language school? How long have you been going there?

4 a in b from c with d for e of

5 Types of music: classical, jazz, calypso
Instruments: guitar, steel drums, trumpet
Celebrations: carnival, festival, parade

6 a carnival b parade c jazz d Steel drums e classical f Calypso

7 a 4 b 1 c 5 d 3 e 2

8 a F b T c F d F e T

Module 3 Unit 2

1 a fastest b better c most successful d not as dangerous e healthier f scariest g the most beautiful h the best

2 a ✘ b ✔ c ✔ d ✘ e ✘ f ✔

3
- a Snowboarding is ~~easyer~~ easier than in-line skating.
- b She's the ~~badest~~ worst gymnast I've ever seen.
- c In-line skating isn't ~~most~~ as dangerous as free running.

4 a playing b do c goes d go e doing f playing

5 a got lost b got in shape c get better d got into e gets angry f get fit

6 1 a 2 b 3 a 4 c

7 ■ ▪ cycling, judo, swimming, tennis
▪ ■ ▪ athletics, gymnastics, karate

8 a It isn't expensive. b Skates, some knee pads (and a helmet) c Los Angeles d France e Free running f There are no rules / people jump across big gaps between tall buildings. g Exciting to watch and more exciting to do h There aren't as many rules. i In the USA and many other countries j People who like running, don't mind getting physical and who can bounce a ball

Module 3 Unit 3

1 1 c 2 c 3 d 4 b 5 b 6 a 7 d

2
- a Jenny told Tom that her parents went abroad.
- b I told my friend that I couldn't meet her after class.
- c She said that this was the best holiday to choose.
- d Tim told me he prefers a relaxing holiday.
- e 'I go to the mountains when I have a break,' said John.
- f Carol said she didn't like hotels.

3 a by, on b by, by c to, in / at d to e in f to g by

4 a exciting b self-catering c sunbathing d historical e resort f paradise g sightseeing h campsite

5 ■ ▪ ▪ paradise, sightseeing, sunbathing
▪ ■ ▪ exciting, exotic, apartment

6 a resort b paradise c campsite d sightseeing e sunbathing f exciting

7 a E b E c E d M e E f M g M h E i E j M

Module 3 Unit 4

1 a want, I'll go b 'll be, don't leave c won't go, is raining d shop, will find e don't have, 'll buy

2 a 'd buy, had b Will (you) give, doesn't run c Would buy, went d lost, would (you) do e would (you) live, could choose

3
a ✗ If I ~~have~~ had more money, I'd buy lots of things.
b ✔
c ✗ If you ~~will~~ find one cheaper, we'll refund your money.
d ✔
e ✗ If I were you ~~I'll~~ I'd choose that one.
f ✔

4 a receipt b model c in stock d An exchange e warranty f fault g refund

5 a fault b warranty c receipt d refund e model, in stock f exchange

6 a helpful b disappointed c angry d suspicious e polite

7 a 5 b 3 c 1 d 6 e 2 f 4

8 1 a 2 a 3 b 4 a

Module test answers

(One point for each answer unless stated otherwise)

Module 1

1 a love b Me too c can't stand d Me neither e prefer

2 a came, was drinking b was talking, arrived c was working, wrote d was having, thought of e was drying, phoned

3
a You don't have to pack a lot of clothes.
b You should take plenty of money.
c You shouldn't worry. It's important to relax. OR You shouldn't worry. You must relax.
d You mustn't be late.
e You must bring your passport.

4 a promise b request c prediction d promise e prediction

5 a growing up b looked after c go into d hang out e takes after

6
a ✘ You really need to be careful or you'll ~~do~~ make a mistake.
b ✔
c ✘ He ~~made~~ did badly in his driving test.
d ✘ Excuse me! Could you ~~make~~ do me a favour?
e ✘ I hate ~~doing~~ making difficult decisions.
f ✔

7 1 c 2 a 3 b 4 b 5 c 6 a 7 c 8 a 9 c 10 a

8 a L b L c B d L e B f I g I h L i I j L

9 a F b F c T d F e F

10 **(Two points each)**
a Stockholm, Sweden
b Music
c Listening to music, watching films and hanging out with her friends.
d Science fiction
e She's friendly but a bit quiet.
f She doesn't like gossiping.
g Work as a volunteer abroad.
h Every day
i In-line skating and skiing
j To write to them and hang out with them online.

11 Give a score out of 20
5 points for accuracy
5 points for vocabulary range
5 points for organisation and cohesion
5 points for content (appropriacy)

Module 2

1 a seen b saw c Did she tell d didn't have e heard

2 a What did you think of it? b If you ask me, c Really? d Me too e Oh, come on

3
a ✘ How ~~many~~ much fruit do you eat everyday?
b ✘ I don't eat ~~some~~ any / much fruit.
c ✔
d ✔
e ✘ I usually have a ~~few~~ little milk in my coffee.

4 1 a✔ 2 a✔ 3 b✔ 4 b✔ 5 a✔

5 a spread b keep c form d keep e have

6 1 e 2 b 3 d 4 a 5 c

7 a booked a table for one b the menu c ready to order d recommend a good wine e the bill

8 a attractive b trendy c old-fashioned d scruffy e accessories

9 **(Two points each)**
1 b 2 a 3 b 4 a 5 a 6 a 7 b 8 a 9 a 10 b

10 **(Two points each)**
a F b T c T d F e T f F g F h T i T j F

11 Give a score out of 20
5 points for accuracy
5 points for vocabulary range
5 points for organisation and cohesion
5 points for content (appropriacy)

Module 3

1 a since b since c for d for e since

2 a the scariest b more c good d the fastest e worse

3 a ✗ 'What did she ~~told~~ tell you?'
b ✓
c ✗ She said, ~~me~~ 'I'll see you later.' OR She ~~said~~ told me, 'I'll see you later.'
d ✓
e ✗ 'Let's go,' she ~~told~~ said.

4 a 4 b 1 c 5 d 3 e 2

5 a do b play c do d go e play

6 a get fit b get angry c get in shape d get into e get better

7 a to b by c in d at e on

8 a refund b receipt c exchange d stock e browse

9 **(Two points each)**
a F b T c T d F e F f T g T h T i F j F

10 **(Two points each)**
a Activity is the new relaxation b Spectacular views with a difference c Party time!

11 **(Two points each)**
a A b P c C d C e A f P g A

12 Give a score out of 20
5 points for accuracy
5 points for vocabulary range
5 points for organisation and cohesion
5 points for content (appropriacy)